"The Object's the Thing. . ."

Also by Rob Cannings

A FIELD GUIDE TO INSECTS OF
THE PACIFIC NORTHWEST
Harbour Publishing, 2018

INTRODUCING THE DRAGONFLIES OF
BRITISH COLUMBIA AND THE YUKON
Royal BC Museum, 2002

SYSTEMATICS OF LASIOPOGON
Royal BC Museum, 2002

"The Object's the Thing. . ."

The Writings of Yorke Edwards
A Pioneer of Heritage Interpretation in Canada

Richard Kool
Robert A. Cannings

Victoria, Canada

"The Object's the Thing..."
The Writings of Yorke Edwards,
A Pioneer of Heritage Interpretation in Canada

Published by the Royal BC Museum, 675 Belleville Street,
Victoria, British Columbia, V8W 9W2, Canada.

The Royal BC Museum is located on the traditional territories of the Lekwungen (Songhees and Xwsepsum Nations). We extend our appreciation for the opportunity to live and learn on this territory.

Cover and interior design by Jeff Werner
Copy editing and index by Audrey McClellan

Library and Archives Canada Cataloguing in Publication
Title: "The object's the thing..." : the writings of Yorke Edwards : a pioneer of heritage interpretation in Canada / [edited by] Richard Kool (Royal Roads University), Robert A. Cannings (Royal BC Museum).
Other titles: Writings of Yorke Edwards : a pioneer of heritage interpretation in Canada
Names: Edwards, Yorke, author. | Kool, Richard, 1950- editor. | Cannings, Robert A., 1948- editor. | Royal British Columbia Museum, publisher.
Description: Includes bibliographical references and index.
Identifiers: Canadiana (print) 20200294164 | Canadiana (ebook) 20200294547 | ISBN 9780772678515 (softcover) | ISBN 9780772678522 (EPUB) | ISBN 9780772678539 (Mobipocket) | ISBN 9780772678546 (PDF)
Subjects: LCSH: Edwards, Yorke. | LCSH: British Columbia. Department of Recreation and Conservation. | LCSH: Canadian Wildlife Service. | LCSH: British Columbia Provincial Museum. | LCSH: Parks—Interpretive programs—British Columbia. | LCSH: Parks—Interpretive programs—Canada. | LCSH: Natural areas—Interpretive programs—British Columbia. | LCSH: Natural areas—Interpretive programs—Canada. | LCSH: Heritage tourism—British Columbia. | LCSH: Heritage tourism—Canada.
Classification: LCC SB484.C3 E39 2020 | DDC 333.78/160971—dc23

10 9 8 7 6 5 4 3 2 1

Printed in Canada by Friesens.

The coming of the salmon is a fairly minor event each fall in the biological economy of the Clearwater Valley, and it should not be made too much of here. But it illustrates well the complex lives that living things may lead. Life has enveloped the earth in wonderful variety. Each kind of life is so complex itself and requires such exact conditions in which to live, these conditions often changing with season or time of life, that there is no word to describe the wonder and beauty and the functional complexity of it all. Words like "masterpiece" fall far short. A masterpiece is but something made by man in his time spared from the essential tasks of living. Yet his living itself vastly outshines in achievement anything that he could possibly do. We take life for granted, because it is everywhere. But surely worth is not a function of scarcity. The return of the salmon to Clearwater is an annual event that continually reminds me that living things are the only wonders on earth.

From the journals of Yorke Edwards, July 1960.

...the naturalist has a duty to society that needs no spelling out. What does need clarifying is whether naturalists are capable of meeting this challenge, for most naturalists prefer action in the realm of nature to action in the society of men. Put more bluntly, perhaps most naturalists would rather enjoy a day in the field than give a day to the task of ensuring that the next generation will have places of high quality in which to go afield.

Yorke Edwards, in a talk to the Federation of Ontario Naturalists, 1964.

A promotional photo from the British Columbia Department of Recreation and Conservation featuring Yorke Edwards in Goldstream Provincial Park, likely from about 1960.
Department of Recreation and Conservation, Government of BC.

Contents

Illustrations

Acknowledgements

We have many people to thank. Of course, we are grateful to publisher Eve Rickert, editor Audrey McClellan and the staff at the Royal BC Museum and BC Archives for their support and encouragement. The educators at the Wye Marsh Nature Centre provided photos, as did Frank Buffam and Bruce Falls. Yorke's daughters, Jane Edwards and Anne Wills, helped immensely and provided wonderful support for this project. Also providing photos and/or information were Bill Merilees, Trevor Goward, Ralph and Clara Ritcey, Grant Keddie, Marg Killing, Lorne Hammond, Robert Bateman and Bristol Foster.

Thanks to Bob Peart for his enthusiastic support, editorial guidance and stories about Yorke and his influence. Present and retired BC Parks staff such as Bill Merilees, Gail Ross and Tammy Lidicoat helped search for photos and provided advice, while Sherry Kirkvold did a close reading of an early draft of the entire manuscript, and both Trevor Goward and Bill Merilees did a detailed edit, full of wonderful insights and critical comments, of the penultimate draft. Bill, Trevor, Anne Wills, Jane Edwards, Bette Cannings and David Nagorsen all provided information for Yorke's biographical chapter, and Bill, Trevor, Anne and Jane also commented on it. Thanks to John McFarlane for providing two papers published in his journal *Heritage Communication*, to Sharon Keen for her assistance in the BC Archives, and to Mark Peck at the Royal Ontario Museum for advice and photos.

We are grateful to all the organizations that gave permission to republish Yorke's articles. The editors also must thank Yorke Edwards himself for providing such engaging and strong writing to work with. Few edits were needed, although we did add some commas: Yorke seemed to be very stingy with that useful piece of punctuation. The quality of his written output was presciently described in 1943 by the editor of *Canadian Nature*, who said, when writing about the teenage York (as he spelled it then) and his illustrator friend, the young John Crosby (who painted all the bird pictures in *The Birds of Canada*), "Their work, however, is exceptional in its beauty and promise." Promise indeed.

Most of the essays presented in this volume were originally handwritten, then typed out either by Yorke or by a secretary. We scanned the typed text and worked with the scanned document to ensure its correspondence with the original.

There are two things we'd like to note regarding Yorke's writings. We are aware that, in 2020, Yorke's language sounds rather sexist and uncomfortably stereotypical about women: all of his pronouns are male ("she" is found only three times in all the essays), and his general statements about humans always refer to "man" (used 60 times, compared to three uses of "woman"). Yorke was a man of his times, and we've not altered the gender balance of his language. The essays also use dated terms like "Indian" and present some stereotypical portrayals of First Nations people that he met. Again, we recognize the difficulties with the language but have chosen to keep the text as it was written.

Yorke as a young man setting mouse traps. Edwards family photo.

Northern Lake

On whose bosom in the morn
The loons will laugh and play
By whose brink the wood thrush sings
Hymns at the close of a day

In whose pines about the beach
The white-throat, fifing loud
Sings of sweet, sweet Canada,
And well might he be proud

In whose waters bass and trout
Live their small lives unseen
On whose hills that stand guard
Grow forests cool and green

On whose surface, as the sun
Sets red beyond the hill,
A shimmering scarlet path
Is stretched, and all is still.

Thy scenery may be surpassed
But nowhere else will be
A lake whose hills are mirrored,
And sometimes mirror me.

Roger Y. Edwards
Rejected, *Nature Magazine*, March 10, 1939

Yorke in the 1960s. Edwards family photo.

Foreword

Bob Peart

EARLY ONE MORNING IN 1974, while attending a nature conference in Guelph, Ontario, there was a knock and whisper at my hotel room door: "I'm going for a walk with two old friends. I'll meet you downstairs in five minutes. Bring your binos." I quickly washed up. We met in the hotel lobby and headed outside, only for me to discover a few minutes later that the old friends were the northern cardinal and the white-throated sparrow. That walk with those "two old friends," the sparrow and that cardinal, was one of my first experiences with Yorke Edwards.

At the time, Yorke was generally accepted as "the father of nature interpretation in Canada," an area in which I was establishing my career. He'd earned this reputation for his pioneering work at BC Parks, establishing a naturalist– and nature centre–based interpretation program in the early 1960s; for his vision for the Canadian Wildlife Service's plan to interpret Canada in the late 1960s and early '70s; and, of course, for his writings. His writings came from his deep love and respect for nature, and focused on his belief that people must spend time in the outdoors experiencing nature first-hand if they are to truly understand the web of life and our place in it.

Over the subsequent years, I got to know Yorke well, and what a privilege that was! We travelled together birdwatching, we worked together on various interpretive and museum-related projects, and I collected and read pretty well everything he wrote. I admired Yorke as a friend and as a gentleman. As you will find in this collection, his writings are thoughtful, descriptive, lyrical and full of the respect he had for nature, birds and other animals, and the province he thought of as home—British Columbia.

His description of what it means to know Canada is powerful and has always stayed with me.

> Canada is rocky seas of mountains and magnificent tables of plain, thousands of leagues of spruce woods and fertile miles of farms, frozen white oceans and cities dominating the Earth as far as the eyes can see. Canada is foggy wet coasts and dry cold deserts, rolling golden grasslands, and valleys ablaze with autumn leaves, lonely surf-girt islands, and towns teeming with people. This land is many lands, each worth knowing. To glimpse this diversity is to feel some of the meaning of being Canadian.[1]

Sadly, Yorke's writings and field notes document a sense of nature that is no longer widely shared or experienced. He describes his trips in the 1960s and 1970s: on BC Ferries going through Active Pass and encountering thousands and thousands of Bonaparte's gulls; the flocks of ducks and geese at Last Mountain Lake in Saskatchewan that took two hours to lift off the land; and—of course—the warblers at Point Pelee, where the trees dripped with multiple species of exhausted birds only yards away.

His writings remind us of what nature once was, and will never be again in any of our lifetimes. His writing offers us a good example of the *shifting baseline*—the fact that each new generation takes what they see when they are young as their normal, the baseline, which leads to the decreasing ability over time to experience nature's diversity as it once was, with the knowledge base of that diversity also becoming lost in the fog of the past. This shifting—this reduction in both numbers and diversity of wild things—conspires against current nature conservation efforts, as the way one sees the natural world determines the kind of world we are willing to live in, live with and advocate for. Without that long view, a perspective people like Yorke have offered, it is too easy for today's public not to appreciate the urgency of conservation, as people simply haven't experienced what has been lost and therefore can't appreciate what is still at risk.

I was never the field naturalist that Yorke was, and I am certainly not the writer he was either, but Yorke's love for the natural world and his understanding of the importance of that first-hand experience—of being right there to draw in with all your senses that cardinal or sparrow—have guided my life and my work. My memories of Yorke encompass more than his pioneering efforts and writings about nature interpretation. They include tramping through wet meadows chasing after that elusive bird, designing nature programs and nature centres that did more than just transfer information, but that also worked to connect the visitor to the outdoors. Most importantly, I will remember our friendly, thoughtful discussions about why the natural world is fundamental to us all and must remain so.

It is important that we honour and celebrate those who have gone before us. This collection of Yorke's writings is just such an honouring, a celebration of a remarkable Canadian. This book is a statement of respect for someone who isn't—yet—that well-known beyond a small circle of admirers. But the fact remains that Yorke, many years ago, set the foundation for many of the conversations that occur today about that essential need to connect and reconnect children and families with nature—to get outside, to play and to explore.

So next time you hear the birds calling in the early dawn, think of Yorke. Then take the time to go outside to listen, watch and visit with some of his old friends.

Bob Peart was assistant director for Research and Public Programs at the Royal BC Museum (1985–1988) and has spent his life working and volunteering to conserve and protect wildlife and the natural world he loves. His time with Yorke spanned a few decades and influenced his approach to conservation education. A number of Yorke's papers collected by Bob served as the basis for this book.

Notes

1 R.Y. Edwards, *The Land Speaks: Organizing and Running an Interpretation System* (Toronto: National and Provincial Parks Association, 1979), 11, http://parkscanadahistory.com/publications/nppac-cpaws/the-land-speaks.pdf.

R. Yorke Edwards (1924–2011)

*Robert A. Cannings**

ON JANUARY 9, 1944, 19-YEAR-OLD Yorke Edwards wrote to Rudolph M. Anderson, chief of the Biology Division at the National Museum of Canada and associate editor of *The Canadian Field-Naturalist* for almost four decades,[†] asking questions on the focus of his nascent career in zoology.[1] Anderson responded three weeks later, apologizing for his tardiness: "I have had to put this letter away twice without finishing, but it is a serious matter to give advice to a young man on his future career."[2] The letter is full of details on small mammal identification, the building of collections and the life of a working

* Unless otherwise noted, all details of the life and career of Yorke Edwards (RYE) are taken from information in Roger Yorke Edwards Fonds, BC Archives (PR-2304). The series MS-3068 contains journals and field notes; MS-3069 includes papers, lecture notes and correspondence; and MS-3071 holds photographs and other graphic material.

† Rudolph M. Anderson (1876–1961) was second-in-command to Vilhjalmur Stefansson in the Canadian Arctic Expedition from Alaska to Bathurst Inlet (1913–1916), leading its southern party and editing the expedition's 16-volume report. He served as chief of the Biology Division of the National Museum of Canada from 1920 to 1946.

Yorke and friends, 1946. Clockwise from upper left: Donald Laurie MacDonald (future professor of chemistry, Oregon State University) and "Doc" Ritchie (Robert C. Ritchie, future pathologist, Banting Institute, Toronto); MacDonald, Ritchie and Edwards in the snow; with the bicycle is John MacArthur (future professor of physics at Marlboro College, VT, and brother of eminent ecologist Robert MacArthur); with thermos and sandwich is J. Bruce Falls (future professor of ecology, University of Toronto); Edwards and MacDonald in car rumble seat; Edwards (holding sandpiper), MacDonald and unknown friend. Montage assembled by Bruce Falls and used with his permission.

zoologist. Obviously recognizing the zeal and commitment in Edwards' letter, Anderson took time from a demanding job to encourage the young man's growth as a biologist. He wrote Edwards several times in the 1940s with information, literature and guidance on publishing,[3] and was instrumental in publishing Yorke's first scientific paper.[4]

Anderson's confidence in Edwards was not misplaced. The eager student grew into a man whose thoughts and energies have helped shape the minds and lives of countless naturalists across the country. For almost half a century Yorke Edwards was a pioneer in wildlife biology, nature education, conservation and museum life, stimulating people to think more deeply about the world and our place in it.

The beginning

Roger Yorke Edwards was born in Toronto on November 22, 1924, to John Macham and Agnes Cornelia (née Yorke) Edwards.* His father was a chartered accountant, his mother a secretary. Yorke was an only child, self-contained and self-motivated. Reading the nature writings of Ernest T. Seton and Thornton W. Burgess plunged him into biology; the colourful Audubon bird charts that hung on the walls of his Toronto school drove him to memorize the plumages of all the species he came across. His first ornithological notebook began in January 1937, when he was 12 years old. Yorke's passion for birds was

* Except on a few unpublished manuscripts written in 1939-40, which he signed "Roger Y. Edwards," he used the name "Yorke," but until 1967 he almost always spelled it without the "e." In a letter to Gavin Henderson (National and Provincial Parks Association of Canada), October 2, 1972, he said, "'Yorke' is right, but for years I never added the 'e'. The confusion following my adding it again about five years ago has been considerable—I am sorry to say."

shared by his high school friend John Crosby, who later became one of Canada's foremost bird artists.* Beginning in 1940, the two rode around Toronto on their bicycles, birding fanatically. To get money for a pair of binoculars in 1941, Yorke painted the next-door neighbour's house, but his "first good binoculars, 7×50," came from his friend Bruce Falls five years later.[5]

Yorke, Crosby and other friends became enthusiastic members of the Royal Ontario Museum's (ROM) Intermediate Naturalists Club; Yorke was president in 1945. Some of these friends are now well-known in biological and naturalist circles, including Robert Bateman (renowned wildlife artist), Bruce Falls (ecologist, University of Toronto) and Bristol Foster (former director of the BC Provincial Museum and BC Ecological Reserves).[6] In the labs and collections of the ROM, Yorke was encouraged in his bird and mammal interests by James Baillie (see "The Grandfather Way", p. 41) and Stuart Thompson. Here were Yorke's origins as a wildlife biologist and museum man.

Yorke wrote a lot, even in those early days. His diaries and field notes are highly organized and filled with exquisite detail, augmented by sketches and photographs; the tone is serious and earnest. He was very clear that observing and understanding nature was his life. Several manuscripts, with titles such as "A Northland Lake," "Some Bark Lake Mammals" and "The Early Nester" (on the nesting behaviour of great horned owls), and even a poem titled "Northern Lake," were apparently rejected by magazine publishers.[7] But there were also successes. One of Yorke's first published articles, illustrated by Crosby, was a result of their intense birding activity. This lovely little piece,

* John A. Crosby (1925-2016) was a staff artist at the Canadian Museum of Natural Sciences (now the Canadian Museum of Nature). He painted the plates for the classic work *The Birds of Canada* by W. Earl Godfrey. He also illustrated the birds on Canadian banknotes circulating from 1986 to 2001.

entitled "Six Wood Warblers," was printed in 1942 in *Canadian Nature*.[8] The magazine's editor and museum staff who reviewed it were impressed.[9]

Blindness in one eye kept Yorke out of military service in the last years of World War II.[10] He spent this time improving his writing, exploring for birds and small mammals, working a couple of summers (1943–44) on the family farm in Agincourt and beginning university. He reminisced that "during the war, hawks and owls about airports lured many a naturalist, complete with spy equipment like binoculars, into the arms of security guards. With luck you got home for dinner, but somehow the experience left you convinced that you really were seriously different."[11]

Yorke's University of Toronto yearbook photo, 1948. Yorke is number 10.
From https://archive.org/details/torontonensis48univ/page/186.

From 1944 to 1948, Yorke studied forestry at the University of Toronto and received his bachelor of science in forestry in 1948. In the summers from 1945 to 1947, he studied small mammal populations for the Ontario Department of Lands and Forests in Algonquin Park. One of Yorke's most significant mentors was Doug Clarke, in charge of wildlife research and wildlife management in Ontario, who hired him for this summer work.* David Fowle, later a professor of biology at York University, was a leader of the student team and a lifelong friend.† While he was at university in 1946, Yorke was also a part-time preparator of vertebrate specimens at the ROM.

To British Columbia

On March 30, 1946, while he was studying in Toronto, Yorke attended a lecture by Ian McTaggart Cowan, from the University of British Columbia (UBC), on wildlife research in the Rocky Mountain National Parks.‡ Yorke was enthralled and

* C.H. Douglas Clarke (1909–1981) was a protegé of R.M. Anderson. He headed wildlife research and management for the Ontario Department of Lands and Forests, eventually becoming chief of the Fish and Wildlife Division. Clarke spoke and wrote extensively on wildlife, conservation and hunting.

† C. David Fowle (1920–1999), born and raised in British Columbia, was biologist-in-charge of wildlife research in the Ontario Department of Lands and Forests. He was a founding member of York University (1960) and first chair of the Biology Department. Edwards hired Fowle in the summer of 1961, mainly to prepare a biological survey of Mitlenatch Island, which had been designated a BC Provincial Nature Park that year.

‡ Ian McTaggart Cowan (1910–2010) was an internationally known wildlife biologist, ecologist, conservationist and educator. He was a biology curator at the BC Provincial Museum (1936–1940), zoology professor at the University of BC (1940–1964), head of the Zoology Department (1953–1964), and dean of Graduate Studies (1964–1975).

eagerly accepted Cowan's invitation in February 1948 to study with him in UBC's Department of Zoology.[12] Yorke arrived in BC that spring, and over the summer he worked on a BC Game Commission waterfowl nesting and banding survey in the Cariboo and Chilcotin regions. Cowan recommended Yorke to Cy Oldham, head of the Parks Division of the BC Forest Service, who hired him to undertake a biological survey of Manning Provincial Park in the summer of 1949, the year the Hope–Princeton Highway was completed.[13] Yorke's supervisor that summer was Chess Lyons, who became a close colleague over the years.[14] In 1950, while finishing his postgraduate studies, Yorke helped curate the UBC vertebrate museum.[§]

Yorke completed his master's degree in zoology in 1950 with a thesis titled "Variations in the Fur Productivity of Northern British Columbia in Relation to Some Environmental Factors."[15] The next year was a momentous one: he accepted a position with the BC Forest Service in Victoria and, on December 1, 1951, Yorke and Joan Thicke were married in Vancouver, Joan's home town.[¶] They had met in Toronto the year before while Joan was working as a microbiologist in the Connaught Medical Research Laboratories.[**]

Yorke's job was to head the newly formed research section of the Parks Division, and from 1951 to 1959 he began studies of wildlife and its management in BC parks. This consisted of

§ The museum was founded by Cowan in 1943 and is now the Cowan Tetrapod Collection of the Beaty Biodiversity Museum.

¶ Joan Claudia Thicke was born on October 18, 1922, in Vancouver. She earned a BA at the University of BC in 1944 and worked as a microbiologist in Vancouver until 1950, when she moved to Toronto. RYE noted in his diary for 1950: "Not a good winter, except met Joan Thicke."

** While at the Connaught Labs, Joan was the senior author on a paper examining the culture of the poliomyelitis virus in the *Canadian Journal of Medical Sciences* 30, no. 3 (1952): 231–45.

"wildlife research, preservation, harvesting, habitat manipulation, censusing, hunter controls, and publishing of popular and scientific articles."[16] Much of Yorke's work was concentrated in the wilds of Wells Gray Park, and his primary research focused on the effects of fire on moose and mountain caribou. His experimental use of controlled burning greatly improved moose habitat. Burning was a novel management tool then, and Yorke and his team often tangled with others in the Forest Service while trying to introduce such innovations.[17]

Some of Yorke's wildlife management papers, frequently written in conjunction with Ralph Ritcey and others, are minor classics, including works on carrying capacity,* aerial census techniques, the effects of snow on ungulate populations and specific studies on moose: herd migration, parasites and diseases, and mark-recapture studies.[18] Yorke's ground-breaking research on caribou in Wells Gray Park should be particularly relevant today, given the endangered status of the southern mountain herds in British Columbia: his investigations included studies of fire and population decline, use of lichens as food, migration, and landforms and distribution.[19] Not all studies were of ungulates; for example, a mark-recapture study of marten estimated range extent,[20] while the usefulness of censusing grizzly bears by measuring tracks was examined in Tweedsmuir Park.[21] Yorke also published on issues in general forestry and resource management, such as the interaction of wood production practices and wildlife management.[22] Such discussions evolved into essays on wilderness and conservation.[23]

* Carrying capacity is the population size a particular environment can sustain given the resources available.

Developing interpretation in parks and museums

Nineteen fifty-seven found Yorke championing a new cause: nature interpretation in parks. How he came to this isn't certain. He'd been thinking about nature interpretation at least since the late 1940s; perhaps it was the publication of *Interpreting Our Heritage* by Freeman Tilden that year that prompted him to act.† In any case, he later wryly noted that the job, in a sense, found him, rather than the other way around. After Yorke convinced Cy Oldham to try park interpretation in British Columbia's parks, Oldham turned the tables on him: "Edwards, you want it, so you do it. You have $300 for supplies and one summer student."[24] Yorke chose Manning Park for the pilot project. Bob Boyd, the chief ranger, who Yorke knew from his 1949 stint in Manning, was supportive of the new effort, but there was little extra money. Yorke scrounged a mildewed tent to go over a discarded tent floor and frame near the Pinewoods Lodge and public parking area. He hired Donald Smith, an Ontario graduate student (later professor of biology at Carleton University in Ottawa), to be the first park naturalist. Inside the tent, they made exhibits of rocks and flowers, bird pictures and beaver workings. A sign announcing "Nature House" hung over the door. Despite the fact that the place was frequently mistaken for a washroom, the park interpretation program flourished. A new building soon followed, and over the years the program expanded, bringing more nature houses, interpretive signs, nature trails and naturalist talks to most parts of the province.[25]

Yorke was ably assisted over the years by several full-time staff, including Ralph Ritcey, David Stirling and J.E. "Ted"

† Freeman Tilden (1883-1980) was a writer, naturalist and pioneer in the documentation of the principles and theories of heritage interpretation. His inspiring works on national parks in the United States are classics of the environmental literature.

Underhill. Underhill was hired as a Manning Park naturalist in 1958 and quickly became indispensable as an inventive interpretation specialist. He wrote much of the interpretive material on many subjects for many parks, but perhaps most importantly, he ran the Parks Branch Display Studio, where exhibits and signs were constructed. Yorke called him "a gem." Some of the well-known artists Yorke contracted to help produce displays and outdoor interpretive signs were Jean André (later to gain fame as the designer of many of the Royal BC Museum's permanent exhibits), Robert Bateman and John Crosby.

By the time Yorke left BC Parks in 1967, there were four nature houses and programs in nine parks; more came later. Yorke described the purpose of the program succinctly as "the enhancing of public understanding, care, and recreational enjoyment of the natural environments preserved in parks." Widely admired, the program set a standard for park education across the country. George Stirrett, the first chief park naturalist for the National Parks Branch (now Parks Canada),[26] frequently consulted with Yorke on interpretation matters. When visiting Miracle Beach Provincial Park in July 1962, Stirrett told Yorke that the new nature house and nature trails there were better than anything in the United States parks system.

Bill Merilees, a naturalist who had a long but intermittent (1960–1996) career in the BC Parks interpretation program and was a lifelong friend of Yorke, recalls:

> In the late 1950s and early 1960s the Parks Branch field operations were exclusively male. It was Yorke who broke this model by hiring Betty Westerborg (now Betty Brooks) to work at Miracle Beach as a park naturalist. This caused a considerable stir within the Branch but, in time, women became the prominent component of the interpretation program and they steadily increased

> their representation in all other spheres of parks operations.[27]

Yorke himself described a talk he gave to the Victoria College Biology Club in 1961: "The girls are campaigning for more field jobs and feel there is discrimination. I agree in principle."

Merilees also recounts another Yorke Edwards first:

> In the 1960s, a very spry, charismatic, youth-oriented senior citizen from Victoria by the name of Freeman King came to Yorke's attention. Regulations of that day prevented seniors from being employed in the Public Service. In Freeman's case, Yorke lobbied and received an exemption, whereby for many years thereafter, a special Order-in-Council was annually signed by the Lieutenant Governor permitting "Skipper," as he was better known, to delight visitors at Goldstream Park each summer.[28]

Yorke was already involved in the museum community in the early 1960s. He was active in the British Columbia Museums Association, founded in 1959 after the province's 1958 centennial inspired the creation of many new community museums. Yorke was elected president (1961–1963) and also edited its magazine, *Museum Roundup*, beginning in 1963. Over the years, and even while he worked in Ottawa with the Canadian Wildlife Service (CWS), he published numerous articles on museums and education in this journal. He was made an honorary member of the association in 1967. Thus, even while he worked for the Parks Branch, he influenced small museums across the province.

He was also influential in the organization of the burgeoning naturalist community in British Columbia. In November 1962, Yorke and David Stirling wrote a proposal for the establishment of the BC Nature Council, the forerunner of BC Nature (the Federation of British Columbia Naturalists), which represents and helps to coordinate the province's many naturalists clubs. Yorke was a founding member of the council, established in May 1963. In late 1964, when construction of the new provincial museum buildings was imminent and plans for new exhibits were required, museum director Clifford Carl turned to Yorke Edwards in the Parks Branch for help. In his diary Yorke noted: "Cliff Carl finally tells me he hopes I'll be on the staff of the new museum—as Curator of Exhibits. The situation is complicated since I now make as much as Cliff. Decisions!" Carl temporarily resolved the problem; he "suggested reviving the position of assistant director and offering it to Edwards in the understanding that he would head the Display Division. An official in the Department of Recreation and Conservation, which was responsible for both the museum and Parks, suggested that Parks loan Edwards to the museum on a part-time basis."[29] In the spring and summer of 1965, Yorke worked out a basic exhibit strategy, but after a few months he decided to return to his full-time BC Parks position.

The halcyon days of interpretation in BC Parks are now long gone. They lasted almost a decade after Yorke stepped down in 1967, but ended when budget cuts and regionalization of Parks programs in the mid-1970s eliminated the centralized organizational model of park interpretation. One telling outcome of this was the conversion of the nature house at Manning Park into a pub. In 1991, Yorke wryly wrote:

> Now the interpretation in Manning Park is different. The Nature House at Pinewoods, after many years of service revealing the unexpected details of the park, is not a nature house any more. But then, in a way it still is, for there is nothing more biological than beer, and I hear that my beautiful House, with

> the low eaves and the simple interior that I specified, is now a pub. As a lover of beer I can't really complain. And alcohol is the work of nature's yeasty workers turning sugar water into grog. Nature still reigns in the House.[30]

To Ottawa and the Canadian Wildlife Service

In the mid-1960s, David Munro, director of the Canadian Wildlife Service, became convinced that the wildlife management, research and conservation initiatives of his organization would be effective only to the degree that they were understood and supported by a broad range of Canadians. He envisioned a series of wildlife interpretation centres stretching from sea to sea, each explaining the distinctive life zone in which it was located. Munro asked Yorke to come to Ottawa and duplicate his provincial achievement on a national basis.[31] Yorke accepted, but agreed to stay for only five years. He recalled: "David dangled more bait than he knew. I was ready to experience again the northern hardwood region of my youth, with its scarlet tanagers and bloodroots, maple forests and winter redpolls. I also had a strong yen to know Canada better, coast to coast."[32]

From 1967 to 1972, Yorke worked on this new national vision.[33] He established a philosophical foundation for CWS interpretive programs, developed interpretation methods, planned the development of a series of wildlife centres and established the first one at Wye Marsh, a rich southern Ontario wetland. Budgets were sufficient to allow innovation, and interpretation at Wye Marsh stressed observation, with a floating boardwalk, an observation tower and an underwater window. The CWS mandate required an even-handed exploration of the management of lands and wildlife and the impact of humans on the landscape, as well as the usual natural history interpretation.[34] Yorke hired Bill Barkley,* who had once worked as a naturalist in BC Parks, to be in charge, and contracted his old friends Ted Underhill and Jean André to produce the centre's exhibits.

After Yorke's tenure, four more centres sprang up across Canada, from Bonaventure on the Gaspé Peninsula of Québec to Creston in the Kootenay region of British Columbia. Work on the transcontinental vision continued until the government changed with the 1984 federal election. Slashed budgets doomed the program; the headquarters and regional units and all five wildlife centres were closed. Some centres completely disappeared; others, such as Wye Marsh and Creston Valley, were repurposed through private/public partnerships.[35]

Returning to Victoria and the Provincial Museum

Yorke returned to Victoria in September 1972 to become the assistant director of the Provincial Museum, then led by Bristol Foster, Yorke's acquaintance from his youthful Royal Ontario Museum days. In early 1975, when Foster resigned to direct the new provincial Ecological Reserves Program, Yorke became director. His museum experience in Toronto, his biological background, his extensive involvement with exhibits and public education in both natural and human history, his work with the BC Museums Association—all prepared him for managing a major museum. Yorke was an experienced museologist who strongly believed in collections, research and "inspirational public programming."[36] He helped guide the development of many of the new building's early permanent exhibits. Speaking to

* Bill Barkley was an Edwards protegé, replacing him as head of CWS interpretation (1972–1977); he returned to BC as assistant director of the Provincial Museum under Edwards and was director from 1984 to 2001.

the Canadian Museums Association in 1976, Yorke emphasized that in producing exhibits, "the challenge is to turn scholarship into entertainment."[37] Under his tenure, which was fraught with periods of government-wide fiscal restraint and budget cuts, major exhibits such as the First Peoples gallery and the natural history gallery *Living Land, Living Sea* opened. Yorke was a writer, and he made sure the museum's publication program flourished. He stressed taking the museum to the province, too: travelling exhibits were a priority, and between 1976 and 1982 an average of six exhibitions visited 15 venues annually.[38]

Although he was a successful administrator of major government programs and a large museum, Yorke was happiest in the field, immersed in the natural world. Shortly after he retired in late 1984, he admitted to his old friend Ralph Ritcey: "Management jobs are a bit like a jail sentence, which I always suspected. I'm glad I avoided 'doing time' as long as I did."[39]

After his retirement, Yorke continued writing and working as a biological and museological consultant, and was designated a curator emeritus at the Royal British Columbia Museum (RBCM).[†] As a research associate, he usually spent one day each week in the mammal collections, mainly researching historical mammal-collecting expeditions that had been undertaken in BC by the provincial museum and other major North American museums. From field notes and published accounts he studied collection localities, calculating geographical coordinates for computer mapping. He made a significant contribution to the species range maps in the RBCM insectivore and rodent handbooks.[40]

Yorke suffered a serious stroke in May 1996. The cumulative effects of additional small strokes and the onset of dementia

† The museum's name was changed from the British Columbia Provincial Museum to the Royal British Columbia Museum on October 13, 1987, when Prince Philip, the Duke of Edinburgh, conferred the designation.

finally ended his writing career. His last major work was a chapter on British Columbia in *The Enduring Forest*, edited by his friend Ruth Kirk.[41] But his final publications date from 2003. He worked hard at the end—every one of the 12 issues of *The Victoria Naturalist* from 2001 through 2002 contains one of his articles. He died on August 16, 2011, aged 86.

Yorke's impact

Throughout his long career, Yorke presented hundreds of talks and speeches on many subjects to many audiences, from schoolchildren to scientific societies, from museum workers and naturalists clubs to politicians and seniors groups. His publication list includes over 400 entries and is impressive in scope. Some of his early writings and papers on wildlife and forestry are mentioned elsewhere in this biography, and many of those dealing with nature interpretation, parks and museums—which were perhaps his most influential—are the main subject of this book. He wrote extensively about research and science in museums.[42] He also wrote widely on his first love, birds: he savoured the complexities of gull identification; hawk migration was a fascination; and birding from the windows and patio of his home overlooking Juan de Fuca Strait was a favourite pastime in later years.[43] He recognized the value of writing for children and worked hard at it.[44] Naturalist newsletters and magazines, including BC Nature's *Cordillera*, which he helped to found, are full of his articles about people and the natural world, birds, ecology and multitudes of other topics. Yorke was a frequent contributor to the Royal BC Museum's newsletter, *Discovery*, with articles on subjects ranging from extinct caribou to the museum's native plant garden.[45] He wrote dozens of book reviews and forewords to books. And he wrote a few books of his own. Among them, *The Mountain Barrier* was a popular treatment of the ecology of the mountains of western Canada,[46] and *The Land Speaks* detailed Yorke's philosophy about nature interpretation and its implementation.[47]

Yorke served on the executive boards of many conservation and natural history organizations: the Nature Conservancy of Canada; Royal Canadian Geographical Society; Wildlife Society; Ottawa Field-Naturalists Club; Canadian Museums Association; Grants Committee of the Museum Assistance Program, National Museums of Canada; Canadian Nature Federation; *Owl* and *Chickadee* magazines; Council of Associate Museum Directors; BC Historic Sites Advisory Board; *Wildlife Review* magazine; *Nature Canada* magazine; BC Forest Museum (now the BC Forest Discovery Centre); Whale Museum (Sidney, BC); Federation of BC Naturalists Foundation; BC Government House Foundation. As a teenager he was president of the ROM's Intermediate Naturalists; later he was president of the BC Museums Association, the Victoria Natural History Society and the BC Forest Museum. He served as editor of the journals of the Canadian Society of Wildlife and Fishery Biologists and the BC Museums Association.

Yorke won many awards for his dedication to the understanding and preservation of Canadian nature, including the Interpretation Canada Award for Outstanding Achievement (1979) and Canada's 125th Year Medal. He was recognized for distinguished service to the Canadian Council on Ecological Areas (1989, 1991). Yorke was an elected member of the Brodie Club (Toronto, 1947) and a fellow of both the Royal Canadian Geographical Society (1984) and the Canadian Museums Association (1980). He was an honorary member of the BC Museums Association (1967) and the Ottawa Field-Naturalists (1980).

Just as Rudolph Anderson's advice to Yorke years earlier convinced him that biology could be his life, Yorke's counsel helped many others on their way, including me. Under his influence, I was a summer park naturalist in BC Parks, I worked at his wildlife centre at Wye Marsh, I inventoried the biological diversity of new parks and I was a curator at the Royal BC Museum. I tried to live Yorke's teachings.

My story is hardly unique. Hundreds of university students who worked as park naturalists in Canada during those years came away infused with his ideas. Today they are biologists, university professors, writers, artists, doctors, lawyers, teachers, parents. Thousands of others who visited parks, wildlife centres and museums, or who read his articles or heard his talks, came away with a bit of Yorke Edwards.

Despite Yorke's resigned cheerfulness on the news that his beloved Manning Park Nature House had been converted into a pub—"Nature still reigns in the House"—we shouldn't be fooled. For nearly 20 years, nature houses had been beacons of environmental education and inspiration, curiosity and wonder. Their loss must have come as a blow to the man whose legacy they should have been.

Such are the reminiscences of a former time. Today we inhabit a quite different world, a world in which breathtaking technological advance goes hand in hand with a deepening alienation from nature—what is sometimes called nature deficit disorder. There are some who say we are on a dead-end path—that we can't walk away from the living world without also putting our own collective future at tremendous risk. Perhaps they are right. What does seem clear is that the ponderings of Yorke Edwards have a role to play even today. Indeed, the need for naturalists and their vibrant experience of the living world has never been greater. Park naturalists in particular can play a crucial role in this age of disturbing, inexorable change. By simply being there each summer to inspire young people to a deeper attachment to nature, they can help a new generation find meaning in the world.

There are some who say it's time to bring nature interpretation back to British Columbia's parks. Perhaps they are right.

Robert A. Cannings is curator emeritus at the Royal BC Museum, where he was curator of entomology from 1980 to 2013 and managed the natural history section from 1987 to 1996. Earlier, he was a biologist and nature interpreter for BC Parks and the Canadian Wildlife Service. He earned a BSc and MSc from the University of British Columbia and a PhD from the University of Guelph. He is a fellow of Okanagan College and a recipient of the Bruce Naylor Award, which recognizes exceptional contributions to the study of museum-based natural history in Canada. On his retirement he received the Royal BC Museum's Lifetime Achievement Award.

Notes

1 RYE to Rudolph Anderson, January 9, 1944, photocopy in Cannings' collection.

2 Rudolph Anderson to RYE, January 31, 1944, photocopy in Cannings' collection.

3 Rudolph Anderson to RYE, December 8, 1942, photocopy in Cannings' collection.

4 Rudolph Anderson to RYE, October 25, 1944, photocopy in Cannings' collection. The first paper was R.Y. Edwards, "Notes on Two Captive Meadow Jumping Mice (*Zapus hudsonius*)," *Canadian Field-Naturalist* 59 (1945): 49–50.

5 RYE personal notes in the collection of Anne Wills.

6 Robert Cannings, "Yorke Edwards: A Natural Thinker," *Cordillera* 4, no. 1 (1997): 7–12; based on personal conversations between RYE and Cannings, 1997.

7 Photocopies of these manuscripts in Cannings' collection. A letter from A.R. Whittemore, publisher of *Canadian Nature*, to RYE, December 24,

1941, indicates a rejection of the owl paper. The poem, "Northern Lake," is reproduced on p. xv of this volume.

8 R.Y. Edwards, "Six Wood Warblers" (illustrations by J.A. Crosby), *Canadian Nature*, March/April 1942: 13–14. See p. 35 this volume.

9 A.R. Whittemore, publisher of *Canadian Nature*, to RYE, March 19, 1941, photocopy in Cannings' collection.

10 RYE to Rudolph Anderson, January 9, 1944, photocopy in Cannings' collection.

11 R.Y. Edwards, "Naturalists and Nature Interpretation" (talk given at the annual dinner of the McIlwraith Field Naturalists, London, ON, December 1, 1967); for complete text, see p. 139 this volume.

12 Ian McTaggart Cowan to RYE, February 11, 1948, photocopy in Cannings' collection.

13 R.Y. Edwards, "Some Early Finds and Follies," in *Reflections of the Past: Manning Park Memories* (Victoria, BC: Ministry of Lands and Parks, 1991), 45–47.

14 R.Y. Edwards, "Chester Peter Lyons," *Cordillera* 5, no. 1 (2000): 3–4.

15 Much of this work was later published: R.Y. Edwards and I. McT. Cowan, "The Fur Production of the Boreal Forest Region of British Columbia," *Journal of Wildlife Management* 21 (1957): 257–67.

16 Fragment of undated RYE *Curriculum Vitae*, photocopy in Cannings' collection.

17 R.A. Cannings, "Yorke Edwards: A Natural Thinker," *Cordillera* 4, no. 1 (1997): 7–12.

18 R.Y. Edwards and C.D. Fowle, "The Concept of Carrying Capacity," *Transactions of the North American Wildlife Conference* 20 (1955): 589–98; R.Y. Edwards, "Comparison of an Aerial and Ground Census of Moose," *Journal of Wildlife Management* 18, no. 3 (1954): 403–04; R.Y. Edwards, "Snow Depths and Ungulate Abundance in the Mountains of Western Canada," *Journal of Wildlife Management* 20 (1956): 159–68; R.Y. Edwards and R.W. Ritcey, "The Migrations of a Moose Herd," *Journal of Mammalogy* 37 (1956): 486–94; R.W. Ritcey and R.Y. Edwards, "Parasites and Diseases of the Wells Gray Moose Herd," *Journal of Mammalogy* 39 (1958): 139–45; R.W. Ritcey and R.Y. Edwards, "Trapping and Tagging Moose on Winter Range," *Journal of Wildlife Management* 20 (1956): 324–25.

19 R.Y. Edwards, "Fire and the Decline of a Mountain Caribou Herd," *Journal of Wildlife Management* 18 (1954): 521–26; R.Y. Edwards, J. Soos and R.W. Ritcey, "Quantitative Observations of Epidendric Lichens Used as Food by Caribou," *Ecology* 41 (1960): 425–31; R.Y. Edwards, "Migrations

of Caribou in a Mountainous Area of Wells Gray Park, British Columbia," *Canadian Field-Naturalist* 73 (1959): 21–25; R.Y. Edwards, "Landform and Caribou Distribution in British Columbia," *Journal of Mammalogy* 39 (1958): 408–12.

20 R.G. Miller, R.W. Ritcey and R.Y. Edwards, "Live-Trapping Marten in B.C.," *Murrelet* 36, no. 1 (1955): 1–8.

21 R.Y. Edwards and D.E. Green, "The Measurement of Tracks to Census Grizzly Bears," *Murrelet* 40 (1959): 14–16.

22 R.Y. Edwards, A.T. Cringan, C.D. Fowle, R.C. Passmore, A.J. Reeve and D.J. Robinson, "Forestry and Wildlife Management – Dual Endeavours on Forest Land," *Forestry Chronicle* 32 (1956): 433–43.

23 R.Y. Edwards, "The Preservation of Wildness," *Canadian Audubon* 29 (1967): 1–7; R.Y. Edwards, "Wilderness Parks: A Concept with Conflicts," in *Endangered Spaces*, ed. M. Hummel, 21–29 (Toronto: Key Porter, 1989).

24 R.Y. Edwards, "First Years of Park Interpretation in British Columbia," *Heritage Communication* 1, no. 2 (1987): 17–20. See p. 284 of this volume.

25 B. Merilees, "The Beginnings of Interpretation in BC's Parks," *British Columbia History* 47, no. 2 (2014): 16–22.

26 W.F. Lothian, Chapter 11, "Park Education and Interpretation," in *A History of Canada's National Parks*, vol. 4 (Ottawa: Parks Canada, 1987), http://parkscanadahistory.com/publications/history/lothian/eng/vol4/chap11.htm.

27 Bill Merilees, text of a tribute to Yorke, given at Yorke Edwards Day in Wells Gray Park, October 5, 2013, Upper Clearwater Community Hall, photocopy in Cannings' collection.

28 Ibid.

29 P.E. Roy, *The Collectors: A History of the Royal British Columbia Museum and Archives* (Victoria, BC: Royal British Columbia Museum, 2018), 197.

30 Edwards, "Some Early Finds and Follies," 45–47.

31 J.A. Burnett, "A Passion for Wildlife: A History of the Canadian Wildlife Service, 1947–1997," *Canadian Field-Naturalist* 113 (1999): 1–183.

32 Ibid.

33 R.Y. Edwards, "A Plan to Appreciate Canada," *Journal of Environmental Education* 3, no. 2 (1971): 11–13. See page p. 227 of this volume.

34 Burnett, "A Passion for Wildlife."

35 Ibid.

36 Roy, *The Collectors*, 328.

37 R.Y. Edwards, "Tomorrow's Museum," *Canadian Museum Association Gazette* 10, no. 1 (1977): 6–11.

38 Roy, *The Collectors*, 394.

39 RYE to Ralph Ritcey, July 12, 1985, photocopy in Cannings' collection.

40 David Nagorsen to Robert Cannings, July 25, 2019, email in Cannings' collection.

41 R.Y. Edwards, "British Columbia," in *The Enduring Forest*, ed. R. Kirk, 109–39 (Seattle, WA: The Mountaineers and the Mountaineers Foundation, 1996).

42 R.Y. Edwards, "Research: A Museum Cornerstone," in *Museum Collections: Their Roles and Future in Biological Research*, ed. E.H. Miller, 1–11 (Victoria, BC: BC Provincial Museum, 1985); R.Y. Edwards, "Science and Technology in Our Museums," in *Science and Technology in Canadian Museums: A Neglected Heritage. Proceedings of a Workshop Held March 19 and 20, 1987, Hotel de la Chaudière, Hull, P.Q.* (Ottawa: Canadian Museum of Nature, 1993), 2–11.

43 R.Y. Edwards, "Notes on the Gulls of Southwestern British Columbia, *Syesis* 1 (1969): 199–202; R.Y. Edwards, "Hawks Migrating Over Vancouver Island," *Cordillera* 1 (1994): 30–33; R.Y. Edwards, "Tropical Birds on McMicking Point," *The Victoria Naturalist* 48, no. 5 (1992):18–20.

44 R.Y. Edwards, "The Living Prairie," *The Young Naturalist* 12 (1970): 1–2.

45 R.Y. Edwards, "The Reindeer That Vanished Forever," *Discovery* (Friends of the Royal BC Museum newsletter) 21, no. 3 (1993): 7; R.Y. Edwards, "Your Live Exhibit, the Native Plant Gardens," *Discovery* 24, no. 3 (1995): 7.

46 R.Y. Edwards, *The Illustrated Natural History of Canada: The Mountain Barrier* (Toronto: N.S.L. Natural Science of Canada, 1970).

47 R.Y. Edwards, *The Land Speaks: Organizing and Running an Interpretation System* (Toronto: National and Provincial Parks Association, 1979).

Yorke Edwards: Interpretation, Inspiration and Love

Richard Kool

Mea culpa

Any reader of any book might rightfully ask the question of any author or editor, why did you do this? So let me confess at the outset: this book is my way of apologizing to Yorke Edwards for not having got to know him better when I could have done so.

I came to what was then the British Columbia Provincial Museum (now the Royal BC Museum) in January 1978, hired as a fresh-faced natural history teacher in the museum's Education Department. Yorke was the fifth director of the museum since its founding in 1886, and presented himself—to me at least—as a serious guy: brogues (described by Wikipedia as "a style of low-heeled shoe or boot traditionally characterised by multiple-piece, sturdy leather uppers with decorative perforations")[1], tweed jacket and tie. My experience of Yorke led me to feel him to be rather aloof in his nature, although I now know that, to many of his acquaintances, he was charming, humorous and warm-hearted. To me, his younger assistant director, Bill Barkley, was far more gregarious and approachable.

While I was aware that Yorke had been a major contributor to Canada's nature and cultural interpretation community, I felt that he hadn't published much in that field (and from the materials in this volume, you can see how much was published and how much written but not published). Even when his 1979 book, *The Land Speaks: Organizing and Running an Interpretation System*, came out, he just didn't make a strong impact on me. I don't know why that was, but it was probably related to my being a young guy at the start of a career while he was an older man near the end of his.

I left the museum in 1990, moved to the BC Ministry of Environment and completed doctoral studies that have allowed me to end my career as a professor at Royal Roads University. I never reconnected with Yorke after his retirement. In my files, however, were many pieces of his writing: handwritten lectures, typed speeches and illustrated plans for what nature houses might evolve into, dot-matrix manuscripts of things he never got around to publishing. As I matured, Yorke's writings seemed to mature with me, becoming more and more relevant and insightful as the years progressed. Every few years I'd think about this wonderful material and ponder what I could do with it. And every few years I'd talk with Rob Cannings about Yorke and his writings, and we would wonder what we might do together with them.

As I wrote earlier, I'm sorry that I didn't spend more time sitting with Yorke, perhaps sharing a drink or two, asking him about the early days of park and museum interpretation in Canada, about where his ideas came from, who his influences were or what his dreams were for the profession. It's too late for that now. But, along with Rob, I can help to bring his ideas about nature and cultural interpretation to a wider forum, where they can be seen by a new generation of interpreters and mined for the insights and wisdom they contain.*

Yorke Edwards and interpretation

For the English philosopher and mathematician Alfred North Whitehead, the rhythm of learning always began with what he called the Stage of Romance: we needed to fall in love with things, Whitehead contended, before we'd go on to learn the details of the topic. This second piece of the rhythm, the Stage of Precision, involved learning the details of the place, the person, the idea, the object. Romance, too, came before putting the object of our fascination into a larger context, what Whitehead called the Stage of Generalization. And from this third phase, we were ready to fall in love again. Whitehead's rhythm of learning, and the progression from romance to precision and generalization, played out in much of Yorke's life and reflects, I think, what interpretation meant to him.

While Yorke Edwards knew a lot about a lot of things, and knew how those myriad details could be incorporated into the "big picture," it is clear to me that, from a young age, Yorke was regularly falling in love with nature. From his earliest publication—written when he was 17 or so—you can feel his keen interest, his desire to hone his writing skills and his real love of the birds and mammals he wrote about. This fascination with

* I began writing this introduction on the ferry in early April 2019, going through Active Pass on the way to Vancouver and admiring the flocks of little Bonaparte's gulls that hang around the passage this time of year. Yorke made many ferry trips and kept detailed records of the birds he saw, and I know the flocks of those attractive swept-winged gulls would have been much, much larger than the ones I saw today. And another necessary apology to Yorke: he loved birds, while I am rather indifferent to vertebrates in general.

living things, the romance he felt for animals as a teenager, led to a love affair with the places animals lived, the landscapes that he wandered through, and the way of life of an evangelist advocating for the natural world and its wonderful creatures and processes.

I can only imagine that every naturalist who ever walked the face of the Earth has also shared Yorke's romance with nature. While not everyone would have investigated the details nor integrated the total picture like he did, romance is what all of those who see themselves as naturalists share. I'm sure that those who don't share our bent can find naturalist-types insufferable at times, always pointing out birds, bees, plants and other biota—biota that the "normal" person might have not a bit of interest in. But Yorke took this romance one step further—one organizational step further; he helped to create a movement, and then a profession, meant to help others fall in love with things, be they organisms, landscapes, histories or peoples.

Yorke Edwards, Freeman King and Steve Cannings, BC Nature Council meeting, Fairview, BC, May 1964. Robert A. Cannings photo.

I wish I could find the smoking gun—the document that Yorke wrote that describes his "aha" moment when, working for BC Parks, the idea came to him that parks were for more than conservation, more than places for nature to hide from humans. The best I can do is quote from his 1965 paper "What Is Interpretation?," where he wrote:

> The first time that I had thoughts like these was in 1949, and I had them in Manning Park.
>
> It bothered me that Manning Park seemed to have nothing as a major attraction that could not be found bigger and better in other places nearby...
>
> So in 1949, I made my first recommendation that there be interpretation in our parks. In 1957, eight years later, we were allowed to give it a cautious try.[2]

Yorke realized that if there was going to be public support for natural areas, citizens needed to feel, at least to a small degree, the same kind of romance he felt for those places. And if they didn't have the inclination that made naturalists do what they did, why not help those poor souls at least get a small taste of the impetus that drove naturalists to stand in the rain for hours waiting for something interesting to show up.

So in the 1950s, Yorke conceptualized and created park interpretation in Canada. Through the mid-1970s, people like Bill Barkley and Bob Peart (both with the Canadian Wildlife Service) and John Woods (Parks Canada), working with the newly created organization Interpretation Canada, considered and then promoted a definition of interpretation that grew pretty directly from Yorke's initial inspiration: "Interpretation is any communication process designed to reveal meanings and relationships of cultural and natural heritage to the public, through first-hand involvement with an object, artifact, landscape or site."[3] This is the definition that Interpretation Canada still has on its website more than 40 years after its creation, a strong testament to those who worked to craft it, and indeed to Yorke himself, who expressed the matter in very similar terms in the first issue of *The Journal of Interpretation* in 1977 (see p. 247, this volume): "[Interpretation] is attractive communication, offering concise information, given in the presence of the topic, and its goal is the revelation of significance."

In spite of these early and important contributions, Yorke just doesn't show up in current texts dealing with what is now called *heritage interpretation* (and that term has its critics).* The American naturalist Freeman Tilden published his book *Interpreting Our Heritage* in 1957, and this, no doubt, was the approach that Yorke was looking for and inspired by, even though he had had these ideas as much as eight years earlier. Though he wrote a modest amount about interpretation, spoke a lot about interpretation and published a small but important book in 1979, the field of interpretation seems to have lost track of Yorke. When I searched for "heritage interpretation" and "Yorke Edwards" on Google in April 2019, I found 43 hits; when I put "Freeman Tilden" in the search, I had more than 6,500 hits. Canadians often take a back seat when compared to American efforts, but I'd wager that even most Canadian interpreters are not aware of Yorke's seminal role in the creation of their profession.

* I'm pretty sure Yorke would *not* have agreed with this Wikipedia entry on "heritage interpretation": "Heritage interpretation refers to all the ways in which information is communicated to visitors to an educational, natural or recreational site, such as a museum, park or science centre. More specifically it is the communication of information about, or the explanation of, the nature, origin, and purpose of historical, natural, or cultural resources, objects, sites and phenomena using personal or non-personal methods." Wikipedia, s.v. "Heritage Interpretation," last edited February 11, 2020, https://en.wikipedia.org/wiki/Heritage_Interpretation.

Freeman "Skipper" King, then in his 80s, in Goldstream Park, 1972.
Photo used with permission of BC Parks.

Yorke's writings on interpretation, what it is and how it should be carried out, are clear, direct and still very relevant more than half a century after he put pen to paper. While Yorke had a range of ideas as to what interpretation should be, I get the feeling, when reading these unpublished or marginally published writings, as to what he saw as the core of the interpreter's work, and what attribute above all else he looked for when he was hiring one.

As I read through Yorke's papers and manuscripts, it was very clear to me that what Yorke valued the most in his interpreters was that they were able to *inspire* others to fall in love with nature. The concept of *inspiration*,[4] it seems to me, is at the core of his thinking and practice, and he mentions it very early on in his writing. In his 1962 paper on interpretation in BC Parks, Yorke says:

> One of the best [interpreters] that I have met (and recently hired) is a 70-year-old man who knows little about many fields of natural history, and in several

> fields, I admit that he is a goldmine of misinformation. But he has one glorious attribute that more than makes up for his short-comings as an encyclopedia, and *this is his ability to inspire people* into becoming permanently and actively interested in natural history. There can be no greater attribute in an interpreter than *an infectious enthusiasm*.* [italics added]

The work of the interpreter is to be an *enthusiastic purveyor of inspiration*. I love that idea. Yorke wrote: "Remember the five words I used, that interpretation 'shows, orients, informs, inspires, entertains.'" These are words that appear often in this volume: *inspires* (43 mentions including inspiration), *entertains* (26 mentions), *shows* (20 mentions), *orients* (15 mentions), and *informs* (5 mentions). *Enthusiasm*, the adjective that needs to go along with all of these attributes, shows up around 20 times; indeed, Yorke's successor at BC Parks, Kerry Joy, wrote in 1970 in a report about visiting the Wye Marsh Wildlife Centre that Yorke had recently opened in Midland, ON, "an interpreter without enthusiasm is like stale, warm beer." Yorke himself wrote in 1964: "Give me these things—know-how and enthusiasm—and I'll hire him even if he has two heads, if he can also get what he knows across to other people."

* This is a reference to Freeman "Skipper" King, who led a group of children in natural history activities in the Victoria, BC, area in the 1960s and '70s. Among these "Skipper's kids" are Nancy Turner (*née* Chapman), Canada's foremost ethnobotanist and a University of Victoria professor, and her late sister Barbara; Bob Turner, noted BC historian and author; Ross McMillan, environmental advocate and lead on the creation of the UNESCO Clayoquot Biosphere Reserve; Andrew Harcombe, retired manager of the BC Ministry of Environment's Conservation Data Centre; Genevieve Singleton, active in bringing bluebirds back to the Cowichan Valley; Carol Berryman, well-known park naturalist in Victoria; and David Gray, arctic researcher, muskox expert and former curator of mammals at the Canadian Museum of Nature. Many of these people worked as naturalists and interpreters in BC Parks in their younger days.

Yorke Edwards (right) and Freeman Tilden (then 87 years old), April 1970, Wye Marsh Wildlife Centre, Midland, Ontario.
Used with permission from the Wye Marsh Nature Centre.

Enthusiastically inspiring people to care

As we enter the Anthropocene Epoch,[5] with its "sixth mass extinction,"[6] transgression of planetary boundaries,[7] climate crisis,[8] and disruption of entire ecosystems,[9] the work that Yorke began—enthusiastically inspiring people to care for the natural world—is more urgent than ever.

I've long felt that the work of teachers is to reveal things that are hidden, while remaining open to revelation themselves. An interpreter is likely no different; Yorke frequently talks about the work of an interpreter being to reveal things to visitors, and inspiring visitors to care for the world and the places and creatures in it. The great medieval Catholic scholar St. Thomas Aquinas wrote that we know things better through love than through knowledge, and while Yorke never used the word *love* in his writings, that is clearly what he was looking for in the interpreters he hired, and what he expected his interpreters to inspire, enthusiastically, in others.

The field of interpretation needs the kind of inspiration Yorke speaks of in these writings And interpreters, with that inspiration, can be charged to inspire those who attend our programs, exhibits and events to love the world, its inhabitants, its creations and products. Yorke's writing makes it clear that he is very much a man with a message for our time too.

We've arranged this book pretty much chronologically, from Yorke's time in BC Parks, then to his work in Ottawa with the Canadian Wildlife Service, before we finally return to Victoria and the BC Provincial Museum. But for a fuller picture, we've included two essays that help to further contextualize Yorke and his thinking. The first is a little essay, "Six Wood Warblers," he wrote as a teenager and published in *Canadian Nature* magazine. The second is a piece from the early 1970s, where he talks about the impact of the Royal Ontario Museum and one of its curators on his life.

Richard Kool worked at the BC Provincial Museum/Royal BC Museum from 1978 to 1991, first as a natural history teacher and then as chief of Public Program Development. While at the museum he also organized and catalogued the dormant palaeontological collection and curated the collection of biological illustrations. He is a professor in the School of Environment and Sustainability at Royal Roads University, where he founded the MA program in Environmental Education and Communication.

Notes

1 Wikipedia, s.v. "Brogue shoe," last modified August 10, 2020, https://en.wikipedia.org/wiki/Brogue_shoe.

2 R.Y. Edwards. "What Is Interpretation?" (paper presented at the BC Parks Training School, Manning Park, BC, 1965).

3 B. Peart, "The Definition of Interpretation" (paper presented at workshop of the Association of Interpretive Naturalists, College Station, TX, 1977).

4 J. Gilson and R. Kool, "The Place of Inspiration in Heritage Interpretation: A Conceptual Analysis," *Journal of Interpretation Research, 24*, no. 1 (2019): 27–48.

5 W. Steffen, J. Grinevald, P.J. Crutzen and J.R. McNeill, "The Anthropocene: Conceptual and Historical Perspectives," *Philosophical Transactions of the Royal Society A* 369, no. 1938 (March 13, 2011): 842–67, https://doi.org/10.1098/rsta.2010.0327.

6 G. Ceballos, P.R. Ehrlich, A.D. Barnosky, A. García, R.M. Pringle and T.M. Palmer, "Accelerated Modern Human-Induced Species Losses: Entering the Sixth Mass Extinction," *Science Advances* 1, no. 5 (2015): 1–5, https://doi.org/10.1126/sciadv.1400253.

7 W. Steffen, K. Richardson, J. Rockström, S.E. Cornell, I. Fetzer, E.M. Bennett, R. Biggs, et·al., "Planetary Boundaries: Guiding Human Development on a Changing Planet," *Science* 347, no. 6223 (2015): 736–46, https://doi.org/10.1126/science.1259855.

8 Intergovernmental Panel on Climate Change, *Global Warming of 1.5°C: An IPCC Special Report on the Impacts of Global Warming of 1.5°C above Pre-Industrial Levels and Related Global Greenhouse Gas Emission Pathways, in the Context of Strengthening the Global Response to the Threat of Climate Change, Sustainable Development, and Efforts to Eradicate Poverty*, ed. V. Masson-Delmotte, P. Zhai, H.-O. Pörtner, D. Roberts, J. Skea, P.R. Shukla, A. Pirani, et al. (Geneva: World Meteorological Organization, 2018).

9 C.H. Trisos, C. Merow and A.L. Pigot, "The Projected Timing of Abrupt Ecological Disruption from Climate Change," *Nature* 580 (2020): 496–501, https://doi.org/10.1038/s41586-020-2189-9.

Yorke Edwards, 1940. Edwards family photo.

Six Wood Warblers (1942)

Canadian Nature (March-April 1942): 41–42. Reprinted with permission.

York Edwards
Illustrations by J.A. Crosby

WHEN THE NEW-BORN LEAVES HANG as a delicate green mist about the branches of their parent trees, and the first violets are showing their shy faces to the sun for the first time, one may begin to look for the Wood Warblers. They come in groups often containing many species, migrating by night and settling in the trees wherever dawn over-takes them. To be in the midst of one of these groups, just as the red sun appears over the eastern horizon, is an experience not easily forgotten. At this time of day, the gorgeous birds, their bright colours enhanced by the ruddy sun, are tiny glowing jewels whose activity never seems to cease.

There are many species of warblers which might be found in such a group, some of which would be difficult to identify. Pictured here are six common species that you are sure to meet and that are easily recognized.

Wood Warblers (from left to right, top to bottom)

Redstart
Black-throated Green Warbler
Black and White Warbler
Blackburnian Warbler
Yellow Warbler
Myrtle Warbler

In the tip-tops of a group of aspens gathered densely about the brink of a small stream, are the favorite haunts of the Redstart. There it flits from limb to limb, at times interrupting its search in the trees to sally out after the insects that hover over the stream in the heat of the warming sun.

In the dense hemlocks that march solemnly up the side of the ravine, the Black-throated Green Warbler gleans his food. There from the emerald depths, if a group of them is present, gleam the many yellow cheeks of this species, forever in ceaseless motion, reminding one of fireflies dancing in the gloom of a dark night.

The Black and White Warbler is unmistakable. These little birds are often found abundantly in the May woods, where they invariably are seen creeping on the limbs or trunks of trees, their smartly contrasting plumage standing out from the brown bark, though not so much as one would expect from such a distinctly marked bird.

The Blackburnian Warbler is startlingly beautiful. His breast is a vivid flame-colour, which, when seen in the red rays of a rising sun, turns to the glowing reddish-orange of a live coal. Against any neutral background the effect is breathtaking, but when glimpsed amongst evergreens, its intensity seems doubled. Your first view of a male Blackburnian will always be among your fondest memories.

One of the commonest of all this family is the Yellow Warbler. He frequents the low trees and bushes that usually border upon unkept fields and pastures, where the sun beams down unobstructed on his bright yellow plumage. Such a colour was never meant for the dark forest, for there so bright a gleam of sunlight would be entirely out of place and spoil the solemn effect of the deep wood. This glowing yellow was meant to be always in the sunlight, and usually is, for throughout most of the day, this bird sings from the top of his beloved bush, where

Yorke Edwards and "Doc" Ritchie, Cedar Woods, Ontario, September 1944. Robert C. Ritchie went on to become a pathologist at the Banting Institute in Toronto and was an active birder and member of the Brodie Club. Edwards family photo.

the sun shines down in all its brilliance. The Myrtle Warbler prefers the bushes that grow in the black muck of small bogs, where he finds an abundance of insects on the shrubs or, failing this, feeds on those that hang on rapidly beating wings over the low trees or shrubs, or fly erratically over the stagnant water.

Pictured on these pages are six warblers only. In a favourable location after a large movement of migrants has taken place the night before, one may obtain as many as twenty species or more. When May returns to Canada, go to a promising open wood and find some of the birds that so resemble butterflies in their colour. It's a fascinating game.

Editor's Note: York Edwards and John A. Crosby are both Toronto high school students, typical of many other enthusiastic "teen-aged lads" who delight in the healthy environment of field and woodland. Their work, however, is exceptional in its beauty and promise.

The Brodie Club, Toronto, late 1948. Yorke is in the middle of the second-to-last row. According to their website, "the Brodie Club is a group of serious and knowledgeable naturalists who enjoy lively discussion, penetrating questions and good fellowship. The club's name honours Dr. William Brodie, one of the greatest all-round naturalists in Canada of his time." Reprinted with permission, Royal Ontario Museum Archives, SC 20 Brodie Club fonds.

The Grandfather Way (1973)

First published in *Museum Roundup* (the magazine of the British Columbia Museums Association) 51 (1973): 50–52. Reprinted with permission.

THE LARGER THE MUSEUM, THE more out of touch with people. Like all sweeping statements, this one has exceptions, but in my experience it is largely true. The problem is as old as man and as big as the population explosion. There is quality and there is quantity, and almost always you can have one or the other, but not both.

The museum is partly a communication system, "talking" to the people through displays and publications, as well as through employees and volunteers. And as always, the best kind of communication is to experience something real with a real live communicator. This is best of all when the relationship is one to one. When I worked in park interpretation, we always felt that the children were short-changed because we could afford no special program for them. And when we day-dreamed about having the best, we wondered if we could find a spry old grandfather who would give us top quality interpretation, in a small way, by taking a child by the hand, just once a day, to lead him into a world of wonder and beauty that he might otherwise never see.

Just one child a day. And who can deny that this small part of a large interpretation program would be, in the long run, the most important part of all. Read Robert Ruark's *The Old Man and the Boy* to get some insight into what I mean.

We museum people love to play the numbers game. The more people through the door the better. And if we can get children coming in school bus bunches—to be more easily processed as bunches—that is better too. But I do not entirely believe it. I agree that museums are for people, and that museums should be for children too, but the numbers game in museums, as in many other places, is a sure way to mediocre service. Serving the public in ever larger volumes seems to be the fate of the democratic way, so for now, at least, most museums seem to be stuck with it. But this does not make the hand-in-hand approach any less important, nor any less attainable. We can have both. I regard the high-quality approach as something we cannot afford to be without.

Museums can be a major force in shaping the lives of young people. I know, because I was shaped. My shaping was not done while I was one of a herd, it was done man to boy.

Early in high school years in Toronto I discovered the museum which in those ancient times was the Royal Ontario Museum and in the new days probably still is. I went there often—as I recall perhaps too often, for looking back I suspect that I was underfoot a lot. But everyone was kind and patient and perhaps I was shy enough about the high status of my museum heroes that my visits were not too long.

My invasion of ROM, and its invasion of me, were piecemeal processes. At first the public galleries were the sole attraction. I devoured again and again the natural history exhibits, and some of my favourites of those times are even now etched into my mind. I remember a diorama with black bears and another with extinct passenger pigeons that were the most wonderful man-made things I had ever seen. And they were pretty good, as I know now after seeing many dioramas. In those days not many Canadian cities had a diorama to show, and those two at the ROM just might have been the two best in the country.

There were also smaller exhibits that I can see quite clearly through the years. They were simple, beautifully conceived communication. One especially good one was mostly a pyramid of blocks. On the small top block was a hawk. Around this top one, on the block below, were several snakes. On the progressively larger blocks down were frogs, then insects, and finally grass. "This is the hawk that eats the snakes that eat the frogs that eat the insects that eat the grass that grows in the earth around us." It went something like that anyway. And through my years as a biologist, that display was my mind-picture of two important concepts essential to understanding the world. One is that all flesh is grass. The other is that there are good and logical reasons why there must be fewer hawks than snakes, fewer snakes than frogs, and so on down the food chain.

In the public gallery I soon made friends. Security guards and the sales lady in the museum shop saw me so much that their curiosity prodded them into speaking to me. Through them I began to suspect that behind the closed doors was the real museum. Perhaps a year later, being increasingly active as a birdwatcher, I was meeting other bird addicts in the wilder fringes of Toronto, and one of them I found to my joy worked at the ROM. Jim Baillie was Toronto's top robin in the bird-chasing set, and his office at the museum became my entrance into mysterious backrooms and storage areas that were the heart of the museum.* At times these places smelled of mothballs and over-ripe specimens and tobacco from over-ripe pipes, but it was all perfume to me. Here I found the latest gossip on people and birds, here was news of the latest books, here were specimens with which to solve biological mysteries, and nearby was the room filled with duplicate publications that became my treasure-house.

I had just discovered the scientific literature and had begun to assemble a mushrooming hoard of books and papers. Several private libraries had just come to the ROM, and these were rich in zoological duplicates that were stored in a small room. This treasure was mine for the buying, and Jim Baillie sold it to me and my friends in heaps for something like ten cents an inch. Not all the treasure salvaged in this way has proven useful. Some day people going over my library—I hope my duplicates can be put in a treasure room available to kids—will come on learned papers with titles like "Three New Species of Earthworm from Sumatra" and "A New Mouse from the Gobi Desert," and they will wonder about my world-wide interests. But it is all very simple. When you are buying literature, much of it very thin, by the inch, just before going for official measurement you grab anything, on a gamble, to bring your pile up to the last exact inch. Jim only charged 10 cents an inch (or was it 25 cents?) but in those days a dime was a lot of money, so you took full measure.

* "For nearly 50 years Jim Baillie worked as Assistant Curator in the Ornithology Department of the Royal Ontario Museum. Although not formally educated in ornithology, his knowledge of birds was unsurpassed. Jim Baillie had the ability to share his knowledge with thousands of people, amateurs and professionals alike, through newspaper columns, scientific publications and informal conversations with countless visitors to his museum office." "James L. Baillie Memorial Fund," Bird Studies Canada, accessed 2015, https://www.birdscanada.org/about/funding/jlbmf/ (site no longer accessible).–Eds.

Jim Baillie with a great auk (extinct since 1844).

Courtesy of the Royal Ontario Museum, © ROM.

Many a museum-struck kid hangs about so much that in desperation someone gives him work to do. This will, so the theory goes, either get rid of him or make him useful. So I eventually found myself working at the ROM. My first job was to boil up an agouti (a hare-sized South American rodent) so I could clean and save the skeleton. Next came a half dozen caribou heads from The Pas. A few weeks inhaling rich fumes from these over-aged specimens proved convincingly that museum work was not all glamour and excitement. And for a long time after I had trouble showing much enthusiasm about stew, either the museum kind or the kitchen kind.

Looking back, I consider myself fortunate to have grown up in a city that had a museum with time for museum-struck kids. I was not the only minor soaking up atmosphere there, and some of us, once our voices changed, were invited to join the slightly exclusive museum-oriented Brodie Club. This enlarged our worlds still more as we rubbed shoulders with the city leaders in natural science. In many ways that museum enriched our days and changed the course of many of our lives. I sometimes wonder if any of its other accomplishments were as important.

Now museums in big cities are not so easy to penetrate. People learn about museums in crowds while processed by programmed guides or sometimes by electronic machines. It is all very organized and it can be impressively informative, but there can be something cold and impersonal and even think-speak about it all. At the ROM I felt that I belonged. In this world of too many people that we talk at with mass communication, there is not much that is warm and human that we can put into the process. I am sure that all our public communication does not have to be that way. We have been brainwashed into thinking we must treat everyone the same. With a little planning we should let the mass production programs roll on, while leaving some time and money for some individual human beings.

I still believe that it would be uncommonly successful to have a kindly grandfather leading children one by one into the green world of parks. And I have no doubt that it would work in museums just as well, for Jim Baillie once showed me that it can be done.

Nature House, Manning Provincial Park, 1957.

Photos used with permission of BC Parks.

Yorke (on right) and colleague, Wells Gray Mountain, Tweedsmuir Provincial Park, 1957.
Photo by Chess Lyons. Edwards family photo.

Parks Branch

BC Department of Recreation and Conservation

Yorke arrived in British Columbia in 1948 to begin his master's degree with Ian McTaggart Cowan at UBC. In 1951, he was hired as a research officer in the BC Forest Service, and it was then that his long relationship with the BC government and BC's provincial parks began.

Annual Report 1957

An initial venture in the field of park interpretation with a nature house in Manning Park was very successful. The nature house had 13,000 visitors in July and August. This first nature house, of humble origin, was housed in a tent. Readily available wild species of plants and animals were shown, and public appreciation indicated a need for expansion of this type of educational facility.

Interpretation in British Columbia's Provincial Parks (1962)

Paper presented to the Third Annual Naturalist Workshop and Training Course of the National Parks Branch, Banff, AB, June 9, 1962.

THIS TALK WAS GIVEN IN SIX PARTS AS FOLLOWS:

I. What the park user sees—A general orientation

A superficial treatment of the interpretation program in the provincial parks of British Columbia, under the headings of

- Park Naturalists
- Nature Houses and their exhibits
- Nature Trails
- Interpretive signs
- Guided walks
- Printed field aids

These topics were illustrated where possible by slides and other materials, such as trail cards, printed pamphlets, etc.

II. Some thoughts for interpreters

A nature interpretation program is one of the most complicated things imaginable if it is broad in scope and uses a number of techniques to deliver its messages to the public. It is so complicated that I am sure that there never will be a really adequate nature interpretation program. The complete program would be too vast to even outline adequately here. But as a partial outline, let me offer the following. There should be a complete and accurate knowledge of most parts of botany, zoology, anthropology, local history, ecology, meteorology and geology. But accurate and detailed knowledge of these is not enough. There must be present an ability to give these facts to people who know little or nothing about them, being at the same time simple and accurate while using few words, and using everyday words. In short, we are describing an interpreter who knows all about everything in the natural sciences, and in spite of his knowledge and of his job to pass on this knowledge, he would never appear to be an intellectual. There will never be the perfect park interpreter, but there is, I think, merit in having an ideal before us.

Sometimes, however, I think that the description just given portrays a deadly dull interpreter. The character that I have just described is a walking encyclopedia with the knack of being one of the crowd. This superman would do fairly well as an interpreter, but I am sure that I have seen better interpreters than he would be. One of the best that I have met (and recently hired) is a 70-year-old man who knows little about many fields of natural history, and in several fields, I admit that he is a goldmine of misinformation. But he has one glorious attribute that more than makes up for his short-comings as an encyclopedia, and this is his ability to inspire people into becoming permanently and actively interested in natural history. There can be no greater attribute in an interpreter than an infectious enthusiasm.

Five years ago I used to look for supermen when I hired people. This was my only yardstick. Now I have two yardsticks, one of them new and labelled "enthusiasm." I use this new one more and more, and the old one less and less. No one ever measured very long on the old yardstick anyway. As long as there was a measurement at all, the person was a reasonably good naturalist, and if he had enthusiasm, intelligence and some background, there was enough ability, or potential ability, to do a good job.

Not every interpreter would agree with what I have been saying. Whether you do, or do not, depends on what you think interpretation is. In such a complex field there are bound to be many viewpoints on what interpretation is. I believe (and this is a definition of sorts) that interpretation deals with things in meaningful surroundings; that its purpose is to give to the public understanding, inspiration and, as [Freeman] Tilden says, revelation with respect to these things and their surroundings; and that the tools of the interpreter are facts and sometimes useful fictions communicated skilfully to produce the desired purpose.

I find in interpreters far more variation in their skill in communication than I do in their store of useful facts and fictions. It is easy to bore the layman with science. Facts are nothing new to him. He is in a blizzard of them every day from newspapers, signs, books, radios, television, night classes, movies, leaflets, fairs, labels, etc. etc.—a deluge. Often the facts of science are beyond the layman's understanding, and he needs partial truths, watered down perhaps, and told to him in a way that relates them to the world he knows and understands. Being a specialist of some kind can be a real handicap when talking to the uninformed. It can be an almost impossible task for the scientist to get down to the other man's level. The specialist is full of his jargon to begin with, and full of details and exceptions and fine accuracies that are unnecessary to anyone but the specialist. Scientists can be the world's worst interpreters. For the same reason, the university student in science can have real trouble talking to people in plain, understandable English. This is a serious matter, for after all it is quite important for the interpreter to be understood.

For what must be the world's newest and greatest example of a fabulous failure in making facts understandable to the public, I recommend the Science Pavilion at Seattle's World's Fair.* This large display cost $9.5 million. Most films in this collection do a very good job, because I suspect that the scientists, of necessity, called in people skilled at taking and editing movies. The other exhibits look expensive, represent much well-meaning effort, but in my opinion they fail. The handbook says that scientists were in charge of making these exhibits. From the exhibits this is obvious. The scientists really knew their fields, I am sure, but they have spent their lives talking to fellow scientists. Most exhibits should have stayed in the scientific journals that they came from. To the average visitor, hurried for there is much to be seen, his feet aching, perhaps with an impatient child in tow, I'm sure that most exhibits remained mysteries. I found them frustrating and eventually irritating. There is far too much detail, too much jargon, too much taken for granted as already known, and often, crime of crimes, there

* This world's fair, also called the Century 21 Exposition, ran from April to October 1962 in Seattle, WA.–Eds.

was no indication of where to start, then how to get to the end—and here I am talking of both the feet and the eyes. I have eight years of university science, and I was frustrated. Imagine what most people got out of it.

The most difficult thing that interpreters must learn is to be simple. Remember that a confused audience is a lost audience (these people are not with you to work hard mentally, and you have no right to expect them to do so), and that most things can be said simply if the speaker (or writer) really knows what he is talking about.

An interpreter must learn to be simple in another way. I find that most of my people tend to interpret the spectacular acres of alpine flowers, grizzly bears, 500-year-old trees. These are relatively easy to interpret, and of course should be interpreted. But I have to remind them repeatedly that there is equal fascination to be found in a leaf, in a pebble, in sand, in a bird's song, in a breeze, in a bit of cloud. These, after all, are the important things, because they are the common things. Interpretation should always have more to say about everyday things than about the unusual.

I've rambled considerably in this rather serious talk, but my purpose was to give you a rough idea of how I think, so you will then be able to understand, better, the program that I direct. Without your being aware of it, I have told you why our exhibits are like they are, why our nature trail signs take the form that they do, and other things, including why, to date, we do not show films. I have given a scanty background of what I believe to be best in interpretation. In this respect, my ideas are always open to change, and they do change. Interpretation is largely a creative endeavour, and there are no rules that anyone can prove are right or wrong. We must have theories; in BC we have tried a few, and with trial and error—many errors—we have evolved principles, or accepted stolen principles, that seem to work. Most are probably at least second rate to another way yet to be thought of. We are careful never to be satisfied, always to search for better ways. Now previously we looked quickly at our program on slides. Let us look more closely at some details on some more slides.

III. A more detailed look, and some principles

Mainly slides, but some signs, pamphlets, etc., illustrating our program.

A. Nature Houses: Tents are the rule initially, with a small permanent building built later. These are nature centres, not museums, for no provision is made for extensive collections.

B. Exhibits:
- Some exhibits used up to 1961, with brief comments on what they were meant to do.
- Some early exhibits that were failures, and why.
- The evolution of two exhibits from 1957 to 1961.

It is policy to try to change or replace every exhibit every year.

C. Nature Trails:
- Our kinds of cards
- Trail "furniture"
- Holders for cards
- Examples of cards, and principles used that govern their content

D. Large Signs:
- The use of large outdoor signs.

E. Nature Walks:

- These are our newest endeavour, and we have little experience yet.
- We think we will favour "stop walks" in some parks.*

F. Printed Matter:

- We are only newly into this field. Our policy is to publish two new pieces a year. To date we have two series (1) Checklists and (2) Aids to identification, which do not necessarily attempt to cover all species in the park. Examples were shown.

IV. Office and shop

A short series of slides with comments dealing with the planning of exhibits, the manufacture of exhibits and painted signs, and the printing of cards for nature trails.

A program such as ours must have a good, well-equipped workshop, and must have in it a magician who understands shop work, art and composition, and nature, as well as the more dignified tricks of the huckster to give the message impact.

Our shop is the foundation of much of our program.

V. Interpretation of history

A few slides and brief comments on our work with history. To date it has two foci: the restoration of Barkerville, and a large series of cast aluminum signs at places of historic interest along our highways.

* Stop walks are nature walks punctuated by stops where the leader discusses particular points and answers questions.–Eds.

VI. Last words

When I put a new interpreter in a park, I am tempted to pour out hours of detailed advice before I leave him to his summer's work. But I never do. There is just too much to say, and in any event, if I have hired the right person, after a few weeks' experience he will be doing well and perhaps able to give me new facts for better interpretation.

But I do give some advice.

If I haven't been able to do it earlier, I hand him a copy of Freeman Tilden's *Interpreting Our Heritage*, and I tell him to give top priority to getting it read.

Then I offer some general advice, which this year we have put on two mimeographed pamphlets. Some of this advice is accepted principle in interpretation, and some merely reflects some of my personal dislikes and idiosyncrasies. Let me read these to you*.

I say these things to you, in closing, as I say them to my staff. You are about to have a thoroughly satisfying summer if you do your job properly. Interpretation is that kind of work. See what you look at, use your imagination, work hard, keep smiling, and you will never go far wrong.

* See "Parks Branch Nature Houses," p. 60.

Bob Boyd (chief ranger) and Yorke Edwards, Manning Park Nature House, late 1950s or early 1960s. Edwards family photo.

Parks Branch Nature Houses (1962)

NOTES FOR STAFF, NO. 1

On duty in a Nature House

REMEMBER WHAT YOU ARE TO DO, and you cannot go far wrong. You are there to help the public know and understand *the park*. So your job is not just to answer questions and drop comments on the exhibits. You are there as a naturalist to stimulate people into seeing and understanding the things about them outdoors. You cannot do this by remaining silently and sleepily in the background. Neither can you do this simply by doing a good job of enlarging on the exhibits alone. Each exhibit is about something in the park and should be talked about as such.

Each exhibit contains only a few morsels of information. You are expected to know much more about each topic, and to relate your knowledge to the park.

Don't force yourself on people. Look available, and give most people an initial smile or greeting. Then leave them alone to get oriented. It is not too difficult to sense whether people want to be talked to or prefer to be left alone. Once you start talking it is more difficult to know when to stop. When to talk, and when not to, is something you must learn, and it will help to have staff members watch one another and compare ideas on a number of situations.

You are not expected to give conducted tours of the Nature House, nor to give prolonged lectures before exhibits, but this is not to say that these should be completely avoided.

Finally, there are small manual tasks that will occupy you from time to time. Sometimes these are interesting to people and give you opportunity to talk. If not, keep your eye on people in the House, and stop what you are doing periodically to walk about, looking available.

Senior Naturalists are encouraged to set most of the rules in each House, but in general these will apply to all Houses.

- Keep neat and clean
- Don't eat, chew gum, drink "pop"
- No blue jeans or equivalents
- Keep smoking inconspicuous
- No bull sessions with friends
- Avoid "upmanship" victories over people
- If you don't know, say so
- Go out of your way to be helpful
- Late nights can be unfair to your job

And above all—smile.

Annual Report, 1958

The park interpretation programme was enlarged. It attracted over 18,000 people to two nature houses—one at Manning Park and a new one at Miracle Beach. Public reaction has been enthusiastic toward these museums, which serve as introductions to the natural features of parks. Associated services, such as nature trails, informal illustrated talks, conducted hikes for large groups, and the placing of outdoor signs at park features of outstanding interest, have shown successes equal to those of nature houses.

Notes for Guided Walks (1962)

NOTES FOR STAFF, NO. 2

(1) Advertise the walk in several places where people will see the note.

(2) State time and place, and give a hint of what will be done. Be imaginative: "to the beach" is dull; "to catch crabs" sounds interesting.

(3) Go over the ground ahead of time; think what you will say; try to see things you have been missing.

(4) Are you in a rut? Was the last one all plant names? Why not something on soil, or old beaches, or the far mountains? Why not the shape of leaves, the veins of leaves, etc. Use imagination! Go to books to check your facts, or to get new ideas; talk to others.

(5) The people are assembled. Too many? Grin and bear it, or try to get some to take another walk in the afternoon. About 30 is acceptable; fewer is better for personal communication.

(6) Don't just lead off like a lead goat before sheep. Talk to them before you begin. Tell them where they're going, a few things they may see. Create anticipation.
(7) Talk to the group as much as possible, not to the talkative characters at your elbows.
(8) Don't just show things. Do things too. Dig a hole (and carefully refill). Break up a cone. Open a clam. Feel spruce needles, etc., etc.
(9) Stop for a rest—perhaps here is the time to do something. Stop where some people can sit. Let things slow down, and maybe a question will come up that was being held back.
(10) Think of new twists for walks. Why not one to make a terrarium? Why not a seine haul, or a whole hour digging in sand, or one on seaweeds? Mix these in with general walks that deal with anything that comes up.
(11) Don't bluff. If you don't know, say so. Then be helpful, inviting the person to find the answer with you, after the walk. Prior preparation, and experience, will give you most answers. But there is no problem if you must admit only a few "I don't knows." If there are too many—back to the books!
(12) The greatest danger is perhaps in overlooking simple things. Remember that most people haven't considered what a leaf is, what bird song is, what a stone is.
(13) When the hour is up, don't just walk away. With planning, be somewhere that is a logical place to stop the walk, tell people the hour is up, but be willing to taper off slowly if some people have questions.
(14) A few don'ts:
    - Don't be too formal.
    - Don't "talk down."
    - Don't let anything annoy you; keep your sense of humour.

- Don't be afraid; by coming they have told you they want to hear what you say.

(15) Do remember you are a leader. Be sure that you measure up to the role, doing the best job possible.

Annual Report, 1959

Park Interpretation
Efforts were concentrated on two parks during the summer season of 1959. These were E.C. Manning and Miracle Beach, where nature houses have been established, housing a total of twenty-six exhibits. Most of the exhibits were constructed at Langford Workshop during the winter of 1958/59.

Three nature trails were also operated, two being at Manning and one at Miracle Beach. This was an entirely new venture, and was considered highly successful.

Two series of outdoor programmes were conducted at Miracle Beach Park. Weekly "telescope" tours for birds and sea-shore searches for marine life were undertaken. They were enthusiastically attended by campers. The problem discovered here was that people joined in numbers too large for the maintenance of contact with the interpretation officer in charge.

A total of about 30,000 people visited the nature houses in the season July 1st to September 7th, with about equal numbers visiting each house. At Miracle Beach a successful unit was a tent featuring the sea, and in which a large salt-water aquarium was especially popular. The Manning Park nature house, for the third year, concentrated upon encouraging more use of the alpine country, a portion of which is now easily accessible by the new public road.

In summation, the interpretation programme continued to be an unqualified success. Public enthusiasm was demonstrated in many ways. Most of this success is due to the keen interest of field staffs and their willing acceptance of long hours.

David Stirling, Miracle Beach Provincial Park, early 1960s. Photo used with permission of BC Parks.

Interpretation Ideas (1962)

Yorke Edwards
Drawings by Raymond Barnes

RK found this document in a dusty cache of files from the earliest days of the Parks Branch. Collected in a green three-ring binder, the pages, each placed in a plastic protector, seems to be an attempt by Yorke to make his vision of what could be one future direction for interpretation visible to those who might be able to approve its development. Raymond Barnes was a young Victorian, good with pen and ink, who Yorke hired in 1962 to be a naturalist at Miracle Beach Provincial Park.

Interpretation is partly a creative process in which the search for ideas is a daily challenge.

The search is not for things to do—the need for these is evident everywhere—it is rather a search for better ways that will say what needs saying more clearly.

Through several years the ideas presented here have come from our "interpretation thinking."

We have no doubt whatsoever that each one of these ideas is one that the public will accept with enthusiasm.

Each one could become a successful reality in British Columbia,

if undertaken by competent people,

in an appropriate place,

with reasonable resources

and encouragement.

R.Y. Edwards
Parks Branch
March 22, 1962

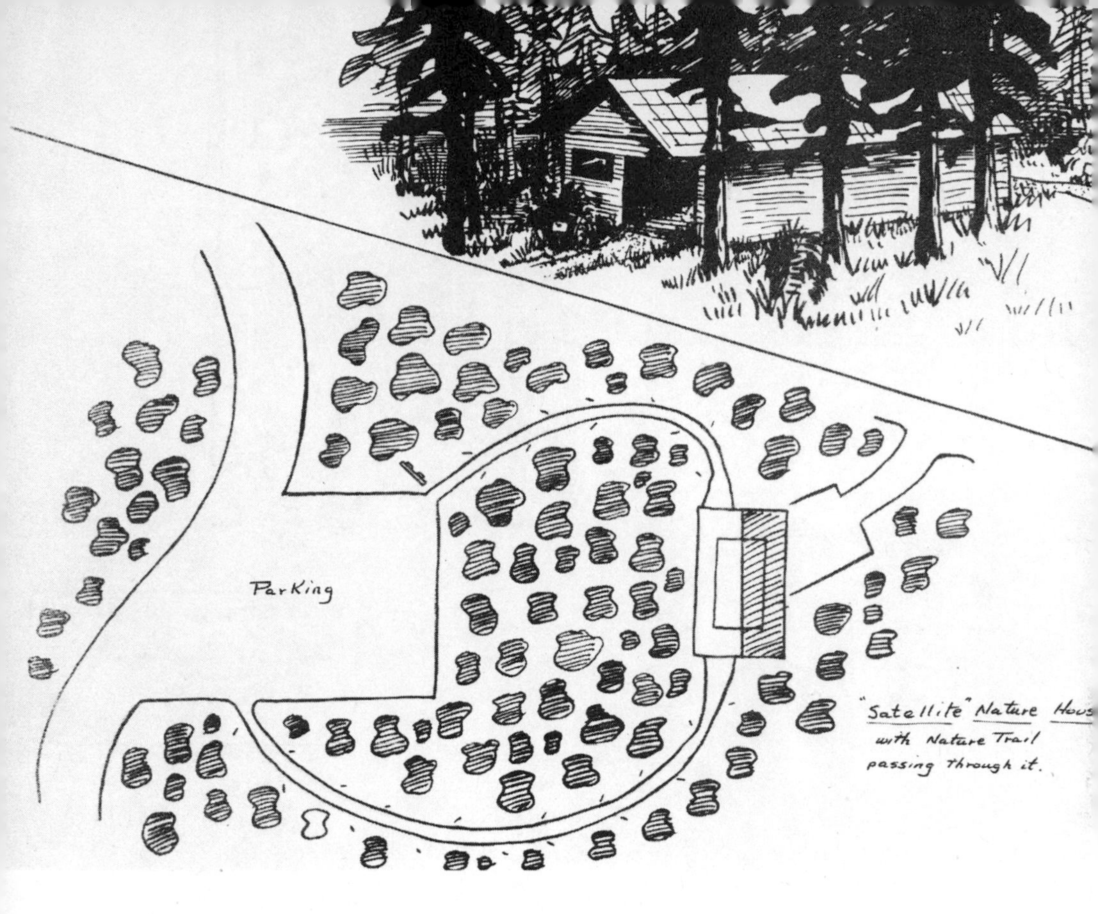

There are some parks where secondary or "satellite" Nature Houses should function.

These should be smaller Houses, open perhaps only half of most days, and with a staff of only one or two.

A possible design is shown. Here, garage type doors on the ends of the building (and perhaps along one side) could open up the floor space, minimizing the feeling of being indoors.

The House shown here is part of a Nature Trail which passes through it.

Secondary Houses could be in small parks, and would function best if a major House was in the same region.

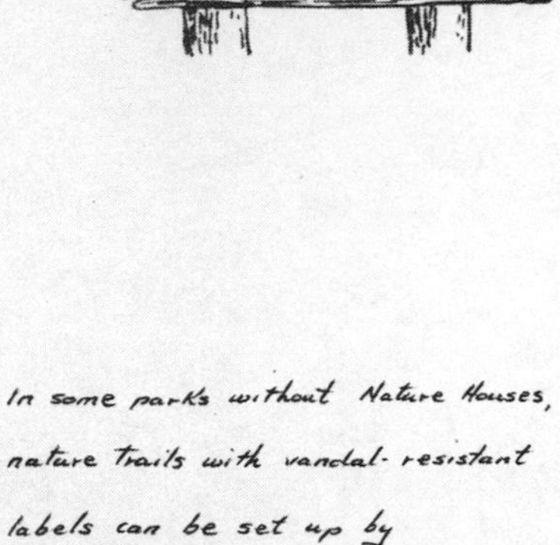

In some parks without Nature Houses, nature trails with vandal-resistant labels can be set up by Interpretation, maintained by park staff.

LODGEPOLE PINE
(Pinus contorta)
- Straight trunks were used for Indian lodge poles.

There is a need now proven by requests from the field for Nature Trails in parks having no interpretation staffs for their maintenance.

We are currently seeking a suitable vandal-resistant label for this type of trail.

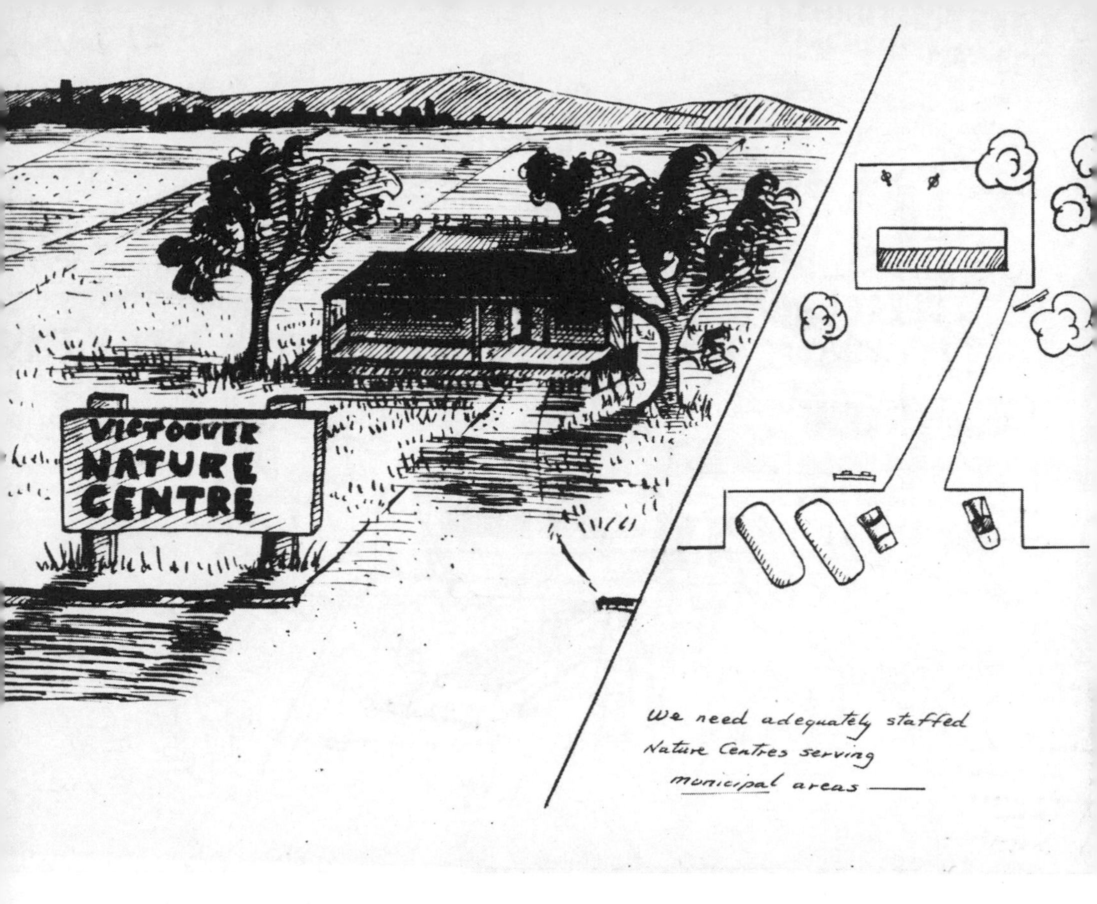

We need adequately staffed nature centres serving municipal areas—and the kinds of services they could offer are almost unlimited.

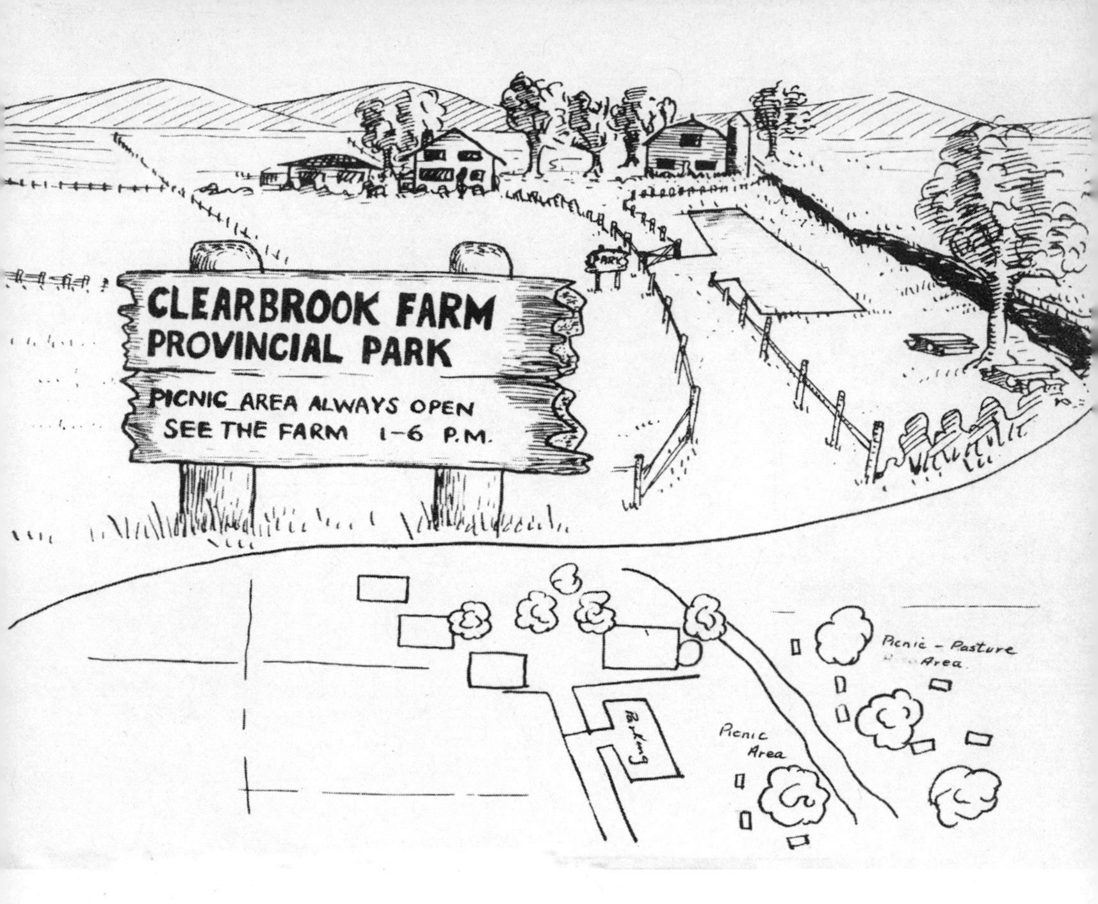

Here is a proven need.

I say this with complete confidence, for I need it myself.

I need a farm where I am welcome to show my children a hay loft, a chicken house and how to make butter. I want them to see cows milked, animals being fed and new lambs.

I cannot easily show them these things, and every child should know them.

The bigger the city, the greater the need.

Our urban voters are increasingly out of touch with rural reality.

Trees built British Columbia.

Trees will nourish our economy in future.

Can we afford not to have an informed public?

The glamour of the Cariboo is its greatest asset, and the cowboy symbolizes that glamour.

We should enrich the memories of the Old West, not let them fade away.

And what subject is more certain to have public appeal?

The southwestern corner of British Columbia has Canada's most spectacular winter concentrations of waterfowl.

Because of climate, it is also the only place in Canada where we can have a living collection of the world's fascinating array of ducks and geese.

On the Severn River in England, Peter Scott has created a world-famous waterfowl park that easily pays its way.

Here on the Fraser Delta could be a conservation project, attractive to tourists, that would be an outstanding educational display.

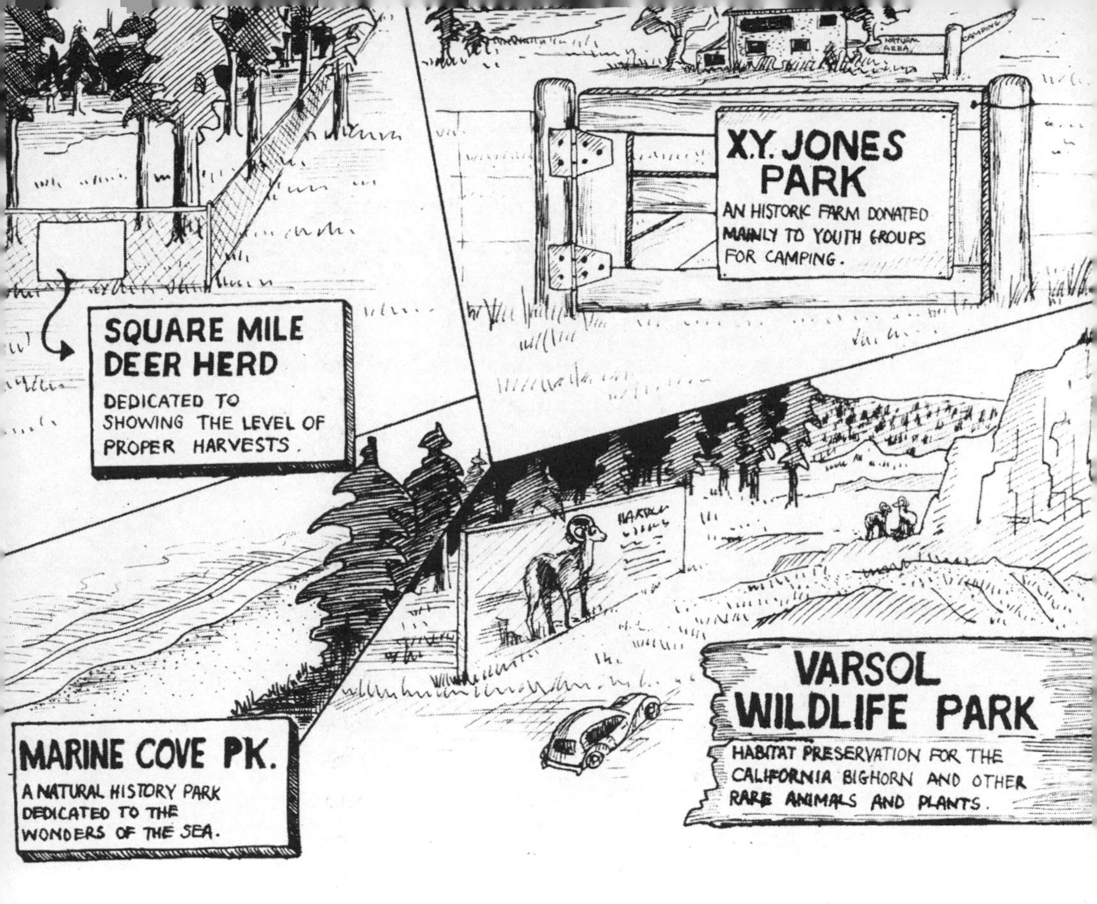

Interpretation is demonstration using *things* that are, as much as possible, in their natural or appropriate settings.

Interpretation to solve conservation problems is much better than words.

An example: *Show* hunters that they cannot harvest a deer herd of 30 per square mile.

Our shores should be a spectacular display of living things for students and tourists, for we have one of the richest coasts on Earth.

Groups need space for camping. Let an old farm fill this need. A minimum of maintenance would be required, and there would be plenty of space to do things—conservation things.

Our unusual wildlife should be protected and displayed in many places. We are neglecting real and unique attractions, like the rare California bighorn, acres of Fraser Delta snow geese, the drama of our salmon runs, the only skylarks in North America, an endless list, with many possibilities.

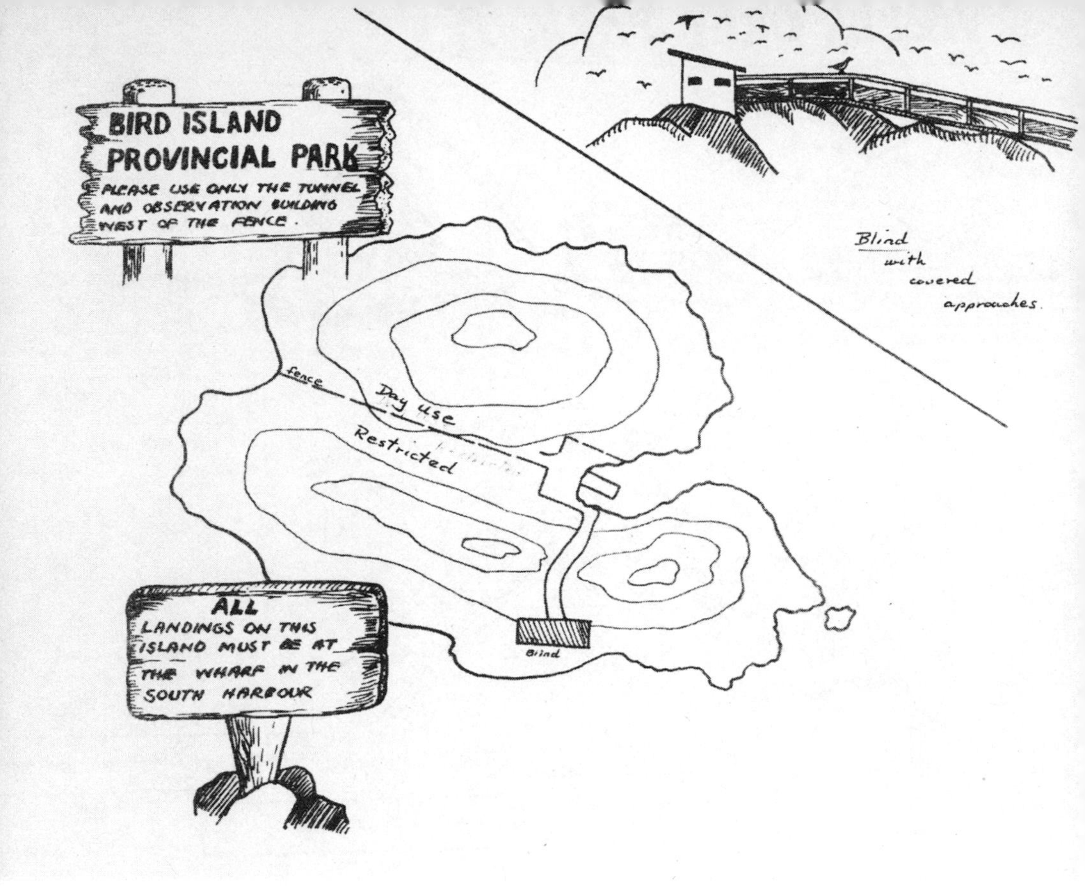

A seabird colony is a fascinating place.

For two or three months each year, these places seethe with activity.

British Columbia is blessed with abundant islands, many of them with large bird colonies. These are often near cities or popular resort areas. They could be unusual public attractions under proper, simple controls and appropriate promotion.

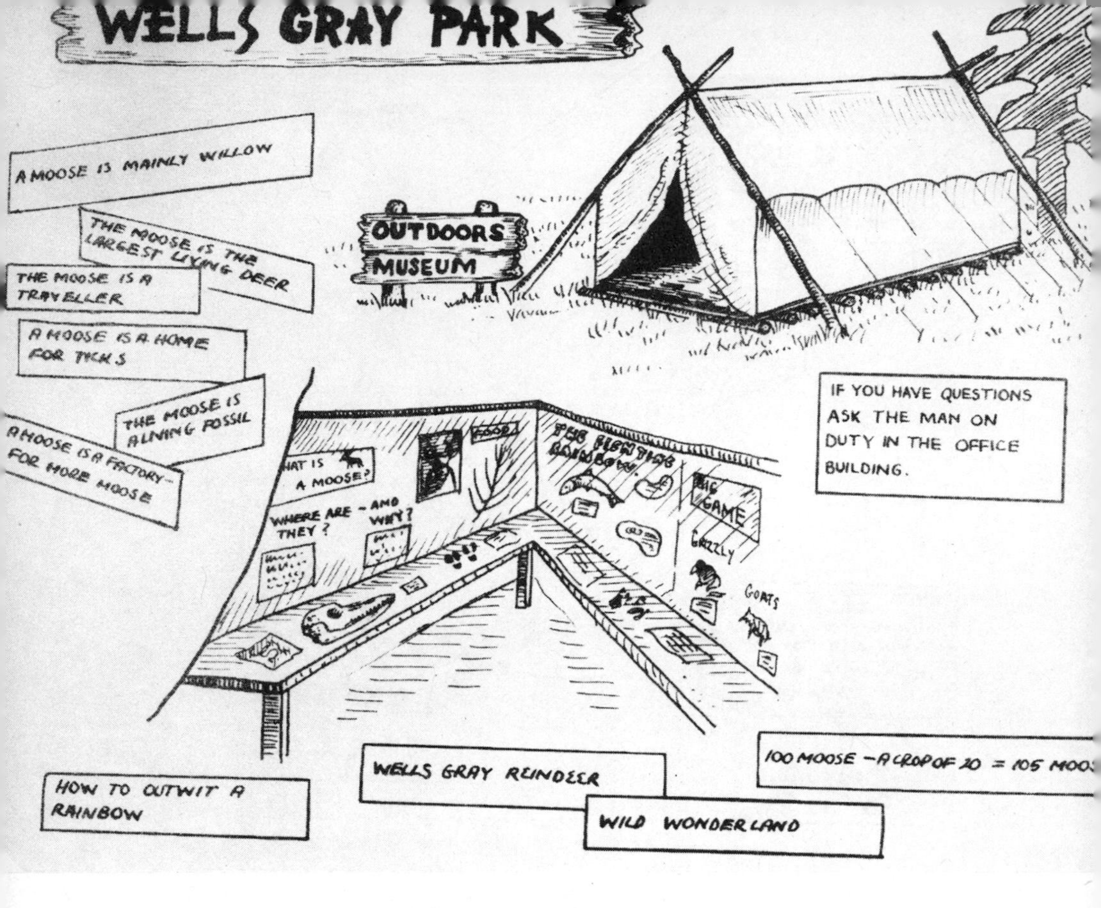

"The best hunters and fishermen are those with the naturalist's interest in the animals they pursue."*

At low cost, here is an opportunity to show sportsmen—and others—the fascination to be found in the wide variety of plants and animals in parks such as Wells Gray.

* While we have not been able to find the source of Yorke's quote, this sentiment was widely felt in sport-hunting circles. For example, "The hunter-naturalist viewed hunting as the best mode of environmental perception, the truest appreciation and apprehension of nature's ways and meanings. Most of them arrived at this philosophy through the combined influences of nature study and hunting experience... The hunter-naturalists evinced a thorough understanding of the ecological basis of natural existence." (From T.L. Atherr, "The American Hunter-Naturalist and the Development of the Code of Sportsmanship," *Journal of Sport History* 5, no. 1 (1978): 7–22.)—Eds.

British Columbia has inspiring alpine lands in abundance, but few people know them.

We need a nature house in the alplands to show people the wonders on the roof of the world.

Canada's Approach (1963)

Paper presented at a panel discussion on the topic "Outdoor Interpretation Through Land for Learning" at the 59th annual meeting of the National Audubon Society, Miami, FL, November 9–13, 1963.

THE REMARKABLE SUCCESS OF OUTDOOR interpretation is not confined to the United States. Other countries are experiencing the boom, and among them is Canada.

Nature interpretation came rather late to Canada. It began in Ontario's provincial parks, largely as a result of the enthusiasm and teaching skill of one man, Prof. J.R. Dymond of Toronto. Since the early 1940s the provincial parks of Ontario have served that province well in providing land for learning more about nature, and how to care for nature. Park naturalists and nature museums, or nature trails, are now to be found in ten of Ontario's parks.

Ontario's example seemed to set a pattern for the rest of Canada to follow. For over a decade, Ontario's program stood alone. Then, in 1957, British Columbia began using its provincial parks for nature interpretation and now has programs in seven parks. After several false starts the federal government in Ottawa started an interpretation program using Canada's national parks, and there are now park naturalists in about 10 national parks. Two additional provinces are beginning to develop interpretive programs, again on park lands, for Newfoundland has a permanent park naturalist, and Saskatchewan has a program of publishing informative booklets that is second to none I have seen.

Nature needs land. There is only one way to preserve nature and that is to dedicate to nature the use of appropriate space on Earth's surface.

Canada, even more so than the United States, has been slow to see the truth in this statement. The reasons for this are obvious. Most Canadians still live on or near a wild frontier, and nature, not yet too badly spoiled, is often part of the view from the kitchen window. But this is rapidly changing as we consume nature at increasing rates, as we grow and prosper and "progress" to no one seems to know where. To date our national and provincial parks have seen most of Canada's nature interpretation. These parks will always be useful in this capacity, but their monopoly is ending. Citizens' organizations, in particular the natural history societies across Canada, are beginning to acquire tracts of wild land, which by happy accidents still exist as natural islands in heavily populated areas. This is the most encouraging development today on the Canadian conservation scene. Conservation by governments is essential, but conservation on a local scale by local people is clear evidence that conservation is not an abstract idea, but is accepted by people as a personal responsibility.

Interpretation in provincial parks has tended to use recreational areas that were not necessarily outstanding examples of preserved nature. Several provinces are now acquiring land solely to preserve the wildlife upon it. Saskatchewan is preserving a prairie dog town and plans to use it for interpretation while it is being preserved. This preservation for controlled public use—use that here means use for education, for inspiration, for scientific study—is the most important concept in years to enter the field of nature preservation. Preserved nature need not be locked away out of reach. With know-how, and careful planning, people and nature can be brought together so that nature does not suffer from the contact. In British Columbia, we have begun to create a series of provincial nature parks, which are meant to be natural nature centres. To date we have purchased two islands, each with colonies of seabirds, and a third park may soon be added in the form of an alkali lake rich in bird life. In these places, studies are under way to find the best way to show people—crowds of people—these natural wonders. Using paths and lookout buildings and boardwalks and blinds and screens of natural materials, we hope to create some nature centres having no man-made exhibits. The best natural history exhibits are those made by nature herself, which is something that the Audubon Society knew long ago. Some of us in the interpretation field are in danger of forgetting this as we do our daily work indoors with exhibits and publications, films, slides and canned sounds. These things are second best, and to be used only when nature and human ingenuity cannot blend into something more useful.

Canada was slow to start but is now an important if small part of the world's nature interpretation effort. If one can predict the future by pondering upon the past, then Canada's progress to date is only a beginning. If you will look north once in a while, I am sure that you will see lands for interpretation doubling and redoubling through the years. We came late as I said, but when we arrived we found an enviable amount of nature still surviving about us. Apparently, many Canadians believe that this good fortune is worth perpetuating.

Annual Report, 1960

Interpretation

Two nature houses (Manning Park and Miracle Beach Park) and three nature trails (two in Manning Park and one in Miracle Beach Park) were open from late June to early September. Nature houses have served a total of 37,000 people, an increase of 27 percent over the total for 1959.

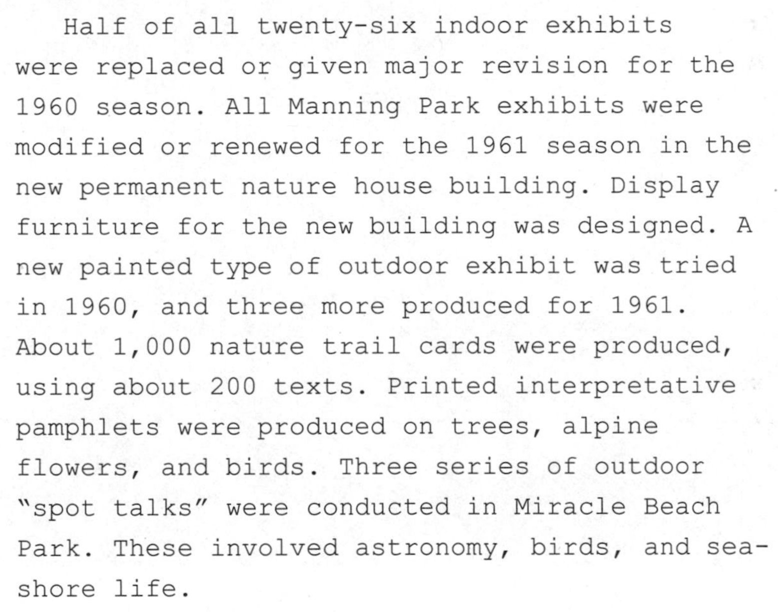

Half of all twenty-six indoor exhibits were replaced or given major revision for the 1960 season. All Manning Park exhibits were modified or renewed for the 1961 season in the new permanent nature house building. Display furniture for the new building was designed. A new painted type of outdoor exhibit was tried in 1960, and three more produced for 1961. About 1,000 nature trail cards were produced, using about 200 texts. Printed interpretative pamphlets were produced on trees, alpine flowers, and birds. Three series of outdoor "spot talks" were conducted in Miracle Beach Park. These involved astronomy, birds, and sea-shore life.

For the fourth consecutive year the interpretative programme attracted more park-users to see more and better interpretative material. The success of this programme continues to be due mainly to the high calibre of staff attracted to this work.

Yorke Edwards in government office buildings, early 1960s, James Bay, Victoria, BC. Photo used with permission of BC Parks.

Interpretation in Our Parks (1964)

Presentation to BC Parks Branch training school, Manning Park, BC, February 11, 1964.

WHAT IS THIS THING CALLED interpretation? For some reason the word scares people, so we avoid using it with the public. Instead, we tell people about "Nature Houses" and "Park Naturalists." The problem is that there is no good English word for this idea, so we make do with some poor substitutes.

Let me tell you what interpretation is by telling you two stories.

I once went to a provincial park for an afternoon's hike with a friend and some children. I did not know this park so I decided that here was an opportunity to learn something. I would pretend to be just another day-user, and in this way learn what a first-time day-user finds in this park. I found out. It was Saturday, one of the really heavy use days, so naturally the office was closed—for it was Saturday, wasn't it? I had gone up to the park's office looking for a map of the park, or better, to pick up a small pocket map to use during the day. I found out later that no one in this park's branch seemed to care whether park users knew where they were in this park. There was no pocket map available for public use; I still don't know if the office had a useful map on the wall.

Now this was a really encouraging start. We had only reached the edge of the park, and all of our experiences to date added up to one clear message from the Parks branch. This was "We don't give a damn whether you use this park or not. Stumble on if you will, but, brother—you're on your own." With a feeling of pending disaster for what we had looked forward to as a happy day, we drove on. Finally, we came to the spot where one of us had once heard that we would find the trail. There was no sign to help us. Recent construction had left a sea of mud and boulders by the road, so I slithered over this and spent the next half hour casting about like a bird dog in the brush, along perhaps half a mile of road edge. I finally stumbled onto the trail. Half an hour later I managed to round up the gang of kids and we started out. The trail was good, and had been worked on within the year, and it would be interesting to know why this trail was worth improving if it wasn't worth a sign so people could find it—even a sign made from a shingle with just one word on it in pencil.

The word "trail" is spelt "T-R-A-I-L." Its message can be excellent interpretation.

So we continued down the trail, never sure where we were, and guessing which way to go at six or eight unsigned forks in the trail. We finally turned back, sure of only one thing—we didn't get to where we wanted to go. Of course, since no one gave a damn where we went or whether we went anywhere at all for that matter, it goes without saying that no one cared whether we saw anything, or knew what we were looking at when we did see something. I drove home fuming, because the park had not improved my day as it should have done; it had made my day into a disaster. This, I might say, happened to me last October, in British Columbia.

Now, let me tell you a happy story. After Christmas this winter I drove 40 miles out of my way through the Arizona desert to see Organ Pipe Cactus National Monument on the Mexican border. I was in a hurry and wanted to cover 500 miles besides taking the side trip to the monument and spending an hour or two there. Signs made it a cinch to find headquarters. There we found a Visitor Center, which is a sort of park museum. It was Sunday, it was Christmas holidays, and the Visitor Center was open. My wife didn't think this was unusual—"Why shouldn't it be open when more people can visit the park?" "In fact," she said, "why should it be closed unless the park is closed?" She had not been with me in October!

We went into the Visitor Center. There was a man there with a smile and he seemed to know all about everything when it came to the monument and what was in it, dead and alive. What he told us was clear and friendly and deadly accurate. There were maps for me, exhibits to help explain what I could see, and small books at small cost giving the things to look for on several loop drives 20 to 40 miles long. These drives were like nature trails, but for people in cars, a really good idea in this open desert country.

I got the happy feeling, in this Visitor Center, that the park staff wanted me to see, enjoy, understand this park. It was an experience to remember. So we ventured forth into the park. We knew where we were, we knew where we were going and we had a rough idea of what to expect along the way. I saw many things, some that were new and mysterious to me—in fact I came to that park to see new things—why else would I come? And before I left that park I returned to the Visitor Center and asked questions, and got simple, accurate, adequate answers.

We left the park at mid-day. But already the day had been a roaring success, and a long, dreary freeway drive passed quickly as we relived our pleasant experience.

So there is the contrast. And the difference boils down to this: Organ Pipe operates as if parks are for people, and as if the staff is there to give intelligent help; Park X shows no obvious evidence of either operating or thinking.

Put another way, one park had good interpretation, the other had none. No, I'm wrong, for the BC park had three signs that I saw: one naming the park at the entrance, one on the door saying "Closed" and one not far away saying "Men." All of these were good interpretive signs.

So what is interpretation in parks? It is *showing* people real things; *orienting* people with directions and facts; *informing* people with well-chosen words; *inspiring* people into the action of learning more for themselves; *entertaining* so that people will come to you to be shown, oriented, informed, inspired and entertained. To do these things an interpreter must know what he is talking about, and know how to say it so that people listen.

Here I should make it very clear that interpretation has two meanings in parks, a broad meaning and a narrow one. Many words are like this. The word "cat" used in the narrow sense means "house cat," but in the broad sense it can be used as a family name to include lion or lynx or cougar or cheetah. In an account of lions we may read, for instance, "that the big cats lie about lazily under thorn trees," and we know that the sentence is not about alley cats.

Interpretation is the same sort of word. The narrow interpretation is the nature house/park naturalist sort. The broad interpretation is pretty nearly everything that we all do in park administration and management and development. Remember the five words I used, that interpretation "shows, orients, informs, inspires, entertains." All good trails and roads in parks should *show, inform, inspire* and *entertain*. Every sign in a park, or every word spoken from park staff to public, must at least *orient* and *inform,* and some may inspire and entertain. Every letter from Parks Branch to the public, every map or leaflet, is part of park interpretation. Even in special-use park areas like beaches, ski slopes, skating rinks, hunting areas, etc., interpretation is present, but the entertainment part in these areas is running away with the others. But we should try to capture people's support, even those coming to the parks only to play games, while pretty well blind to the park itself.

In 1962 in Seattle, the Assistant Director of the huge US National Park Service, Daniel Beard, said: "In a few years interpretation will constitute the major activity of the United States National Park Service." He was talking about interpretation in the narrow sense. In 1963, in Monterey, I heard Dan Beard speak again. He said, in effect, "What I said in Seattle I now take back. Interpretation has always been the major activity of the United States National Park Service." He was talking, of course, about interpretation in the broad sense.

Now at this point some of you, especially those of you who still think that park interpretation is some kind of lacy frill appearing in some of our parks, will think that I'm blowing up my own job. Let me make one thing quite clear. I'm not saying interpretation is important because I happen to be paid for doing interpretation. The truth is the other way around. I'm in interpretation because ten years ago I saw that interpretation has to be the biggest and most interesting thing in park work. I don't have to blow up interpretation. It's already too big for comfort. I do have the task of showing some of you the truth of interpretation's importance, and that is why I am here now. The park interpretation idea is not very old, but it is nearly as old as the period that large numbers of people have been using large parks.

The United States National Park Service had their first interpretation program in Yosemite National Park, in California, in 1920. This was probably the world's first park interpretation program. It came from ideas gathered before the Kaiser's War [World War I], in Norway, England and especially Switzerland, where local governments offered naturalists' services to schools and resorts. Since 1920, many state governments, municipal governments and private organizations have started interpretation programs, and there are now hundreds in the United States and Canada, but for 44 years the US National Parks have led the way. Their interpretation organization is gigantic. In 1962 they employed 1,600 interpreters, and these met 40 million park visitors in that year. In one of their out-of-the-way parks, Olympic National Park, which is just across the Strait of Juan de Fuca from Victoria, their interpretation staff, budget, amount of equipment, is larger than we have for all BC parks. Last summer, we employed 11 interpreters who met 100,000 people.

Some of you have had to live with park naturalists in your parks lately. More of you will have this experience in the future. I want to give you some hints on how to work with a park naturalist and keep smiling. Just as surely as the sun rises every morning, you are going to behave like normal human beings towards these interpreters, and be bothered by things they do; wonder at times who is crazy—you or them; wish that they would go away and leave you alone; and, we hope, also bask with them in the praise heaped on our parks, and on our interpretation program, by the enthusiastic public. We are all of us, you and park naturalists, and everyone else in this outfit, trying to do the same things. We are employed by the public to look after the public's parks, which is *protection*; to help the public to see their parks by giving them trails, road signs, etc., which is *providing access*; and to open the minds of people to what they are missing in their parks, which is *interpretation*. In our day-to-day work, we usually lose sight of what we are doing, and this is dangerous. For example, a road that we are making is *not* supposed to be a chute from A to B, nor merely a first-class road with all modern fads built in. That road must be first-class *park* road, and the only purpose for that road, if we are not wasting public funds, is to help people see and enjoy more of their park, and to see and enjoy their park more. Both quantity and quality are involved. Everyone connected with making that road is doing what the park naturalist is doing, helping people enjoy their park, and if everyone involved isn't aware of this fact, watch out. The public is in for a fleecing! The public won't get the quality—the *park* quality—that it should. Whether you are talking about roads or trails, concessions or signs, nature or guided tours, campsite maintenance or fire protection, the enjoyment of the people is the only concern of we who look after parks. The end we are working to is to serve the park visitor, and everything else we do is just a means to that end.

This is your end just as much as it is the park naturalist's end. He gets most of the glory, I suppose, by being paid to meet the public, but I suspect that he earns glory, what little there is of it. If you don't believe me, change places with him some time. One reasonably busy day should be enough to convince you for life.

So you and the park naturalist will inevitably have your differences and frictions and problems, but I suggest that some mutual respect, some frank discussion of problems and some agreeing on the best way to disagree when there is no other way out will solve most problems. I have found that solving problems with other people involves only two things: first, working hard to see the other point of view; then talking it over in a spirit of being after a solution, not a victory. It's amazing how often big problems just vanish when you give them an airing.

Perhaps it will help you to understand park naturalists if you know what I look for when hiring them. The perfect park naturalist is a superman that will never exist. But he does exist in my mind, and he is the standard to which each candidate is compared. Appearance is not too important except that he is clean, fairly neat, stands straight and keeps his hands out of his pockets. Regular shaving and fairly regular haircuts help. He should be able to talk to people, alone or in bunches, with no distracting mannerisms and a look of enjoying himself. He must have enthusiasm for the work. He must be full of accurate names and facts and general knowledge on trees, shrubs, herbs, mosses, lichens, fern, liverwort, grasses, the stars, geology, insects, spiders, mammals, snakes, amphibians, fish, the weather, etc., etc. So it really boils down to—I hire the guy who understands the natural world about him. And if he knows a lot, I'll try to pay him a salary that recognizes his years of preparation for the job and that rarest of all things that most such people have—enthusiasm. Give me these things—know-how and enthusiasm—and I'll hire him even if he has two heads, if he can also get what he knows across to other people. Obviously, this guy is a specialist, and as a result he may not give a damn about fire pumps, hoses, cats, cars, the cook's problems and who Mabel is going to favour tonight. To him, this may be deadly dull stuff—just as you may think his interests are dull. Everyone to his own peculiar interests and may they all combine to make better parks.

If there is one thing a park naturalist must have it's a great mental storehouse of details. He is expected to know all about everything, and while this is impossible, he will be trying. He will be cramming himself with hundreds of facts on hundreds of plants and animals and other things. On top of this, I frequently follow him around nature houses and nature trails complaining about dust, dirt, damage, signs not made, signs made wrong, signs made right that look wrong, exhibits that need changes, and his staff doing a dozen things poorly. The park naturalist has a complicated world to interpret, and we've given him a complicated operation to interpret it with. If he comes unravelled at times, or in his desperation seems to be wanting a lot of help, look upon him with understanding, for the job has got him down for a day or two.

It will help to remember that the park naturalist does what he does for only one reason—to give people greater enjoyment of their parks. Your job has the same purpose. When you help one another, you are both really doing your jobs.

The park naturalist, more than most other park staff, is in the front line, actually in touch with the public. Therefore, the image that the public have in their minds after visiting one of our parks is apt to be the park naturalist. So you can appreciate that I try to choose with care, and I'm not too concerned over whether he has hair on his chest, whether he is good with a shovel, or whether he is anything at all unimportant to the job. Doing the job is what concerns me. He can sleep to noon, if he wants, if the job begins at 1 p.m. He can write bad poetry or paint worse pictures whenever he wants in his own time. But, if he gets into stupid trouble of any kind I'll fire him, just as I told him I would when I hired him. We can't afford to have our image a menace to society. Whether we like it or not, the park naturalist is apt to be symbolic of the branch staff, and the image must be as good as possible.

So interpretation is a major part of running good park systems all over America. Other countries are now asking for advice on how they should begin. Our own program is a small one, just as our Parks Branch is on the small side, but in both our parks and our interpretation this gives us the chance to be high quality. If you don't have many, it's easier to be good, and BC today has the reputation of having better interpretation in better parks than you will find anywhere else in Canada and in lots of places in the United States. I think this is a good thing. If we all think so, it will stay that way.

We can sum up interpretation and its importance with three thoughts.

Interpretation increases people's enjoyment of their parks by showing, orienting, informing, inspiring, entertaining. It does this through park naturalists, nature houses, nature trails, outdoor theatres, conducted walks, outdoor signs and displays, and printed matter.

The value of interpretation is measurable only by the number of people wanting it. This is also the only measurable value of parks. In a country such as ours, there is nothing more important than what people want. This puts parks, and park interpretation, in line for a very bright future, because people like both.

Annual Report, 1961

Interpretation and Research
The interpretation programmes in Manning and Miracle Beach Parks had a total attendance of over 50,000 people during the summer of 1961. The new building in Manning Park undoubtedly contributed to a 38-per-cent increase in visits at that park. The nature centre attendance figures were 39,000, an increase of 6 per cent over the 1960 figures. Nature trails (three in Manning, one in Miracle Beach) were used by an estimated 11,000 people. Conducted walks were stressed this year...A total of twenty-one walks provided pleasant outdoor instruction for 850 people. By the use of adequate promotion, the Miracle Beach Park programme attracted over 100 people per walk.

The newly constructed Manning nature centre contained twenty-six freshly designed and constructed exhibits. The Miracle Beach nature centre was under canvas for the last time. Four of its eleven exhibits were new...

The interpretative programme, begun in 1957, now serves four times as many people as in that first year; cumulatively the total is now over 150,000 participants. Data were gathered on people using large, wild areas in parks in a continuing programme to study the use of wilderness and near-wilderness. Focal points for study were Wells Gray Park and Black Tusk Meadows in Garibaldi Park.

Interior of Miracle Beach Nature House, 1964. Photo used with permission of BC Parks.

Interpreter Ted Underhill and an unknown staff member in Manning Park Nature House. Photo used with permission of BC Parks.

The Role of the Park Naturalist in Park Inventory, Planning and Management (1964)

Paper presented to the Third Federal-Provincial Park Conference, Victoria, BC, October 1, 1964.

SO THAT BOTH OF US can warm to the subject, I will begin, as is traditional, with a few platitudes. Fifteen minutes gives me no time to be subtle, no time to brainwash you gently before slipping across my own ideas. So here it is, brief, blunt, dogmatic and, therefore, vulnerable.

Talks about parks are dangerous things. Talker and listener are often completely out of touch. It may sound like English words, but the words do not add up to much sense if—without knowing it—talker and listener are thinking about different kinds of parks. Perhaps we can avoid this kind of misunderstanding here.

My remarks on parks will be concerned only with those parks in which nature is an important value of the park. By "nature,"

I mean wild land, whether a plot or a whole countryside, that is more or less unmauled by men; or land that is being left alone to heal from a man-handling in the past. The parks that I am talking about include many—perhaps more accurately most—of the national and provincial parks of Canada. Even the bits of parks nearly hidden each summer under canvas villages are usually encouraged to remain as natural as possible, and so even these may have some natural values. It makes little difference to the philosophical approach if the nature present is tattered and if it must be viewed on all sides through lines of family washing. So long as there is the desire to preserve and to use some nature, I am talking about that nature, even in our Coney Island park lands, in our asphalt desert park lands, in our cancerous townsite and commercial centre park lands, in our canvas bedroom park lands, and in the park lands considered simply as scenic wallpaper to be watched from mechanical vehicles, or from expensive hotels, or while knocking a small white ball into 18 fairly large holes in the ground. To the extent that any park has nature that is valued, I am talking about that park.

Park interpretation is the process of showing people that the things in their parks are stimulating and interesting and enjoyable and meaningful to understanding their surroundings. Do not underestimate these things. These are the kinds of experiences that make life worth living, and what can be more important than things that do that? Someone once told me that interpretation is the frosting on the park cake. At the time I found the analogy disturbing, and I soon concluded that this was because the analogy was wrong. Interpretation is no frothy frosting. It is rather the process of serving the park cake so that the cake fulfills its purpose and so that people experience full and proper use of the cake. The Park Naturalist is the interpreter of nature in parks. This term "naturalist" is not a label to be pinned meaningfully on just anyone. A naturalist worthy of the term has a knowledge of nature, and an attitude toward nature, that sets him apart from all others. The naturalist understands nature. It's as simple as that. So it follows that being or not being a naturalist can have nothing at all to do with how a man is trained to make a living. I know people whom I would hire as park naturalists who are housewives, teachers, farmers, welders, salesmen, foresters, geographers, lawyers, surgeons, civil engineers, physicists, mathematicians, mechanical engineers, dentists and the list could go on and on. The term "naturalist" can go with almost any skill or training. It is an attitude and a background of knowledge, and only these things.

So what of the role of the Park Naturalist in park inventory and planning and management, to quote from my title? I do not think it is important whether he participates in these things or not, beyond, of course, doing his job as interpreter to the public. Dealing directly with the public is the primary function of the Park Naturalist if one spells that term with a capital "P" and a capital "N," and this work should keep him more than busy enough. But at the same time I also believe that a naturalist, this time spelled with a small "n," whether he be on the staff as a forester or as a labourer or as a Park Naturalist, should be in every park office to advise from a position of strength on just about everything to do with parks. For there are two ways in which to run the kind of park that we are talking about: with a naturalist, or in ignorance. This reasoning is so logical to me, and so conclusive, that I cannot think of anything more to expand the idea.

But there is a side issue, and that is: What are the dangers of not using a naturalist's skills? I shall mention but a few. There is always the danger of acquiring mediocre park land. For example, I once heard of a park agency which considered the most important attribute of park land to be flatness. What interesting parks they must have had. I have also seen parks with outstanding attractions completely ignored as important by a succession of reconnaissance teams, surveyors, site planners, developers and maintainers. I have seen construction do unnecessary damage so unbelievable that no one involved could possibly have had any concern for park values. Examples are machinery churning over alpine meadows or over equally delicate prairie; gravel taken from famous geological features; rare species destroyed; scenery scarred; trees killed because smothered in fill; and roads too wide, too straight, too expensive and completely unrelated to the job—the park job—that they were meant to do.

I have seen park plans with buildings located where they destroyed valuable park features, and plans which left some spectacular nature in place but made it impossible to locate developments for an interpretation program. And I have known parks where the ugly brown of shrubs killed by brush killer was the main feature of the park scenery, where magnificent trees were cut down because they "might be" dangerous, and where ideas on how to treat wild vegetation seem to have come from a fussy formal gardener. But we all have seen sights like these, for every park system must have its ghastly mistakes from the past stealing public enjoyment from the present. My thesis is that a naturalist will catch several times more of these kinds of mistakes, before they are made, than will anyone with any other kind of background.

To sum up then, and while doing so to present the case from a slightly different viewpoint:

(1) Our only measure of the value of parks is the magnitude of their public support, for all things are valuable only because people think them so. This support of parks is probably proportional to the quantity and quality of the public's enjoyment of the parks.

(2) Interpretation is the process of increasing the quantity of people having high-quality experiences in the parks.

Interpretation therefore quite automatically increases public support of parks, and hence increases the value of parks.

(3) Interpreters cannot be expected to do much of a job in poorly chosen park lands made poorer by rampaging bulldozers. The better the quality of nature, the greater the possibility of high-quality nature interpretation. The development of a park can help or hinder interpretation, and even ruin forever the possibility of having it at all.
(4) Therefore, simply to have park quality, the thinking of a naturalist is essential.

Also, in order to have effective interpretation when desired in our parks, the interpreter or his equivalent must have a strong voice second to none in the choosing of park lands, in evaluating the importance of park resources, in park planning, in park development and in park maintenance. Otherwise you will get second-rate interpretation.

It all boils down to this. If you want good parks, use a naturalist. If you do not like naturalists, use them anyway, for they are the lesser of two evils. In the light of this reasoning, the major question is: How many organizations concerned with natural parks in Canada have a naturalist in a strong position influencing the inventory, planning and management of their parks? If there are many, I will be surprised. But at the same time, I hope that you can surprise me.

Annual Report, 1962

Interpretation and Research

Interpretation programmes continued in Manning and Miracle Beach Parks, and were initiated in Shuswap Lake and Goldstream Parks. Three nature centres had a total attendance of over 54,000, and 142 conducted walks were attended by 3,400 people. No estimate was made of the use given five nature trails in four parks. Nature centre use increased by 40 per cent over that of 1961.

The Shuswap Lake Nature House had a successful first year, serving about 16,000 people. People's reactions were interesting. Formerly a new house was approached with cautious curiosity. Now most people know what a nature house has to offer as a result of familiarity with the two older houses.

In Manning, Miracle Beach, and Goldstream Parks regular walks, conducted by park naturalists, were offered to the public. They were received with enthusiasm. In Goldstream Park there was no nature house, the interpretation programme consisting almost entirely of frequent conducted walks. During the summer the naturalist there led eighty-nine walks, a total of over 2,200 people.

The Miracle Beach Nature House was in its new building for the first year. Eighteen new exhibits were planned and made to furnish it.

The new Shuswap Lake Nature House, under canvas this year, received seventeen new exhibits. An experiment with heavily plasticized labels on nature trails was conducted in Goldstream Park, and results were encouraging. The aim is to perfect a tough, damage-resistant label for use on trails given infrequent servicing. In 1962, after cautious trials in previous years, large, colourful, plywood signs at features of interest were made for five situations. These were placed in Sproat Lake, Miracle Beach, Okanagan Lake, and Mount Seymour Parks. Some of the more exposed were heavily damaged, as expected. The experiment has suggested how to reduce damage by using different materials and by placing the signs in what are now recognized as low-damage positions.

Miracle Beach Nature House.
BC Archives I-07042.

The Scientific Basis of Natural History Interpretation (1964)

Paper presented to the Fifth Annual Naturalists Workshop, held at Palisades National Parks Training Centre, Jasper, AB, July 5, 1964.

WHEN I BEGAN TO THINK ABOUT the title given to me by Dr. Stirrett, it was soon evident that everything I have to say on this subject can be boiled down to three sentences, as follows:

- The business of science is the business of dealing in facts.
- Research is the process of uncovering new facts, and is a process invariably needed by any scientific endeavour.
- Interpretation, as a field demanding accurate facts, must be scientifically based, and must be accompanied by research if it is to have good quality.

These three thoughts are the bare bones of my paper, and what follows will merely pad out this skeleton.

Not long ago, when I was in a mood for daydreaming, I went in my imagination on a guided nature walk with Canada's finest interpreter. On this walk were enacted all the errors, all the misinterpretations, that I have seen park naturalists use to contaminate the poor, unsuspecting public. It was fun to mentally construct this walk, an exercise in recalling bits of information from the past, but it was frustrating too, for the really bad error, the really mixed up ideas, are so illogical that one is unable to recall them easily, if at all. Those that do come readily to mind, the errors of the logical sort, are almost understandable, but they are still errors, and so are not to be taken lightly.

My misinterpreter was full of confidence in his errors. This, of course, is much worse than errors made after warnings that errors are possible because knowledge is fragmentary. In other words, it is not too serious to err, but it is very serious to be ignorant of one's own ignorance. We are all ignorant in many fields of knowledge. This is inevitable, but to be unaware of ignorance is an extremely dangerous condition in a person explaining scientific facts to the public.

On my imaginary walk, my guide was in rare form. When an orange-crowned warbler flashed across the path too fast for even a Peterson to name it for sure, my guide stated emphatically: "Yellow warbler! Everyone see the faint red streaks on the breast?" When the same bird sang a few seconds later, everyone was given a short and authentic-sounding talk on the song of the chipping sparrow. The talk was acceptable enough in itself, but it was a disaster since it was about the wrong bird.

The group passed an old shed, and attention was called to the "flies" coming and going from spaces between the shingles. Our guide had the wrong order of insects. They were Hymenoptera, not Diptera, and they may have looked superficially like bluebottle flies, but they were really carpenter bees, carrying pollen into the spaces that were their nurseries.

We pressed on. Flowers were everywhere, for we seemed to be in an alpine meadow. Somehow, this fellow made all

Compositae into daisies, whether blue or orange or yellow or white, unless they were small enough to be called dandelions, or large enough to be sunflowers. He made all Composites fall smoothly into this major revision of the family—the fleabanes, groundsels, ragworts, hawkweeds, arnicas, asters, balsam root, to mention a few.

Our guide was a confident geologist. All rock light in colour and of igneous origin was granite.

And to our hero, grasses were grasses, which was not so bad, but sedges were grasses too, and this was bad.

At one point the little group went into a damp wooded valley. It must have been on the Pacific coast, for the trees were big and tall and draped in mosses, and ferns hung over the damp trail. Our guide launched into an informative story of warm winters and heavy rainfall and resulting forests of huge evergreens. It was obviously a tale he had told many times before, and it seemed a bit automatic. Then we were shown just how automatic it was. As he moved along, talking, he broke stride to avoid something on the path. He rattled on as unswerving as a taped message, and he never missed a beat as he stepped over a giant slug, one of the wonders of the Pacific rainforest, the largest slug in the world, a lovely khaki colour and seven whole inches long. The people were so impressed with the slug that none of them heard what the guide was saying for minutes. But he talked on, and he moved along, and he made not the slightest effort to capitalize, as a naturalist and interpreter, on this unusual opportunity. There was no question of the trees and their mosses waiting while the slug was admired and commented upon. The guide had simply let himself become a machine that ran best if left alone to run its course. Or perhaps he did not know much about slugs—but anything at all would have been appropriate if accompanied by some honest wonder at its size.

Towards the end of the hike, our hero had everyone watching a hummingbird that was really a hawk moth. He quite easily got into the wrong phylum.

Without scientific facts and a certain amount of scientific accuracy, nature interpretation is not just useless, it is downright destructive, filling minds with misinformation, old wives' tales and dangerous nonsense. It was balderdash as fact that keep the Dark Ages dark, surely proof enough that misinformation can be far worse than no information at all. Mere ignorance says "I don't know," and this is acceptable enough occasionally from an interpreter. But misinformation says "black is white," and thereby sows the seeds of confusion, incompetence and a poisonous infection of all ideas touched by the nonsense stored as fact.

There will always be two kinds of facts: those known to man and those yet to be uncovered. The facts accumulated by man through his short history are our greatest inheritance from the past. This body of knowledge is easy enough to acquire, once it is threshed out of the unknown and made palatable by an educational institution. Yesterday's hard-won fact through research is today's easily acquired fact from a book. We all have a store of facts, not all from books either, for from personal experience we have added many facts to our book knowledge. As naturalists, this book knowledge plus the facts from our personal experience makes us desirable as nature interpreters. In part at least, hiring a nature interpreter is hiring thousands of accumulated facts. The potential interpreter will already know facts such as the colour of a robin's egg and the cup of mud that is part of the robin's nest; such as the migratory behaviour of the monarch butterfly, which survives winter as a species by keeping south of winter's reach; such as the difference between "jack pines" in the east and west of Canada, and the western one is better called lodgepole pine; such as that rattlesnakes are not found in Jasper National Park, but are found in the extreme south of several Canadian provinces, four to be exact. These are the sorts of facts that qualify you to try to become a good interpreter, and with study, both of books and nature, you can increase your qualification.

This general sort of knowledge is your general strength as interpreter. With careful observation and some midnight oil, one can readily acquire more of this sort of scientific fact than an interpreter ordinarily uses. But you may arrive from Ontario well equipped in this respect and still be just an apprentice while interpreting a place like Banff National Park. There are a specialized set of conditions in every area which require special knowledge. In Banff, for instance, the Rocky Mountain bighorn sheep is a glamorous special feature of the park. General knowledge on these sheep is not enough in Banff. The sheep demand emphasis in detail, and intensive research must provide the facts for interpretation. In British Columbia's provincial parks, moose are unusually common in Wells Gray Park, and sand dollars are a feature of Miracle Beach Park. Interpretation of these parks would demand special research on these species to satisfy the special public interest created by their prominence and abundance. In Manning Provincial Park grow two plants, neither abundant, but each with the glamour of rarity to go with interesting appearance. Here the spectacular red rhododendron and the stunted timberline tree, alpine larch, demand special research for their interpretation and perhaps, incidentally, for their survival as well.

Two kinds of research are essential to a good interpretation program in parks.

One is the inventory sort of research. This is the job of recording what the park has in the way of geological features, plant and animal life. No interpreter can do much of job without knowing what he is dealing with, so this sort of research usually precedes interpretation work. In a large park, this task of inventory is never really done. A good initial study usually terminates the need for intensive research of this inventory sort, but through the years new species come to light, new localities get added to range maps, and population changes are bound to occur. The job of inventory in a park is never quite done.

The other sort of research is more intensive and usually aimed at park features of special interest. In many parks, for example, glaciers demand research in order to know what they are doing. Common or spectacular species of plants or animals need more than knowledge if our treatment of them is to match their importance in the park. This is the sort of research mentioned in connection with Banff's bighorns.

Be careful lest this word "research" mislead you. Nowadays, every scientist has his picture taken in a white coat and beside an impressively large microscope, and everyone thinks that research must involve computers and radioactive tracers. Even in this atomic age, we are by no means far enough out of the jungle of ignorance that just standing and staring may not be very good research. Much research in parks for interpretation will be this stand-and-stare sort, with of course a good brain working away behind the staring eyes.

Research is not needed for interpretation alone. Research is needed for being intelligent about park administration. There is a saying that "you cannot have public understanding of a park if the park is not understood." I would like to add that people protecting the park, people planning the park, people developing the park, people managing the park—in fact all park personnel in general—cannot have much hope of knowing what they are doing if research at various levels has not shown what is in parks, and what is important in parks.

You cannot run properly anything as complex as a park without understanding it, unless you count on perhaps 50 per cent of your decisions being disastrous. In my opinion, this is not good enough.

What I have been saying to you will make no sense at all if you regard our parks as simply miles of three-dimensional wallpaper—in other words, as just scenic surroundings in which to do things quite unrelated to the surroundings.

Many people think of parks in this way. They sweep through a park saying, "OK. I've seen it. On to the next one."

What fabulously expensive wallpaper!

We have inherited this attitude from the 19th century, when lack of research, hence of knowledge and understanding, led to many errors in managing our parks. In Canada this 19th-century attitude has persisted half way through the 20th century.

That that is now over is proven by our being here today.

It is our job as interpreters to show people that parks are not just wallpaper along roads, along chair lifts and outside the windows of expensive hotels. Parks are a million million bits of fascinating nature, and these bits are doing interesting things, and all of these things do, of course, sometimes add up to impressive scenery, and in some parks this summation to good scenery is not the exception but the rule.

So it boils down to this.

Without facts, the interpreter is powerless.

When we hire an interpreter, we expect to get an impressive quantity of facts along with him, as part of his mental baggage, and often as real baggage in the form of good reference books. Before the interpreter can do a really good job, however, the park office must give him two things:

- Personal experience in the park
- The results of research in the park

The research is needed, and some of it is getting done. But we need more if our parks are to move deeper into the 20th century.

Annual Report, 1963

Interpretation and Research

Park naturalists conducted daily interpretation programmes through the summer in four parks—Manning, Miracle Beach, Shuswap Lake, and Goldstream. Using nature houses, nature trails, and guided walks, this staff made over 125,000 contacts with park-users.

Nature houses in Manning, Miracle Beach, and Shuswap Lake Parks served 56,800 people, most of these in July and August. Trial periods of operation in June and September revealed that there can be sufficient use in these months to justify keeping the houses open.

For the first time, sample counts were taken of use given to the six nature trails. Estimates, from carefully gathered figures, indicated use by 66,100 persons. One trail is especially heavily used. On some days, Beaver Pond Nature Trail in Manning Park receives a person a minute.

Guided walks are being given increasing emphasis in our programme. Walks in Miracle Beach and Goldstream Parks were conducted daily, and long walks were offered several times a week in Manning Park. A total of 4,700 people was led on these walks.

A biologist spent much of the summer on Mitlenatch Island Nature Park. His two main tasks were to study glaucous-winged gull behaviour and assess present holiday use of the island. Present human use is surprisingly heavy, considering the park's location, and a small-scale interpretation programme is clearly justified...Similar, but much briefer, surveys were made of a small range-land lake near Lac la Hache Park, and in Mount Robson, Little Qualicum Falls, and Elk Falls Parks.

What Is Interpretation? (1965)

Presentation to BC Parks Branch training school, Manning Park, BC, 1965.

BEFORE YOU START TO DO something, it helps to know what you are going to do. It does sound a bit ridiculous, perhaps, that anyone would do something all day on most days for many years and not know what he is doing or why he is doing it. But don't laugh. We may be talking about you.

You work in parks. Tell me what a park is. Tell me what parks are for. Tell me what people want from our parks. If you're typical, you don't have ready answers for these questions, and the first answers that come to mind are not going to mean very much.

In order to understand interpretation, it is necessary to understand parks and what people want from them. In fact, I'm going to say quite a lot about parks and people before I can talk about interpretation at all.

What do people get from our parks?

What do people want from our parks? It's easy to give a quick answer to this question, but perhaps the quick answer is not the right one.

Do people want recreation? Probably they do, but what is recreation? Recreation is too general an idea to be very useful. In fact, "recreation" is one of those words of fuzzy meaning that helps our lazy minds do a lot of fuzzy thinking. To say people want parks for recreation is to say nothing useful. We must look deeper.

People want tenting space from parks, you say. I don't believe it. British Columbia is full of tenting places. Tenting space is tenting space in a park or out of it. Most people have space on their own lawn to pitch a tent; why go to a park for it? Tenting space can be no major attraction of parks.

People want skiing from parks, you say. Why in parks? This land of mountains has ski slopes everywhere. There is nothing unique about hills or ski tows in parks.

Do people want parks for fresh air? BC is full of it.

Exercise? Why go to parks for it?

Swimming? Why go to parks for it?

Photography? Walking? Birdwatching?

Vegetating? Sunshine? Drinking beer? Burning gas in the family car? Boating? There is no scarcity of places in our province to do all of these things, and there never will be. People do these things in parks, and these are usually quite acceptable activities in parks, but nothing about these things in parks is necessarily a special attraction that may not be a much bigger and better attraction outside of parks.

It's beginning to look as if parks are ordinary places that we could easily do without. But this is not true. All over the world, man has created large, wild parks. You will find them from the

Congo to Iceland, and from Scotland to Thailand. This suggests that something about parks is needed by man everywhere. It seems clear also that parks—wild parks of our sort—must have something that no other kind of land can give. This must be so. If it is not, then we do not need parks. Parks are justified only if they give people something not available on other lands.

I can find only one thing in our parks that makes them something special, and that is wild land. We protect this wildness in parks, and our planners minimize damage to it. As people tame more of British Columbia, this wilderness in our parks will become even more attractive, even more valuable. Today, our parks attracting the most people are in or near tamed areas. When most of British Columbia is tamed like New York State or California, our parks will be bulging like theirs are today.

I can find no other special feature of parks. If you can find some I have missed, I will be happy to hear about them, because I don't like to carry around faulty ideas.

What is wild land?

Wild land is not just land with trees on it. It must be land unsullied by man.

- Cultivated lands are not wild lands; they are exceedingly civilized lands.
- Logged hills are not wild hills; they are industrial hills.
- Lands grazed by cattle or sheep are also industrial lands.
- Waters dammed by man are industrial waters.

Wild land is land not changed by man. There is not much land left in southern Canada that is still wild by chance. Most of what is left has been kept wild on purpose in parks.

What is wild about wild land? Everything. The geology is unscarred by man; the air and water are unpoisoned by man;

and most important of all, the life on the land is wild, hence not affected by man.

Parks are mostly wild land. Think for a minute about what things make a park. Any park anywhere consists of these things:

- rock and soil
- weather
- plants and animals

Often found in parks in addition are people and development, but these may be absent.

Mostly parks are just rock and soil, weather and living wild things, or wildlife. In short, parks are bits of nature. Our parks are bits of nature. The Parks Branch has the job of looking after these bits of nature.

The attraction of nature

Our ideas to this point have led to the conclusion that people come to our parks because of unspoiled nature. Not that they all realize this. I suspect, for example, that most people who like to camp in parks are only dimly aware that the atmosphere about them is the only unique attractive feature.

Unspoiled nature is the only unique feature about our parks. In most city parks, of course, this is not true. Here, public space alone is attractive and unique. But space is no real problem anywhere near most of our parks.

Why should people be attracted to parks because of nature? I don't know, and no one knows for sure, but one thing is clear from evidence gathered from all over the world: the more people get crammed into cities—in other words, the more people are cut off from nature—the more they want nature, and the more they are willing to work and pay to have nature. This is not just someone's idea. This is a proven fact. But why this should be so, we are not sure. Part of the answer is that we are all looking for "kicks" in our lives. Most people want more out of life than food and shelter and sex and alcohol and the latest motorized tin can from Detroit.

These are all right, but a steady diet with nothing else is apt to lead to the loony bin or to an overdose of sleeping pills. There usually has to be something else in life.

It helps to have something in your life that proves you are a useful human being. And there are only two important things that make a human being different from a horse or a mouse or a butterfly. One is hands; the other is the human brain. Of these, the brain is by far the more important.

So to prove you are a human being, you use your brain. You learn things. This learning is something every sane person does every day, and it is pleasant to do. We see new movies, read new magazines, try new hair tonics, travel to see new places, play new games, learn what new cars look like, read new ads, learn how to fix the rattle in an old machine. We have hobbies of all kinds. A hobby is a kind of study, whether it's birdwatching or girl watching, boat building or photography, wine making or collecting stamps. In all of these things, we use our brains for "kicks." It is a fact that your brain is the only thing that can give you a "kick."

People like to use their brains. Dozens of tourist surveys have shown that the places tourists aim for are historic sites, museums and parks. They do not go to these places to be bored. They are looking for interesting things to make their lives interesting, and they know that these places are interesting places.

It will help to think a minute about things that are interesting. How important, how valuable, are interesting things? Aside from food and shelter, interesting things are the most important things in our lives. Only interesting things can make life interesting. An interesting life is what makes life worth living. It's as simple as that. Interesting things are as valuable as our lives. I can think of few things as valuable to me as the interesting things that make life pleasant and satisfying and worthwhile.

Nature offers endless things of interest to people. To get something out of nature you don't have to be a birdwatcher or a rockhound or a butterfly chaser or a flower admirer. These people get the most out of nature, perhaps, but the hiker is soaking up the general atmosphere of nature, and so too are the trail rider and the mountain climber. And the guy who sits all day in one of our campsites sucking on beer bottles is possibly getting as much from the nature that our planners have carefully left around him as he is getting from the alcohol in the bottles.

Wild land has an atmosphere that people can enjoy from a car or on skis or while putting up the family tent. Most people call it scenery. Scenery is real stuff, and people like it well enough to tell governments to preserve it. We do this in parks. And of course scenery, in wild places, is just a word for nature in the distance. The scenery in Manning Park is only plants and animals sitting on a foundation of rocks and soil under the lights and shadows of a sky full of weather. Any way you look at scenery it boils down to this, although the way these things are put together is important too, for this is what decides whether the scenery is good or bad.

Many people like this wild scenery of parks. Some really look at it, and a lot of people just like to be with it, eating, walking, sleeping, skiing, riding or just sitting. Like wallpaper in their houses, the scenery is all around them, and they sort of know that it is there, but they don't really look at it very often.

But parks are pretty expensive if they are only wallpaper. Surely they are more than just wallpaper to surround us while we do things we do quite as well, or even better, somewhere else.

Enter Interpretation

The first time that I had thoughts like these was in 1949, and I had them in Manning Park.

It bothered me that Manning Park seemed to have nothing as a major attraction that could not be found bigger and better in other places nearby.

I decided that the only difference, the only thing that made Manning Park something different rather than a hoax, was that in future it would be wild and the other places would not. Wildness, which is nature unspoiled, is the only difference, and Manning's only special attraction. I also decided that while most people liked nature unspoiled, they did not really get very much out of it. After all, you can get just so much from wallpaper.

So in 1949, I made my first recommendation that there be interpretation in our parks. In 1957, eight years later, we were allowed to give it a cautious try. The problem ever since has been to find enough qualified people with enough time to keep up.

But what is interpretation? It is a combination of at least six things.

- It is a guiding service.
- It is an information service.
- It is an educational service.
- It is an entertaining service.
- It is a propaganda service.
- It is an inspirational service.
- It is all of these things put together in different amounts.

And the purpose of all of these is to get people to enjoy nature not just at a distance as scenery, but close up as rocks and trees, flowers, grasses, insects and birds. Interpretation's job is to reach people as they spend a whole minute looking at 50 square miles of scenery, and to show them happy hours poking about in just an acre of that scenery.

Scenery watching is a fine thing, and some people, like landscape painters, can use nature quite efficiently in this way, but most people think that they are through with scenery once they have glanced at it. If this is true, our parks are an expensive luxury that we cannot afford. It's people like these who drive to a park, stop once in the park, then jump into their cars to drive on to the next park. They will tell you later about the parks they have seen. They saw them all right, as wallpaper.

People want to know more about nature, but most people don't even know that they want to know more, and many that do know, don't know how to go about it. Every year we see clear evidence that this is so. We interpret nature in BC parks to over 100,000 people each summer, and we find that the best way to understand people is to watch them. For that matter, what other way is there?

We have people who once didn't know a robin from a cedar coming back every year to learn more—about their parks. Every year parents bring us children who somehow caught fire last summer, or the summer before perhaps, and they have taken something a park naturalist said or showed to them, and they have built it into a lifetime interest that will give them a lifetime of pleasure. It really makes no difference what this interest is. It can be anything. It can be in bugs or flowers, in birds or rocks, in spiders or pine cones, and no matter what the interest is, it is valuable because it will bring a lifetime of pleasure. There can be nothing more valuable than this, and like most really valuable things, money can't buy it.

Every year we see more people in our parks enjoying the details of nature with cameras or packsacks or binoculars or magnifying glasses, or maybe just with a child in tow. Often we know these people from previous years.

These people are the users of our parks, the intensive users, enjoying to the full the things that the park is made of.

I have said that interpretation is a guiding service. One of our major jobs is to tell people where to go in the parks to do the things they want to do. Sometimes we actually lead the way to things of interest on conducted walks.

I have said that interpretation is an information service. We answer questions and we give information that we are not asked for.

I have said that interpretation is an education service. We avoid acting like teachers in classrooms, but one of our most popular tasks is using pleasant methods to improve people's knowledge of their parks. Speaking generally, the more people know about parks, the more they want to know, and many people get their holiday "kicks" from collecting understandings of what makes nature tick. We do not aim at educating deeply. We aim only at opening the doors in people's minds so they will go elsewhere to fill up the space inside. We do this with nature house exhibits, with outdoor signs, with nature trails, with guided walks and with evening slide shows.

I have said that interpretation is entertaining. It has to be. We want people to come to us, and if what we had to offer was not entertaining, they would not come. Fortunately, most people find that interesting things are entertaining things. For obvious reasons, we avoid many entertaining approaches because they do not help people understand parks. We could pack people in using bubble dancers or Mickey Mouse cartoons, or free feature movies; but our job is not to pack people in. It is to help people get more enjoyment out of their parks. The entertainment factor must not run away with the main task to be done.

I have said that interpretation is a propaganda service. We know that by helping people understand nature, and hence understand parks, these people take better care of nature, and so of parks. We reduce vandalism, and some things that we tell people are purposely aimed at reducing vandalism. We also, quite openly, get people to stop littering parks with garbage; to reduce wear on parks by walking on trails and roads; to reduce dangers in parks, as from bears or getting lost. And, unavoidably, we are telling a conservation story that people take home with them to use everywhere, not just in parks.

I have said that interpretation is an inspirational service. The extent to which we inspire people is the real measure of our success. I would rather inspire one person than bore a thousand, or merely entertain a hundred. This most important task is the hardest task of all. One doesn't inspire by formula; one does it with infectious enthusiasm, or by firing imaginations with the spectacular, the beautiful, the sheer delight of new understanding. Some people do this better than others. Really, the subject matter has little to do with it; it's more a matter of how it is done. I would expect a really good interpreter to be inspiring if he were talking about a drop of water. This inspirational aspect of interpretation not only changes people's lives in wonderful ways; it also has a major influence on the future of parks. People inspired about wild nature, so inspired about wild parks, are the people who want parks badly enough to defend them when they need defending. Interpretation builds up a loyal following of these park users. The most successful park systems in the world have a large body of inspired supporters. Interpretation has done much of the inspiring.

I suppose that park interpretation or nature interpretation explained in its simplest terms is this: it is opening the eyes of people; it is sharpening the noses of people; it is tuning the ears of people; it is sensitizing the touch of people. We each have a number of antennae out to pick up signals from our surroundings—our eyes to pick up light, our ears to pick up sound, our noses to pick up odours, our skin to pick up touch signals. These wonderful instruments are useless unless their signals are received. Most of us do not receive very much. The job of interpretation is to open the minds of people so they can receive—on the world's best receiver, the human brain—the interesting signals that parks are constantly sending.

The purpose of interpretation is to help people enjoy their parks. I did not say its purpose is to help people enjoy themselves in parks. This can be quite another matter and may involve all sorts of activities best carried out elsewhere. The difference is very important.

So while entertaining, we give directions, hand out information, educate a bit and even spread a little beneficial propaganda. If we do it right, we will inspire a few people so that the park becomes a special place to them, and their lives will never be quite the same again.

This is the aim of interpretation in the parks of British Columbia. We try our best to achieve this aim. If we never quite make it, we know that we are getting some results, for we can see them every summer as we watch people in our parks.

Annual Report, 1964

Interpretation and Research

Throughout the summer, park naturalists conducted daily interpretation programmes in five parks—Manning, Miracle Beach, Mitlenatch Island, Shuswap Lake, and Goldstream. Using nature houses, nature trails, guided walks, and an outdoor theatre, this staff made over 132,000 contacts with park-users.

Nature houses in Manning, Miracle Beach, and Shuswap Lake Parks served 62,000 people, most of these in July and August. A record day at Miracle Beach nature house on Labour Day saw over 1,500 people jam into the building.

Nature trails were maintained in Manning (two trails), Miracle Beach, Goldstream, Shuswap Lake; Emory Creek, and Skihist Parks. They were used by an estimated 70,000 people.

Guided walks, outdoors, were daily features in Miracle Beach and Goldstream Parks, and frequent attractions in Manning Park. Over 4,100 people participated.

A new feature in Manning Park was an amphitheatre, an outdoor theatre where park naturalists gave 40 late-evening talks, using slides, to more than 2,500 people. Some evenings the theatre was filled to capacity.

Fifteen new indoor displays were constructed and installed in nature houses. Numerous outdoor signs and displays were made and placed. Three new pamphlets were produced—one on nature houses, one on blueprinting natural objects, and one on star identification.

A survey of stands of large trees located in parks or recreational reserves on Vancouver Island revealed an only fair preservation of samples of the forest that made British Columbia famous. One stand has trees rivalling the record height for Douglas firs in the Province...

Twenty-six parks not mentioned above were variously surveyed and assessed for their possible future interpretative needs.

Annual Report, 1965

Interpretation and Research

During the year, park naturalists conducted interpretation programmes in nine parks—Manning, Miracle Beach, Mitlenatch Island, Shuswap Lake, Goldstream, Wickaninnish Beach, Ellison, Okanagan Lake, and Haynes Point. The programmes were new at the last four parks mentioned, and at the last three a new kind of programme was offered two days a week in each park by a park naturalist travelling on a regular schedule. Naturalists interpreted parks to over 150,000 people through nature houses, nature trails, guided walks, and outdoor talks. Additional interpretation was done through outdoor signs and displays.

Nature houses were visited by more than 64,000 people, mainly through July and August. Miracle Beach nature-house attendance set a nature-house record with a total of 28,000 visits.

Nature trails were maintained in Manning (3 trails), Miracle Beach, Shuswap Lake, Goldstream, Emory Creek, and Skihist Parks, and briefly in Crooked River Park where an experiment failed. They were used by an estimated 70,000 people.

Guided walks, most of them from one to two hours long, were offered on regular schedules in all nine parks having park naturalists. These were new ventures in Wickaninnish Beach, Shuswap Lake, Ellison, Okanagan Lake, and Haynes Point Parks. About 7,000 people were led on 413 walks, with the most patronage being in July and August.

Evening outdoor talks, offered in only Manning Park last year, were given in six additional parks this summer—Shuswap Lake, Wickaninnish Beach, Ellison, Okanagan Lake, Haynes Point, and Goldstream Parks. Only Manning Park had facilities to show slides. Other "theatres" were impromptu gatherings about a camp-fire. Naturalist staff talked to over 11,000 people, using about 15 titles on 236 talks.

Consistent with the policy of keeping nature houses fresh and interesting, 11 new indoor exhibits were planned, manufactured, and in place for the summer. A new programme of outdoor display signs at the entrances to parks was expanded from the two experimental displays of past years to a total of 12.

Annual Report, 1966

Interpretation and Research

In 1966, park naturalists experienced increases in public use of all interpretation programmes that were greater than any previous year. Every phase of every programme in every park accumulated participation figures that were typically much greater than those of previous years. Some increases were well over 100 per cent. Walks, talks, and nature houses served 103,500 people; nature trails and outdoor exhibits were used by an estimated 70,000; and parks offering mainly natural visual attractions, such as MacMillan and Petroglyph Parks, received an estimated 65,000 people. Although numbers are not reliable indicators of our success in interpretation, they do indicate that about 240,000 people were associated with interpretation programmes.

Through the summer, park naturalists conducted interpretation programmes in nine parks. Nature houses in Manning, Miracle Beach, and Shuswap Lake Parks offered a total of 65 exhibits. Of these, 16 were new, having been made the previous winter in the interpretation shop. Attendances at each of two nature houses exceeded the previous record total of 28,000. Miracle Beach nature house set a new high mark of 32,000, or about 400 visitors per day.

Regular walks in nine parks (721 walks, 10,000 participants) showed people a wide assortment of natural features, from nesting gulls to scorpions, and from boa constrictors to giant forest trees.

Regular evening talks, often around a campfire (307 talks to 18,000 people), were given in nine parks. Two programmes were new, those in Miracle Beach and Mitlenatch Island Parks. A new permanent amphitheatre was constructed in Shuswap Lake Park. Talks in other parks were in informal and often makeshift settings, except in Manning Park, where slide shows in an amphitheatre were a daily feature.

Nine nature trails operated in seven parks. These offered numerous small signs describing trailside features, using approved texts from a collection now numbering 365 different messages. A new nature trail was built and used in Mitlenatch Island Nature Park. In Manning Park, Mule Deer Nature Trail was constructed, complete with a bridge across the Similkameen River, and will be in operation in 1967. Also to be open next year, in Spahats Creek Park, is a short nature trail through beautiful old timber. This trail was located and inventoried this year. In Manning Park the popular highway-side red rhododendron stand was made more accessible with a parking area and an outdoor display from which a loop trail leads through the stand.

Inventory of natural features in parks is essential for interpretation. In selected parks this work continues whenever possible, consisting mainly of listing species present and noting their abundance. Nine parks are involved, ranging ecologically from alpine areas to bunchgrass slopes, a marine island and an alkaline pond in grassland.

Interpretation programmes can be no better than the people involved. Our interpretation success to date is the result of highly qualified and enthusiastic staff being attracted to this work.

NATURE HOUSE ATTENDANCE

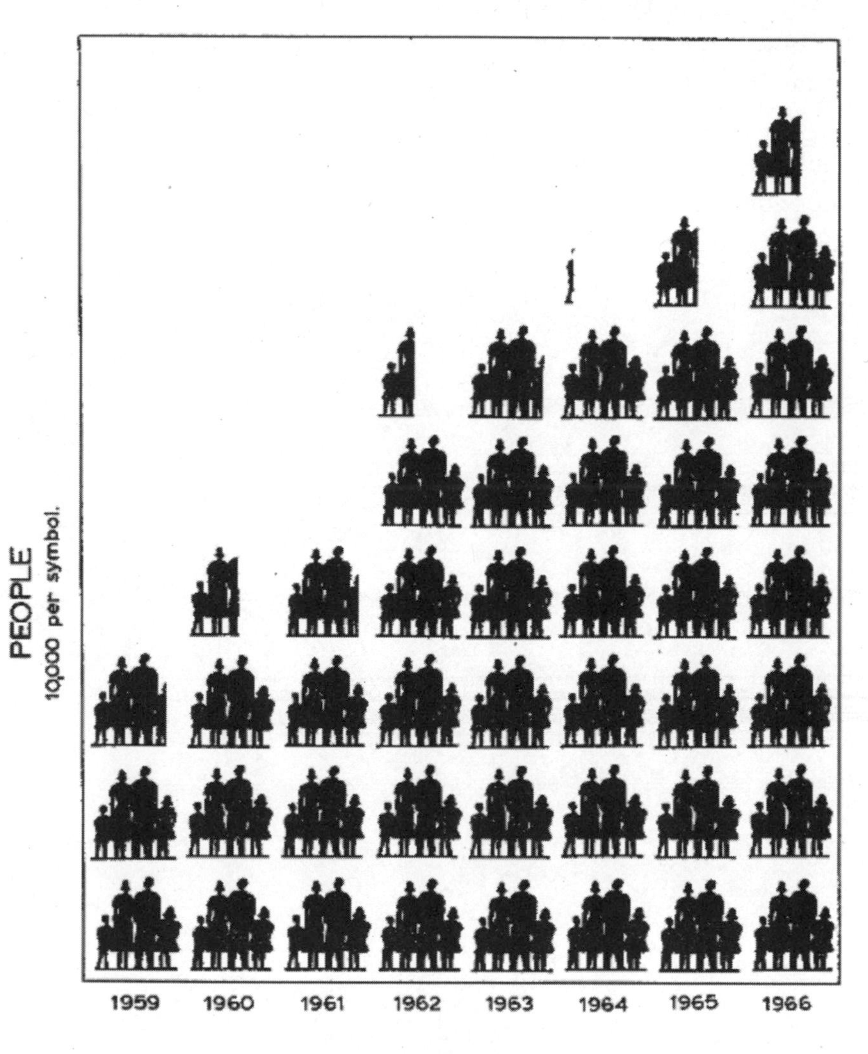

From the Department of Recreation and Conservation, Annual Report, 1966.

Yorke Edwards was the second editor (1963–1967) of *Museum Roundup*, the magazine of the BC Museums Association. In that context, he contributed this small note about the kind of work that his interpretation staff was doing in Manning Park.

The following is from the report of the Manning Park Nature House for 1965, and describes the best kind of exhibit, the kind that lets the visitor actually experience something historic:

"Another temporary display was carried out by David Neilson and David Gray. They made some kinnikinnick tobacco from dried Bearberry leaves, mixed it with some real tobacco, rolled it into cigarettes, and put up a sign telling about kinnikinnick, and offering smokers a real live Indian tobacco cigarette. People were very interested, and kept us busy making cigarettes—and they all smoked them to the bitter end." Reported by David Gray.

From *Museum Roundup* 25 (1967): 6.

Sign at Wye Marsh Wildlife Centre, Midland, ON. This oil painting, created for the centre in 1968 by Hugh Monahan, was copied and enlarged for the entrance to the centre. It shows a flock of American black ducks landing in the waters of the marsh. Edwards family photo.

Canadian Wildlife Service

In general, 1967 was a year of excellent progress for the Section. We did have one very serious loss. Mr. R.Y. Edwards, Park Officer i/c Research and Interpretation, left in midsummer to join the Canadian Wildlife Service. It should be recorded that our programme has been shaped by Mr. Edwards since its inception 10 years ago, and it is largely to his individual credit that today the programme is widely regarded as one of the leaders of its kind in North America.

Department of Recreation and Conservation, Annual Report, 1967.

Yorke's work in the BC Parks Branch did not go unnoticed. In 1967, he was enticed by the Canadian Wildlife Service (CWS) to move to Ottawa to create a series of wildlife centres representing the major biotic regions of Canada, showing the wonder of Canada's natural history to Canadians through innovative and engaging interpretation.

David Munro, director of the CWS, developed the idea of this national network. In 1968, Munro, along with John Livingston (one of Canada's great naturalists, then at York University), Ian McTaggart Cowan (wildlife biologist and vertebrate taxonomist at the University of BC, who had been the vertebrate curator at the BC Provincial Museum in the 1930s), William Gunn (who created an enormous archive of nature sounds), Andrew Macpherson and William Whitehead produced a CBC-TV documentary *A Place for Everything*. It was the transformation of this series from the realm of television to the creation of physical structures and animated programs on the ground across Canada that Yorke was now asked to enact.

Naturalists and Nature Interpretation (1967)

Talk given at the annual dinner of the McIlwraith Field Naturalists Club in London, ON, December 1, 1967.

MY SUBJECT IS NATURE INTERPRETATION, but first I want to talk about naturalists, and about some of my experiences as a naturalist. After-dinner speeches should not be too heavy, and while long enough to be worthwhile, not long enough to make the chair too hard. The problem here is that long for one person may be short for another, so forgive me if I make your chair uncomfortable.

Forgive me, too, for talking of myself. I know my experiences best, and I use them in the hope that they are something like other people's experiences. Maybe I'm an average naturalist, if there is such a thing.

And forgive me for working in a message or two. I enjoy trying out original thoughts, especially if someone will disagree with me.

Scenes then

In my younger days I was willing to concede that naturalists are a bit queer. I have since changed my mind, but that, for the moment, is another part of the story. Since I have been a naturalist from my early teens, the uncertainties of youth, and the wishes to conform that are so strong in our youthful years, were with me for a large part of my naturalist life. To be different at that age is to feel queer. I felt that way, but I couldn't help myself, for I was a naturalist and that was that.

The result was some painful experiences—painful at the time, that is—but looking back they are simply amusing now, and should have been at the time as well.

Field clothes are often a bit on the worn out or disreputable side, or at least they were in the days when money was scarce, and the city naturalist frequently found himself on city buses and streetcars. Sundays were good times to get out with binoculars, notebook and an assortment of equipment in a packsack. The early morning rides out were usually uneventful. The city still slept, aside from a few shift workers and the occasional all-night-party people, but the return trip was another matter. The ride back was among crowds of people dressed in their best and on their pious way home from church. Never was civilized man so stiffly civilized. And there we were among them, tattered, often wet, usually dirty, and hung with queer equipment. We were acutely aware of disapproving glances, and we seemed to get special reactions when the weather was wet and heavy field clothes gave off their special perfume, or when the packsack held a special treasure, like a gull or a mole that was very dead and on its way home for careful indoor study. Toronto was still the "good," or at least thought it was, and in a small way we were probably the hippies of those days—in some minds at least.

Sometimes the early mornings were exciting too. Walk the quiet streets at 5 a.m., even in those days, and you were suspicious simply because you were there. A motor coming slowly up behind was often a police cruiser. I explained the hobby of birdwatching to so many policemen that I got pretty good at it. But even at my best, my audience still looked unconvinced when I was through. I was sure that my efforts just created a new kind of suspicion. After all, to an ordinary person, anyone who rises before dawn just to look at birds could be queer in other ways too.

Even at civilized hours, nervous housewives seeing us sneaking about with binoculars occasionally called for help, with the result that a big policeman marched upon us, scaring rare birds; and during the war, hawks and owls about airports lured many a naturalist, complete with spy equipment like binoculars, into the arms of security guards. With luck you got home for dinner, but somehow the experience left you convinced that you really were seriously different.

When I went into Canada's wilder places, I thought that things would be different. In the far Chilcotin of British Columbia, where the grizzly bear still caught salmon in icy mountain rivers, and Indians had only a veneer of civilization over their old and often better ways, I felt far away from long-faced Sunday people in noisy street cars. But I soon found that queer in Toronto is queer in the Chilcotin too. We were a government party sent into the backwoods ranch country to do a survey of waterfowl populations. Our arrival caused a panic. The miles between far-flung ranches have a moccasin telegraph that joins them, and we were from the Game Department. Soon every rancher was busy hiding evidence. Green moose hides and fresh venison were buried hurriedly over a large part of that wild country in that month of May. But we had nothing to do with law enforcement. And we were regarded with a new kind of suspicion when we finally convinced people that we were there just to look at birds. In that country, anyone who didn't mend fence, cut wood, punch cattle or cut hay all week, to get drunk on Saturday so you could recover on Sunday, was definitely queer, especially if you wasted time just looking at birds and such things. I can remember telling a rancher that I was also collecting mice for the university. He looked at me like I told him I could fly like a bird. I let the matter drop, but he didn't. The story soon got around, as news will in a country where news is scarce. Of course, no one believed it, so I was glad I hadn't told him that I was collecting fleas as well.

As some of you will know, the naturalist in an unknown country has a duty to science, and while he may not be much of a collector at home, in faraway places he may enthusiastically take up traps and a gun and collecting jars and a plant press. It was this way in the Chilcotin. And one of the spare-time activities I worked at most was collecting small mammals—mainly mice, shrews and squirrels. Mostly I trapped them, but I wanted to have a large series of chipmunks, so I often carried a .410 shotgun with me. A favourite place near camp to hunt them was along the telephone line. This was a primitive strand of wire that crossed half of British Columbia from Williams Lake in the Interior to Bella Coola on the coast. The Japanese scare during the war had caused it to be built. And through the dreary pine forests it cut a sunny swath that chipmunks loved. Piles of wood from clearing the swath made chipmunk fortresses.

On a memorable evening in July it was hot and sticky, for thunderstorms had hung all day over the nearby Rainbow Mountains. The mosquitoes were plentiful and aggressive. I decided to leave camp in search of a breeze, and as always took binoculars and the little shotgun. Two miles from camp, near the telephone line, I spotted a chipmunk on a pile of pine bolts. I did a long, careful stalk, crawling in the dust, hot, sticky and feeding mosquitoes. When I fired, the chipmunk vanished. I was sure he had departed this world instantly, so assumed he had fallen deep into the heap of pine. Hot, perspiring, dirty, freckled with squashed mosquitoes, and now rather out of sorts, I burrowed into the woodpile. The wood flew, and I was soon on my knees, my head deep into the crater I had dug. Then, quite suddenly, for some reason I knew I was not alone. My position was undignified, but with as much dignity as I could assemble, I backed out.

Gazing down on me from horses were the steady eyes of two Chilcotin Indians.* As Indians will, they showed no expression, they didn't move and they were absolutely silent. For some reason an explanation from me was essential and urgent. The truth seemed unbelievable, so in my confusion I clutched suddenly at an idiotic fiction. I put on a sickly smile and said, "I'm re-piling the wood." As if this covered the situation and closed the conversation. I bent to the task of rebuilding the pile. They watched in stunned silence. Then rode on their way.

I was never good at instant white lies, and this was one of my worst. Soon the whole Chilcotin would know that the crazy looker at birds and hunter of mice also liked to burrow into woodpiles and then re-pile them. But what would you have done? I was hunting cute little chipmunks with a weak little gun not much better than a toy, and I had just had a tiny chipmunk outwit me. Hot and bothered, and caught in the act of doing something pretty hard to explain, I suddenly was cowering under the steady gazes of two of the tribe's best hunters. These were stalkers of the mighty grizzly bear and relentless hunters of the tireless mountain caribou. Big rifles hung in their saddle scabbards. Was I to tell them the story of the chipmunk hunt?

* Today, the name of this First Nation is spelled Tŝilhqot'in.–Eds.

But as is often the case, I had fooled no one. A rancher told me later that the Indians had watched my stalk as I burrowed through the dust and bushes, then shot at the woodpile. This was puzzling enough to them, but the show I put on after that had the local Indian population theorizing for weeks.

It was Tom Squinas who finally solved their mystery.* Tom had the rare combination of being both Indian and somewhat extroverted. He began coming to our campfire and accepting mugs of coffee. He didn't say much, but he seemed to have decided we were safe. One evening he came when I was skinning a shrew. He was convulsed. No doubt thinking of the beaver he had skinned the winter before for $100 each, he looked at the little shrew, smaller than his finger. "Ho," he said, "him not worth much!" And in his world, it wasn't. I showed him my collection then, 40 or 50 mice and shrews, chipmunks and squirrels, a rabbit and a porcupine and a weasel or two. He didn't understand, although it did help solve for him the mystery of the woodpile. And I'm sure I stayed just as queer to him as I had ever been. About all I had done was convince him that I was probably harmless.

The scene now

This is the way it was, but things have changed in recent years. This is partly because being a naturalist is now about as common a thing as being a duck hunter. People do not really think unusual hobbies are queer; they simply don't understand anyone doing the unusual. The naturalist, and among all naturalists

* Squinas was a Tŝilhqot'in chief from the Ulkatcho First Nation at Anahim Lake. In 1951, on horseback, he explored the rugged territory between Anahim Lake and Bella Coola, searching for the best route for a road through the Coast Mountains.–Eds.

especially the birdwatcher, is now no longer an unusual element of our society. When government bureaus run national surveys to count naturalists, and when a large car manufacturer uses birdwatchers to help sell one of America's most expensive cars, there can be little doubt that these are now "in" groups.

To most people there are two kinds of things: the familiar and the unfamiliar. The familiar is accepted without question; the unfamiliar is suspicious. I can think of nothing more ridiculous and useless than a man devoting a large part of a day to whacking a small white ball about a big lawn so he can put the ball into 18 fairly large holes in the ground. But golf is familiar, so we accept it. I'm sure that an intelligent being from outer space would find many of our popular hobbies and games too dull or too artificial, but I would bet that he would be a keen naturalist. Naturalists are involved with real, basic things. Few interests concern matters of such substance.

Not only have people and their ideas changed through the years, but I have changed too. Much of my change is based on one great truth that I stumbled on while doing a little private research on car washing. I once worked in an office where cars seemed to be the chief topic of conversation, and most of my colleagues drove cars that always shone. By comparison, I found it difficult to consider a car more than a motorized tin can with wheels, and my cars were always dirty. All my life, my days have been too short to do all the fascinating things that there are to do, and taking time to wash a car is about as low on my list of things to do as the list goes. I even begrudge the time to run a car through a commercial car wash. So I decided to investigate. My little office research project soon uncovered a fact that startled me. Most of my associates polished their cars every weekend, and they did it mainly because they were bored and didn't know what else to do. A second fact I uncovered was somewhat suspect. Many of these men considered their hunks of motorized iron to be some kind of status symbol. So part of the weekly cleanup was really a shining up of one's status.

My car wash research was the turning point of my life as a naturalist. Suddenly I understood my fellow men far better than ever before, for I realized that most of them do not have interesting things overflowing their lives with happy hours and pleasant activity and accomplishments, however minor. Small wonder that naturalists are considered to be different. But it was my resolve to help these poor devils that changed my life. I went into the field of nature interpretation.

So here, in a shaggy dog sort of way, I arrive at the point of my talk.

Nature interpretation

Nature interpretation is a scarce, suspicious, new sort of thing, like naturalists once were, and the first step toward getting it accepted is to clearly state what it is. The word "interpretation" is here a handicap, but we are stuck with it. This is not interpretation in the sense of translating the mysteries of an unfamiliar language into one's native tongue. This is the translation of the mysterious jargons and complexities of science into everyday terms that are attractively presented. It has one feature that usually makes its task both easy and successful, and that is that interpretation tells its story right where the thing talked about can be seen or smelled or heard or felt. With advantages like this, small wonder that nature interpretation is so often successful.

Most of you, if you know about nature interpretation, have learned about it in parks. In the parks of North America, and especially in the national parks of the United States, the methods and objectives of nature interpretation have evolved and grown for 40 years. It is now active outside of parks, invading city greenbelts, nature sanctuaries, summer camps and even schoolyards.

The confusion over what nature interpretation does that is different is understandable, for it is nothing really new; it is rather a new combination of familiar things. It has borrowed bits from museums, public relations, information services, showmanship, public speaking, advertising techniques, education and theatre. The result is like none of these things most of the time, but when there is a need it can swing into temporarily being entirely one of these things quite gracefully and successfully. Usually, however, interpretation is using appropriate methods to introduce people to new understanding, while inspiring them to go beyond the introduction on their own into what might be called education. Interpretation gives well-chosen morsels of the feast available, the morsels showing clearly the quality and the scope of the feast that is there for the taking. This is how interpretation makes naturalists of people, and I have watched many people discover a new interest in the world about them through nature interpretation.

To those people already naturalists, nature interpretation offers valuable services. When I first went into the American desert, I felt like I was on another planet, so different was the landscape and its living things. To me, a new landscape is frustrating until I can begin fitting together understandings of what makes the place look like it does, and what living things dwell there. The desert didn't frustrate me long. The Americans have done a superb job with parks in their arid southwest, and an equally good job of interpreting them. For some reason I especially remember Organ Pipe Cactus National Monument, 330,000 acres of desert on the Mexican border in Arizona. Arrive there, and a convenient nature centre offers displays on what makes the desert dry, how plants and animals live in the desert, what plants and animals live there, and a bit of history. An attendant nearby knows most of the answers, and he will sell you books and leaflets to further your enjoyment of the desert. Nearby was a car-sized nature trail. This was a good one-way road with periodic stops clearly indicated. A printed pamphlet keyed to the stops soon had my family looking on the desert with new interest and a new resolve to know more. Interpretation had us involved in the desert. Interpretation had done its job.

Misinterpretations

Another task of interpretation is to get people to forget the load of misinformation that many of us carry about. As a boy in Ontario I remember learning about hoop snakes rolling downhill, black snakes chasing people across fields, milk snakes taking milk from cows, and a lot of other nonsense so improbable that it was difficult to remember.

Whenever I think of nature fictions, I think of the lady who took her small child into one of our nature centres in British Columbia. The child was a bit frightened by it all, and the mother leaned down and was heard to say, "Don't be afraid, dear. None of it is *real*. This is a nature centre." Nature is all fiction to some people.

Others want it to be fiction, but the fairy tale can be ruined by reality. One day a woman confronted a BC park naturalist with this one. "Why," she said, "does nature have to be spoiled by snakes?"

Another woman rushed in one day and asked, "Is this where you take blood samples?"

There seems to be no limit to the confusion, even in adult minds, and one wonders what nests of errors are hidden there.

A classic example of this sort of mental chaos is in the essay of a small city boy who wrote about the cow. Even if you have heard it, I'm sure you can enjoy it again. He wrote:

> The cow is a mammal. It has six sides, right and left, upper and below, also backside and inside. At the back it has a tail on which hangs a brush, and with this he [*sic*] sends flies away so that they don't fall into the milk. The head is for the purpose of growing horns and so his mouth can be somewhere. The horns are to butt with and the mouth is to moo with. Under the cow hangs milk. It is arranged for milking. When people milk, milk comes, and there is never an end to the supply. How the cow does it I have not yet realized, but the cow makes more and more. The cow has a fine sense of smell and you can smell it far away. This is the reason for fresh air in the country. A man cow is called an ox. A cow doesn't eat much, but what it eats, it eats twice so that it gets enough, and when it is hungry it moos, and when it says nothing at all it is because its insides are full up with grass.

This was a mixed-up boy with a lot of facts, but somehow they didn't go together very well. We all have our confusions (not this bad I hope), and one task of nature interpretation is to straighten out these fables.

Future interpretation

Nature interpretation grew up in our parks. It is now ready to step into other situations, like telling conservation and land use stories right out on the land where the story has full meaning.

Another task for it to do has special meaning to naturalist groups such as this. Near Victoria, British Columbia, in a large patch of preserved forest, is a small and popular nature centre. That forest, and that nature centre, were fought for, obtained and now looked after by the Victoria Natural History Society. Thousands of people every year enjoy that forest and enlarge their enjoyment in the nature centre. Children do most of the trail work and most of the supervision of the centre as well.

If British Columbia can do this, I think Ontario can too, and in several places.

The naturalists are numerous now, and our society knows that we are here. Our image will be big or small in proportion to our service to our communities, and I can think of nothing more rewarding to naturalists than showing people nature and in the process creating more naturalists. Naturalists especially, I believe, should be active in nature interpretation. Many are. But very few are reaching people who are not already naturalists.

A touch of evangelism is our greatest present need.

Frank Buffam, Manning Provincial Park, 1960.
Courtesy of Frank Buffam.

Educational Measures Dealing with the Conservation of the Natural Environment (1968)

Paper presented to the International Federation of Landscape Architects at the Bonaventure Hotel in Montreal, QC, June 20, 1968.

Introduction

IT HAS BEEN SAID THAT a teacher affects eternity, for there is no end to his influence on men. This puts the teacher in the special position of influencing the behaviour of men far into the future, and of being a force for good or evil, depending on the content of the teaching.

Teachers are not just the people instructing in our schools. Those in schools are the agents of formal education from kindergarten to postgraduate studies at university, but this formal education is only one of many educational influences upon human thought and behaviour. When we think of education we think of schools, but this is a narrow view. Most of the education that shapes our lives comes informally from social contacts, from publications, from television and from other influences on thought like displays and movies and radio. In a very real way, many people are our teachers, and most do not reach us in schools.

The word "conservation" is a dangerous one, for it has many meanings, and some are as different as black and white. The trees that the forester wishes to cut down in the name of conservation, the park planner may want left standing in the name of conservation. There are many such conflicts possible, and anyone working at land management soon learns that the word "conservation" is a constant source of confusion and misunderstanding. In my title, a better word might be "preservation."

The world of naturalists and outdoor enthusiasts and wild wilderness supporters is full of platitudes. I suppose most such worlds are. You have just heard an unusual and stimulating paper in which many of these platitudes were held up for inspection. We need more of this approach.

My approach will be much more conventional. Education is my main theme, and I elected not to get much involved with illuminating sacred cows.

Ordinarily I am against beginning a talk with definitions, but I kept the title given to me, even though it contained three words with debatable meanings. These are "education," "conservation" and "natural." All three require brief examination.

I plan first to comment on these words, then to examine briefly the need for untamed landscape. Next, I wish to look quickly at the forces opposing improvement to the quality of our surroundings. Finally, I will examine the educational media that are today enlarging the public awareness of beauty and diversity and intellectual adventure in our wild and partly wild landscapes.

Our surroundings—our environment—can be completely wild in one extreme, or almost completely man-made. Between these extremes can be every conceivable blend of the wild and the tamed. Some wild elements are always present. Even in the glass and concrete world at the heart of a large city there is a sparrow on the pavement and clouds in the sky overhead. Both the sky and the sparrow are partly influenced by man, but both have also a degree of wildness. In this way there is some wildness everywhere. This degree of wildness in the landscape is at its highest possible value in wilderness areas, but even when we live in large cities, wild elements in our surroundings frequently touch our lives.

These wild parts of our world have come to be known as "natural." The idea is not a good one. Man is surely natural, so what he does is natural. He is not, I hope, unnatural. He is part of nature. It is much better to think of wild (or untamed) elements in the landscape than to get involved with attempts to divide the world into natural things and the others—whatever they are.

The need for education

Man came originally from green living places, and there can be no doubt that man needs a measure of untamed things and untamed places in his life. Proof of this need is to be seen everywhere, in man's interest in gardens and in other animals, and in his large and frequent expenditures of time and money to get away from cities on weekends and to seek vacations in variously wild landscapes.

At the same time, man is the most destructive biological force that the face of Earth has ever seen. Using increasingly powerful machines and chemicals, man easily destroys vegetation, exterminates animals and changes the very surface geology of Earth. His increasing powers of destruction have kept pace with an even more frightening increase of population. The world is filling up with people.

All life is basically selfish. Survival through the ages has demanded an essentially selfish attitude. To sustain life, the individual has taken what he needed, or wanted, from his surroundings. Originally there was no reason to be gentle with the landscape. It seemed endless, and the people in it were few, so the small destruction a man and his crude tools might cause had little influence on the countryside. All this has changed. Billions of people with hugely expanding powers of destruction now swarm the Earth. Unless there is careful use of these powers, and much unselfish concern for the welfare of others, the face of the Earth must degenerate. Selfish modification of the landscape, when undertaken by billions of people, is destructive change too extensive to visualize.

Like all living things, man must take his needs from the surface of the Earth. But if the limited surface of this planet is to support men with some measure of dignity, some measure of beauty, some measure of relief from monotony, man must preserve some of the wildness that is the original condition of landscapes.

In preserving these wild things, it is not enough to save bits of wilderness land in their almost completely wild conditions. I have no doubt that these parks and preserves are priceless areas that we must save. But while I believe that such areas are essential even when remote, and that we are in danger of having far too few of them, I consider it far more important to preserve some of the wild character of our everyday landscapes where it can enrich the daily lives of people. This is much harder to do and can be much less spectacular when done, but in the long run it must accomplish more. The need here is to keep trees in cities, and birds in those trees. And to keep squirrels, not as beggars of crumbs from people, but as meaningful users of the trees. The need is also to keep some marshes and forests in agricultural landscapes, and to keep wild ducks and turtles in the marshes, and wild deer in the forests. The need is to preserve some old forest in landscapes used mainly to produce forest products, and to preserve some of the plants and animals that must have old forest if they are to survive at all. These sorts of things are the challenges. Men can have these sorts of landscapes if they wish to have them. As in all matters of quality, it is simply a matter of values and of knowing enough to make intelligent evaluations. Without knowledge—gained through education—there is not much hope of high-quality landscapes that enrich the lives of men.

The counterforces

The task of educating people to preserve diversity in their environments is discouragingly large, and it has an alarming number of counterforces acting against its success.

It is large because the number of people is large. In even the small population of Canada there are 20 million people. The problem of reaching 20 million people is gigantic enough, but the task is not just to reach them. The task is to teach them.

The counterforces are potent and diversified. Some of the most important follow.

Some innate characteristics of men are involved. We are all inherently self-centred. The man preserving the landscape in his own neighbourhood may be a wrecker of the landscape elsewhere. To some degree, most of us are involved in this "uglification" of the land. Social courtesy is really confined to only a few situations. We say "please" when asking and murmur apologies for inconveniencing, but at the same time we scatter our refuse on the property of others, and pollute public land and water and air without much sense of wrongdoing. I live on the edge of a city near a greenbelt. Not many people there refrain from putting unwanted materials onto the public lands. Here sticks, stones, dead plants, grass clippings and heaps of earth are accepted pollutants of the public area.

Paper and similar refuse is not thrown there, but it is never picked up when found there. In North America, well away from one's own property, junk and household garbage are considered by many people to be properly discarded onto public lands. Small wonder that many public places have the same scenic charms as garbage dumps.

Also, society puts no reliable values on trees and birds, on quiet wild places, on pleasant form and colour. When a tree by a road is someone's delight, how does he defend it from the engineer making money by widening roads? How can colour and motion, form and shadows, the sanctuary of orioles and the drama of the changing seasons counteract the engineer's statements of traffic flow, convenience and greater safety?

Also, the process of formal education has done little to equip the eye to see beauty, or to help people maintain pleasant and diversified surroundings. To a sizeable part of humanity that this education has touched, one result has been a firm conviction that learning is boring, not very useful, painful and to be avoided whenever possible. New trends in our schools are beginning to correct this unfortunate side effect of the old teaching methods. But in the meantime, we have a population that is shy of learning. Fortunately, the learning processes that are entertaining, absorbing or otherwise pleasant are not usually recognized as education.

Finally, the most persuasive, ubiquitous educational activity in much of the world today is advertising. In industrialized and commercialized countries, this mass educational activity on an unbelievably large scale works endlessly at the minds of people. Playing on selfish desires, this unparalleled influence on human thought and behaviour creates considerable materialism and an almost pathological preoccupation with money as a yardstick for values. This condition, more than any other, has created a discouraging climate of opposition for those striving to give people surroundings that are interesting, beautiful, diversified and alive. Too often, dollars make it easier to have them dull, ugly, monotonous and dead.

Biology can demonstrate conclusively that animal quality is a reflection of environmental quality. This is a law affecting all life. Man has been slow to see this influence upon his own quality.

The effective education

In North America today, there are five forms of education teaching the values of untamed environment. The one with the greatest potential of all is not among these five. Learning in the home from family knowledge and tradition is not a major force in conservation today because the current crop of parents is largely uninformed. This will surely be the most important media of the future. But until an accumulation of awareness grows to become family tradition in many homes, five other avenues of learning will be the principal influence on public thought and action. These five will also be the main sources of the family tradition yet to come.

They are:

(1) the schools of today, including their satellite activities
(2) clubs catering to hobbies, and their educational programs
(3) television
(4) books and other publishing
(5) interpretation programs, mainly in government parks

To deal with these in turn:

Schools have always had a few inspired teachers capable of enthusiastic teaching on landscape quality. Usually this inspiring use of the classroom was augmented by field trips into the landscape itself, where the teaching took on real meaning because of personal contact with the environment. These trips into the real world out of the make-believe worlds of classrooms were often the stimulating and involving experiences that first opened young eyes to the meaning and value of diversified environment. Usually these trips were unofficial, undertaken in the teacher's own time and at his own expense. As is so often the case, these teachers were the dedicated, pointing the way and paying the bill to do so. Now, in some places at least, their success has resulted in official action.

The Province of Ontario, for example, encourages school boards in that province to acquire semi-wild lands on which to teach natural science, to build buildings, to accumulate equipment as necessary and to appoint staffs to the areas. The first and most famous of these natural science schools is on Toronto Island. Every Grade 6 student in the Toronto area has an opportunity to spend a week living with his classmates on the island, while the pleasant activity of exploring the world of wild things profoundly affects his view of his surroundings.* This is education of the best sort. Not many of the children consider it education, because it is fun.

Several other Ontario cities are following Toronto's lead, and others appear ready to begin. I consider this new trend in science education to be the major hope today for producing the citizens of tomorrow able to make intelligent decisions on environmental quality. Once a child has held a wild bird for banding, has measured and identified trees, has understood the needs of a wild plant, and has helped to put life on land that had no such life before, that child is more aware of the scope of nature, and is equipped to begin his understanding of his role in this living world. This outdoor education is surely a major offensive in the battle for people's minds. Without such programs we are in danger of being convinced that our major roles in life are merely as consumers of goods and services. How boring such living would be.

The new education reveals the most important thing on Earth—life—as fascinating to explore, and as satisfying to be involved with as another living thing.

Natural history societies, youth groups of various kinds and other voluntary organizations of people do a fine job across Canada of spreading the gospel of quality in the environment and of preserving diversity in the environment. Perhaps their most effective medium of communication is, again, through outdoor activities. One of the most successful

* The school on Toronto Island was established in 1960 by the Toronto Board of Education. Students from grades 5 and 6 in downtown Toronto would spend a week there. Today, teachers of grades 5 and 6 "from the inner core of the City of Toronto" can choose from a range of programs, which "continue to focus on giving students experiences which allow interaction with and appreciation for nature." "Island Natural Science School," Toronto District School Board, accessed December 2019, https://schoolweb.tdsb.on.ca/islandoutdoor/ (text since changed).–Eds.

is in Victoria, British Columbia, where the local natural history society sponsors a junior group. That group is a model of its kind. Those children do things. Led by an energetic man old enough to be a great-grandfather, these children have a forest that they manage for public enjoyment and study, they have weekly field trips full of adventure and action and understanding the outdoors, and they operate a display centre—a nature house—that is dedicated to explaining the world of nature to the public. Mainly through the efforts of one man, who somehow has the magic of a Pied Piper so that children follow with delight, hundreds of children have been happily oriented in their world, and their world has wide horizons and is filled with endless interesting variety.

Television's educational potential is very large, but most of it has yet to be realized. Much television that is educational and outdoor oriented uses techniques as old as the storyteller or as stereotyped as the B movie. There is much that holds attention, for television does this well, but there is little content to inform, to inspire, to remember because it is worth remembering. The educational function of television as a commercial tool is impressive today, but its role as an improver of men has so far been very limited—and in the opinion of some authorities has been negative.

Books and other publications dealing with our topic of interest are in impressive volume. However, a major weakness is that they are read mostly by those already interested in their message. Education is largely ineffective if it reaches mainly the educated. Most of us live in a constant blizzard of printed materials on a bewildering number of subjects. We are forced to be severely selective in our reading, so we select the interesting, which usually means that we select areas in which we are interested. This is not an efficient way to spread new ideas. There are some exceptions, of course. Front-page headlines on today's pollution crises are increasing public awareness of our surroundings, and books like Rachel Carson's *Silent Spring* enlarged rapidly the environmental knowledge of countless millions of people.[1] But usually the spread of knowledge through voluntary reading is a slow and inefficient process, and we must remember also that much of the literate world associates serious books with the miserable experiences of formal education.

Interpretation programs, mostly in government parks, are a rapidly growing influence on people's attitudes toward wild environments. In these attractive programs, millions of people annually are experiencing displays, audiovisual programs, campfire talks, conducted walks, nature trails and related methods for helping people understand the wild things about them. Like books, this educational method, which largely involves voluntary participation, does most of its communicating with people who are already convinced. Those that need the message most are apt to stay away. They have no interest, so they fail to expose themselves to becoming interested.

But some do come, and some do see the world through new eyes as a result, while, of course, large gains are made in improving the knowledge of the already converted. Certainly there is usually no lack of participating people, and in my experience too many people are the rule. Like television, here is a fairly new teaching method that has yet to reach its full potential. It is maturing quickly, however. Interpretive programs are found throughout North America today, and they will become more numerous. The interpretive approach is unusually effective, because it must be entertaining, inspiring and involving as well as informative, and its greatest strength is that it reveals the meaning of the environment while right there in the environment. Small wonder that nature interpretation is effective.

In all of this talk about education, one thing has bothered me. In our world, the word "science" is becoming deified, and scientific facts are becoming the controls on our lives. But these are things from a logical, precise, cold and dehumanizing world. We have the power to make our surroundings every bit as frigid and monotonous and dead as we wish, or, alternatively, we can maintain a living, beautiful, inspiring world of men to live in. Science and its facts are valuable parts of our lives, but so too is the pleasure from the songs of birds and the joy of finding a rare wild flower in an interesting landscape.

For many years I have been convinced that the most important conservation education of all is that which shapes the abilities and thoughts of land managers and land planners.* These can be the greatest enemies of wildness in the environment. Some landscape planners that I know approach wild landscapes with many of the same ideas that they would use to plan a formal garden. It is easy to forget that the more the land is landscaped, the less wild it is; and the best wild things must always be those created with no interference from man.

It is not easy to preserve wildness in our landscapes, and the main reason for this is that it takes wisdom and courage to be engaged, to be creative and then to honestly conclude that the wildness there cannot be improved. Unfortunately, it is in man's nature to want to gild the lily.

The last sentence ended my paper when I came to Montreal several days ago. Now I must add a comment after listening to some of your deliberations. As a Canadian, and as a naturalist who has spent much of his life concerned with some of the wilder parts of Canada, I have not been well informed on the profession of landscape architecture. I am delighted at what

* A pioneer of modern ecology, Aldo Leopold, expressed a similar sentiment when he wrote in a 1937 paper, "The real substance of conservation lies not in the physical projects of government, but in the mental processes of citizens." A. Leopold, "Conservation Blueprints," *American Forests* 43, no. 12 (1937): 596–608.—Eds.

I have seen and heard here. I now feel much less alone in my convictions on landscape quality.

I am sure that your stature will grow, as it has been growing, through education, for the best way of all to educate people on the good things that you can do is to show them the good things that you have done.

Notes

1 Rachel Carson, *Silent Spring* (Boston: Houghton Mifflin, 1962).

Original exhibits at opening of Wye Marsh Wildlife Centre, Midland ON, 1970. From left: Doug Haddow (naturalist), Judy Wilson (office administrator), Fran Westman (naturalist), Bill Barkley (biologist-in-charge), Gene Stratton (building and grounds development and maintenance). Edwards family photo.

Interpretation and the Public (1968)

Paper presented at the annual meeting of the Canadian Society of Wildlife and Fishery Biologists, Ottawa, ON, January 10, 1968.

Background

TO PUT MY TOPIC IN perspective, and to also run the risk of boring you with a bit of personal history, I am going to tell you why I am specializing in interpretation. This seems the simplest way to give you my opinion of the importance of interpretation, and my opinion is not lightly held, as my one-minute autobiography will make clear. If you will think back to college days, we who were concerned with the management of the Earth's real wealth had bull sessions on land management. With the enthusiasm of youth discovering new ideas, our talk ranged from walruses to white pines, and from wilderness to slum renewal.

Yet the discussions, whatever the topic, usually ended on much the same note: namely, that intelligent management was being hampered by public ignorance and inertia, and that more education was the only hope. We seldom explored who was going to do the educating. It seemed to be up to someone else, and with the naive faith of youth, we assumed that since the need was obvious, the authorities—whoever they were—would clear the path to our rosy future.

Later I found myself involved in a small way with research and management in the wildlife field. Both are stimulating and challenging fields, but after ten years of these I was still coming up against the action-stopping conclusions of the student bull sessions. More public understanding was needed. I was not happy with research that achieved mainly a stack of reprints, and the limits on management were usually people instead of a lack of knowledge about resources. A positive approach seemed to involve communicating with the public. So when my frustration coincided with my office endorsing a trial-run interpretation program, I changed hats without even leaving my desk. My temporary venture into the field of interpretation is now in its 11th temporary year.

These autobiographical notes seemed a better way than most to orient interpretation with the various land use fields. I could think of no more forceful way to indicate my ideas on the importance of interpretation nor on the potential of interpretation. For my opinion on its importance I could offer no words whatsoever—simply its planned domination of my life. As demonstration of my faith in its future, I can offer the fact that it made me forsake Victoria for Ottawa. What greater faith than this, not, of course, because Ottawa is so bad, but because Victoria to me is a unique and very special place.

What is interpretation?

Most of you, I hope, are familiar enough with interpretation to know that I'm not talking about language translation. So as an interpreter, I am not the fellow between an English tongue and a Russian tongue making meaningless sounds meaningful. But it has occurred to me recently that the difference is not very great. I stand between the scientist or specialist and the non-scientist and non-specialist, trying to translate specialized language and thinking into clear understandable English. With help, I hope to do the same with French. And in doing this translation I also must take the careful monotone of science and inject more attractiveness into the message. There is no point in talking if no one comes to listen.

Interpretation grew up and filled out in the US national parks. From there it has spread to many other park systems. If you have been touched by interpretation, the chance is overwhelming that the contact was in a national, provincial or state park. Even today, in many circles, interpretation in the natural sciences is in danger of being thought of as park interpretation alone. This is a restricted view that shortchanges a highly useful, wide-ranging approach to communication. It suggests Marshall McLuhan's remarks on IBM. Their major breakthrough, according to him, was the realization that they were not in the field of making office furniture; they were, rather, in the field of processing information. It does help to know what you are, and it does help to decide on the directions of your goals.

Interpretation is highly effective in parks, interpreting understanding of the outdoor environment, of the wisdom of proper use and of the values depending on park preservation. But interpretation's approach has a much wider arena available than parks alone, and a much larger audience potential than just park visitors. And this will become apparent if we examine the methods of interpretation.

The methods of interpretation

Interpretation is not public relations, not publicity, nor education, nor an information service, nor a propaganda machine. It does have areas in common with these, however, and it may have identical objectives. The main differences here are in the methods used, and the best way to compare them is with examples.

Suppose that a restaurant has added a gourmet dinner to its menu, and the public is to be informed about this new and outstanding service. To do this:

- Publicity might hire a sound truck, a girls' band and space in the local newspaper.
- Public relations might mail engraved invitations, see that a uniformed doorman was at the carpeted doorway and persuade a columnist to write about the dinner.
- An information service might have a famous chef write a booklet on the history of the dishes served and include the recipes involved. A short film for local audiences could use the book for script content.
- Education would set you down and lecture you about the aesthetics, ethnic history, nutrition and social significance of the dinner, all these being given as separate subjects.
- Interpretation would let you wander informally about a table, where you could sample bits of the food as you read brief labels telling what you are eating while trying also to fix something interesting in your mind about each dish. A short talk might relate the dishes to better-known foods.

If you want to eat a meal, you are on your own. As in anything, the complete experience usually comes from personal initiative and effort.

Note that interpretation was the only approach that required some of the food, and the interpretation is best if the sampling is done in the proper atmosphere of the dining hall. Within the hall, no holds are barred. Interpretation steals communication ideas and methods from any field with an effective approach worth stealing. Interpretation has pirated ideas from publicity, public relations, information, education, advertising display, printing and publishing, theatre, museums, public speaking, radio and television, and others.

The difference that makes it interpretation is that it communicates about something that is right there, so the audience is given a sample experience. When interpretation tells you about a Douglas fir, it wants your head back and your eyes looking up into the crown of a Douglas fir tree.

Interpretation today

Interpretation is becoming increasingly common in our world. Historic buildings, repaired and furnished, can reproduce the environments of the past, and reconstructions when honestly done can be almost as good. The teacher who brings a weed into the classroom to help teach the parts of a plant has brought a bit of reality into the pretend methods usual in education. He is interpreting, although both his interpretation and his effectiveness would be greater if he would take the children outdoors to the nearest clump of living, transpiring, growing weeds.

Real objects are good, but they do the best job when in a meaningful setting. This is why interpretation in museums has limitations. No matter how graceful and well-made, a Grecian bowl isolated in a glass box and set out in a modern institutional room is a rather meaningless thing. It is probably better than no bowl at all, but even this is debatable. The bear in a cage in a zoo is comparable to the bowl. Here is a real object—a bear—and the stage is set for interpretation. But even if we disregard the fact that most zoos communicate very little, and that often this is erroneous, there can be room for much misunderstanding if people, because of zoos, think of bears as neurotic, peanut-begging hulks shambling about stark and filthy cages. The bear, after all, is rather meaningless in such an environment, and few people are able to make allowances for this fact.

So interpretation uses real objects and meaningful environments, and while one or the other may be preferable to neither, both together are best.

Interpretation today is still found mainly in parks and historic sites. From these, it is beginning to invade museums and historic structures. It has, of course, existed in education for centuries. Not under the name of interpretation, but rather as an effective teaching method found here and there as a result of the initiative of good teachers. I suspect that changes are afoot now, but not long ago the teacher that brought objects to the classroom and took the class to objects and environments was a rare, creative thinker, unusually concerned about effective teaching.

One of the early pioneers in this sort of teaching was Liberty Hyde Bailey, who as early as 1903 had ideas that sound progressive today.* His influence was great, for he published and was widely read.

So this is about the present extent of organized interpretation. The big expansion, I believe, is just about to begin and

* Liberty Hyde Bailey (1858–1954) was an American botanist and horticulturist who authored, in 1903 and through several editions, *The Nature-Study Idea: An Interpretation of the New School Movement to Put the Young Into Relation and Sympathy With Nature* (New York: Doubleday, Page, and Co., 1905). "Nature-study, then, is not science. It is not knowledge. It is not facts. It is spirit. It is an attitude of mind. It concerns itself with the child's outlook on the world" (p. 6). This book, which all interpreters should try to read, can be found at https://www.biodiversitylibrary.org/item/62717#page/19/mode/1up.–Eds.

will involve the whole range of using the land and its products. Modest beginnings are functioning today. The Peace River dam site has an observation building for the public, exhibits on making the dam that use the best interpretation I have seen in years, and guided tours that get you involved with the dam as an immediate environment. A forest products company in Quebec has a nature centre to promote public understanding of the forest. Nature trails in Washington State, maintained by a lumber company, tell the story of forestry and the forest. Land users are beginning to be concerned about public understanding, and they are beginning to revise their opinions on how to spend their communications dollar to get a satisfactory result.

If the medium is the message, and even if it isn't, if you want to communicate about forestry or water or wildlife to the extent that people feel involved, what better approach than using trees or water or wildlife in some of the communicating.

The techniques of interpretation

There is nothing mysterious about interpretation. It simply uses the most effective methods available to try to infect its audience with interest, enthusiasm and revelation. The end sought is personal involvement that is independently undertaken. The interpretive phase is intended to be mainly introductory, followed by some subsequent help when there are difficulties.

There is some mystery, however, in how people vary one to another in their ability to be effective interpreters. The ability to interpret effectively is partly innate, partly learned. Every aspiring interpreter brings a different innate ability to the task, and here, of course, one or more innate excellences can often outweigh some deficiencies. The assets desirable are rather obvious, like ease with people, effective language, infectious enthusiasm, ingenuity, ability to see the viewpoint of others and so on. Some are not so obvious, like the ability to simplify a complicated story so it is both understandable and still essentially accurate, and the ability to make factual messages effective to audiences containing people from many backgrounds, many levels of education and many interests.

It is, of course, impossible to please everyone, and a built-in part of the interpretation job is to resist pressures to become too superficial on the one hand, and too technical or scientific on the other. Each limits effectiveness, for excessive simplicity says nothing, while language fit for a scientific journal is much the same to most people—it says nothing understandable. The interpreter is constantly turning to the expert for facts, and if he does his job well, he can be under fire frequently for changing the wording of the factual message. The resulting dialogues can be good for both expert and interpreter when both have a sympathetic understanding of the other's objectives. Without this understanding, not much results but heat.

So the interpreter tries to communicate only a bit of knowledge and understanding, hoping that he will kindle a spark that will grow into full interest and deep understanding. Using the light touch in order to be attractive, interpretation hopes to inspire a lasting interest as a result of trial involvements with situations and things. And to the extent that the facts offered must be attractive and understood, interpretation must simplify and glamorize the message that it passes on. While in theory this modification is dangerous, in practice I find that most specialists regard the result as more or less acceptable.

The public response

A fact that few communicators have realized is that the roads of North America in summer are jammed with people actively seeking interesting experiences. Commerce knows it. People in park offices know it. Aside from the heavy programs of park interpreters, and a blizzard of promotional literature for motels, resorts and various tourist traps, there is not much communicating with these experience-hungry people on their summer exodus from the cities.

Park interpretation has shown what response can result from efforts to reach them. Typically, park interpretation is swamped by people, often to the extent that the result is ludicrous. In the crush of humanity there is not much hope of getting very close to nature. Too often these programs are mediocre because volume of attendance has seriously affected quality of message. Statistically, interpretation has a low optimum audience capacity. If you want a high count of noses, don't use interpretation, use radio or television or advertisements in magazines. But if you want maximum influence of the individual for each dollar spent, consider interpretation among your best methods.

In British Columbia, a nature house attracts about 35,000 people in a two-month summer. This results in a fairly relaxed and uncrowded program. This, remember, is in an area of sparse human population. I shudder to think of the potential in an area like southern Ontario. Midland, where the Canadian Wildlife Service will have its first centre, is within 450 miles of 55,000,000 people. I'm not familiar with driving habits in eastern North America, but in the west we considered 450 miles a leisurely one-day drive. So we estimate the tourist potential of our centre at about one-quarter million a year. Add to this the use by local residents, and the school potential from much of southern Ontario, and one wonders if much nature can survive within sight of the centre.

Our estimates may be conservative. The Algonquin Park Museum receives each summer use by more visitors. Its attendance has been growing for decades, so by now it must be approaching the 200,000 mark.

The public hunger for worthwhile attractions is clear. I wonder that natural resource managers have been so slow to take advantage of the situation. Only parks people among the land managers have done much to exploit it. Could it be that the others consider the public a nuisance, to be avoided as much as possible? Whatever the reason, the good old days when you could successfully take this attitude are vanishing. Whether managers like it or not, people are becoming involved with their natural resources—as they should be. And the manager of these resources, who is often an employee of the people, can expect more of the people's noses in his—or their—business. An interpretation program is a pleasant means for meeting this public halfway.

The future of interpretation

It is fun to let the imagination race a bit and to explore possibilities in the years ahead. I have done this, briefly, with interpretation. Since I am certain of interpretation's dazzling future, I doubt that I have had the time or the insight to do its future justice in my descriptions. I am sure that it will be much more exciting than I can envisage at the moment. But I do see some changes.

- I see an impressive flowering of simple, self-guiding nature trails, especially where available to school classes and weekend family groups. Vandalism has held this activity back, but a few solved problems will cause a flood of activity.

- I see schools and school camps virtually stampeding to interpretation. Ontario, at the moment, is making impressive progress here.
- I see increasing numbers of interpretation programs near our cities, sponsored by both municipal and private agencies.
- I see natural resources departments in governments, and land management industries, using much more interpretation, often with elaborate techniques. Here, in industry at least, the money spent could give impressive returns, and there will be tax incentives for interpretation spending akin to those for advertising.
- I see park interpretation, the present stronghold of the field, becoming relatively conservative, relatively low cost, but still being a highly successful fraction of the total interpretation effort. The reason for this difference is that park land use imposes severe limits on the interpretation techniques that are appropriate.
- I see forest interpretation that explains forestry methods and that moves the public through different kinds of forests and through all levels of a forest, including the sunlit crowns, where much of the biological action is, and including into the ground, where most of the raw materials are.
- I see people—the public—taken under water to watch pond life, taken into bird nests, following the hunts of predators, entering the world as sensed by insects, observing innate animal behaviour, following nutrients through food chains, watching animal populations explode and crash, walking into a piece of wood as if small enough to enter the cells.
- I see people watching trees grow, experiencing the apparent scarcity of deer at 30 deer per square mile, seeing the results

of marsh management, observing the biological effects of different levels of grazing, and watching how wild fish in wild places react to lures and baits and people and boats.

- I see people walking on elevated walks in many places, over marshes and swamps and lakes and meadows, not only to be above the wet, but in dry places too, simply to preserve the natural habitat.
- I see public towers widely used to look across flat areas, like prairie or marshes; and I see helicopters to enable the far-off, vertical perspective that so enlarges understanding of the landscape.
- I see relatively common use of electronic devices to enable the public outdoors to see where their eyes alone cannot see and to hear where ears alone cannot hear. Think of the possibilities here of television, infrared, sonar, radar, radio and a confusion of devices for measuring winds, temperatures, moisture, movement and so on, and doing it from afar.
- I see a few good programs able to help especially keen people look into the wild lives of wild creatures seldom seen by anyone. Have you, for instance, ever watched a wild and undisturbed flying squirrel?
- I see historical interpretation where you almost become part of historic events—recreated, of course—and where, at long last, a generation of Canadians will learn that Canadian history is fascinating. The wonder to date is that successive historians have been so uniformly poor as to make it so uniformly boring. And remember that, most history books to the contrary, the important history is really historical human ecology.
- I see many interpretation programs so popular, and so unable to do a worthwhile job with mobs of people, that

attendance will be at a controlled rate into which, if you wish, you can fit by previous appointment.

- And I see these predictions so conservative when compared to what really is coming that I must stop demonstrating my inadequacy.

It is obvious, I think, that I'm sold on interpretation. If you think it sounds interesting, and if you want to know more—drop that bored professional look, become an eager tourist and move in on an interpretation program. I try to do this every year. See some exhibits, walk some nature trails, tag along on guided walks, listen to campfire talks. Don't stop at one. See several. See the work of three or four agencies, for some are better than others. Don't be a fussy old woman disturbed by a few inadequacies, or twittering about a few slips of fact, but look at the effect it is having, look at the total result it is getting. You owe it to yourself and to your profession to know, first-hand, what interpretation is and how it can help you with your objectives.

References

Bailey, Liberty H. *The Nature-Study Idea*. New York City: Doubleday, Page and Co., 1905.

Edwards, R. Yorke. "Park Interpretation." *Park News* 1, no. 1 (1965): 11–16.

Tilden, Freeman. *Interpreting Our Heritage*. Chapel Hill: University of North Carolina Press, 1957.

Wallin, Harold E. "Interpretation: A Manual and Survey on Establishing a Naturalist Program." *Management Aids Bulletin* no. 22. Wheeling, WV: American Institute of Park Executives, 1963.

The Future of Recreation on Wild Lands (1968)

Excerpted (with permission) from *The Forestry Chronicle* 44, no. 3 (1968): 24–29, https://doi.org/10.5558/tfc44024-3. The Canadian Institute of Forestry has published *The Forestry Chronicle,* a professional and scientific forestry journal, since 1925.

SOME AGENCIES MANAGING WILD LANDS have been communicating with the public for half a century and have perfected impressively effective techniques. The US National Park Service and now a host of smaller park organizations reach millions of people annually with attractive methods for helping people understand the landscape. An important feature of these programs is that they take place right outdoors on the land and the message is about something real and right there as you stand in the landscape, not about something unreal or imagined. We need more of this approach. People are beginning to think that nature and its preservation, its use, its conservation, its many popular aspects live only in slick magazines, in books and on picture screens. They know this really is not so, but they behave as if it were, and this is as bad as believing it. Public ignorance and the lack of public involvement is a major land use crisis facing land managers today. We simply must get more people understanding their surroundings and, as a result, able to comprehend land use problems.

It would be beyond the scope of this paper to dwell on the problems, aside from the recreation ones, that our soaring numbers of citified citizens, out of touch with the countryside, are going to cause in all resource management. Let me say, however, that these investors, these consumers, these voters, can be terrifyingly ignorant of national needs.

I am going to devote some time to the need for informing people as a major contribution toward alleviating the recreation crisis. If I were a forester interested in spreading understanding of forestry, I would change a few of the words and the message could be about the same.

Interpretation solves problems

The difficulty seems to be people, and people would be no problem if they did the right things. The interpretation method that has evolved in our parks, and which is now sweeping through our museums, is the surest, most effective method known for informing people about the outdoors, and for doing it so people enjoy it. Much of North American man, it seems, roams our highways every summer seeking new experiences, and some of us wonder how to reach him. All the while, nearby park interpretation programs are groaning under the load of too many people. Their conducted walks are so crowded that the naturalists cannot keep in touch with their audiences, and most people cannot see what is being talked about. Campfire talks have standing room only. Nature centres are jammed like sale day in a department store. The public thirst for new experiences involving new information is proven by these conditions. I must add that you do not have to be a park naturalist long to learn that interpretation actually does what it is designed to do. Its message reaches people. Results are easily seen in any good program that has been operating for a few years.

North Americans are wasteful of the land and its products. Visitors from Europe and Asia are astounded at our partial uses of resources. The recreation resource is no exception. A hugely increased number of people could use the recreation lands used now, and used properly there could be more enjoyment to the individual, less wrecking of the resource base and large reductions of maintenance costs.

Interpretation holds the key to this better use of our recreation lands, and better use is a partial solution to the coming crisis. We note that other resource fields are beginning to talk of better use too. A well-known example concerns the water resources of the United States. Here, Stewart Udall has pointed out that there is really no shortage there; the problem is one of improper use creating an apparent shortage.*

* Stewart Udall was an American politician and secretary of the interior from 1961 to 1969. "Among his accomplishments, Udall oversaw the addition of four national parks, six national monuments, eight national seashores and lakeshores, nine national recreation areas, twenty national historic sites, and fifty-six national wildlife refuges. . . . A pioneer of the environmental movement, Udall warned of a conservation crisis in the 1960s with his best-selling book on environmental attitudes in the United States, *The Quiet Crisis* (1963)." Wikipedia, s.v. "Stewart Udall," last modified August 4, 2020, https://en.wikipedia.org/wiki/Stewart_Udall.—Eds.

Interpretation—Something new

Interpretation is a ponderous term with, as yet, no popular synonym, but do not let the word mislead you. Interpretation deals with people's knowledge, and their attitudes and enthusiasms. It attracts them with its helpful, entertaining approach. The star that it reaches for is to inspire people. It is not just education. It is not just an information service. It is not just demonstrations or showmanship or a guiding service or an outlet for propaganda. It is all of these things at once. Its aim is to send people forth inspired by new understanding and enthused about more involvement with the fascinating new world revealed to them. Interpretation, when well done, has the light touch. It cannot afford to be ponderous, and anyway, the realm of the ponderous is already crowded in the communications field. Interpretation sows seeds, skilfully chosen, imaginatively treated, that will grow into inspiration, revelation, involvement and, in some cases, a new lifelong passion. And it works—not always, but often enough to be impressive. It works often enough that staff members working in good interpretation programs are usually fulfilled types with well-groomed egos.

How to inform people

Interpretation has the solutions to most of recreation's challenges through the next three decades.

We need a populace more interested in and informed on the natural things that together form the wild landscape. Interpretation is highly successful at doing this.

We need a populace that understands land use problems so it will support measures to preserve its resources while using them intelligently. Interpretation does this, properly, for it begins with building interest in and respect for the fundamental parts of the landscape.

We need a populace that does not spread its garbage across the land while avoiding paths and hacking at the vegetation as if no other man would pass that way. Interpretation, by creating delight and understanding, creates respect. We could use more of it in our time.

We need a populace with vandalism scarce and strongly regarded as a crime against society. Interpretation builds public opinion by creating involvement, and it does this by opening the minds of people to understanding, leading to appreciation and respect.

Park interpretation is widespread today and requires little modification to interpret the other uses of land. In interpreting recreation use or range management or forestry or any other land use, the great strength of park interpretation remains intact, and that strength is the strength of truth. Our lives have become full of fakes—pictures, substitutes for the real thing, even real things that have been put into meaningless situations. Interpretation operates on the spot with real things that are in meaningful surroundings. This is the strength of nature interpretation, and this is why inspiration and revelation can so often be its result. This is why a life touched by interpretation may never be quite the same again because of the new interest that makes it fuller, and happier.

Land use, as well as the land itself, is open to interpretation. There is a meaningful story in the worn-out vegetation of an overused campground, or in the soil erosion caused by human activity, or in the too many people jamming a beach. These are ecological situations that can be made fascinating, revealing and meaningful. I can think of nothing easier to interpret than a managed forest, whether recreation is involved or not, with its beautifully rounded picture of land, plants, animals and man in harmonious interrelationships.

The uniqueness of all interpretation, anywhere, is that things are made meaningful. Here is a scarce commodity in our modern world of men—the meaningful. People thirst for meaningful things in their lives. Interpretation caters to this need. If we do not use it lavishly to help solve our recreation problems, and our other land use problems too, we deserve to be swamped by the tide.

Interpretation is not just a good cure; it is so far about the only cure available to us. Most other measures are merely treatments of symptoms.

When we are dealing with the ills of public wealth, diseases cured are surely preferable to symptoms masked—especially when the cure is cheaper.

Wye Marsh Wildlife Centre, Midland, ON, 1970. Edwards family photo.

Interpretation in Your Museum (1968)

Paper presented at the annual banquet of the British Columbia Museums Association, Vernon, BC, September 13, 1968.

IN THE FIELD OF HISTORY, one can sum up interpretation by saying that it tries to involve people in the past, and if you can involve people—in history or in natural history—so that they can mentally become part of it, glimpsing what it was like to be there, then I suppose you have reached the ultimate in communication.

There is much confusion over interpretation, both what it is and what it does. An example might help you to see its differences from related things. Suppose that a popular local museum, your museum, decided to put on a temporary feature exhibition called "Moustache Cups" or "How Grandpa Kept His Whiskers Dry." The museum wanted no one in the area to miss the exhibit, so it asked for ideas from five men on how to inform the public. These five were a publicity man, a public relations man, a man skilled at museum information, a teacher who, of course, was in education, and an interpreter.

Publicity said the only effective way to publicize the exhibit was
(1) to hire a sound truck to cruise the streets,
(2) to use a girls' band in a parade on opening day, and
(3) to put black paper moustaches on the girls, the sound truck and the museum building.

Public relations suggested:
(1) a local moustache contest with a moustache cup the prize;
(2) hiring a red carpet, an entrance canopy and a uniformed doorman;
(3) having a formal opening involving well-known people; and
(4) getting as much space in the local press as possible.

Information's idea was to
(1) supply newspapers with a good, accurate story on moustaches and moustache cups;
(2) produce an attractive and informative pamphlet on moustache cups; and
(3) produce spot announcements for radio and television telling of the exhibition, and including something about the cups.

Education offered to organize
(1) a series of public lectures on "How Human Anatomy has Influenced Ceramics" (properly censored, of course);
(2) a study, much publicized, on "The Moustache Cup as an Art Form"; and
(3) slides showing these cups, which would be shown in local schools.

Interpretation suggested:
(1) organizing a preliminary tea where people actually used moustache cups while wearing, if they wished, inexpensive false moustaches provided for the occasion;

(2) encouraging local potters to make moustache cups and sell them at the museum;
(3) dividing the exhibit into three parts:
   - one showing cups and their variation
   - one showing moustaches and their variation, as well as their prominence in historic times
   - one showing how a moustache cup actually handles a moustache—this could be done, to offer one simple idea, by showing the cup applied to the moustache and allowing the viewer to look through the bottom of the cup; and
(4) if possible, allowing exhibit viewers to handle a cup and even drink from one while moustached, as in the preliminary tea.

Notice that interpretation alone tried to get people actually involved with the cups. Interpretation always tries for involvement. Notice also that interpretation went directly to the point of what is a moustache cup, why was it necessary, and what role did it play in the lives of people.

Objects used by man in the past played a part in history. The part may be no larger than that of keeping a moustache out of tea, but little things like this are the essence of history. The history that I am interested in, and the history that I believe is the really important history, is the past lives of ordinary people. Many little things, like moustache cups, made these lives what they were.

Some need it, some do not

When you museum people begin to think about the question of interpretation in museums, there is at first only one simple problem. You must decide whether you want interpretation, or whether you do not. It is a question, really, of what your museum is trying to do.

If the function of your museum is simply to collect, you have a perfectly sound museum policy. If, in addition, you simply let the public look at bits of the collection, you are conforming to accepted museum behaviour. When you largely ignore the public or simply display your collection with a minimum of effort, you do not need interpretation. At the same time, this minimum service to the public should result in minimum public support, which is not serious if you have friends in high places or a wealthy patron with a generous purse.

Most museums, however, need considerable public participation because they would die without enthusiastic public support. Many museums also feel that it is one of their purposes to involve the public in their work.

If you want to reach the most people with exhibit halls that are attractive, entertaining and enlightening, you need interpretation. In all probability you already have it, or at least touches of it here and there, for one of the good features of interpretation is that each individual exhibit can have none, or a little, or much. It is probably best if some of your exhibit units have none, and only a few are major attractions because they have much. Once you have decided to push the use of interpretation, each exhibit then requires the decision of whether it will have interpretation, and if so, how intensive it will be.

If museums are to survive and to achieve the success that they deserve, at least some of them must specialize in reaching the public. It is really not enough to just provide public floor space with historic objects scattered about it. Unless the museum somehow says something revealing about these objects, only the few people already informed will get much out of such displays. An old stereoscope, just lying there under glass and labelled simply "stereoscope," is meaningless to those who know nothing about what stereoscopes do, or about why people had them. But one set up so it can be looked through—even if behind glass so it cannot be touched—and if a label says it once was in every parlour for entertainment, and if an old advertisement shows people in a parlour using one, then the thing becomes understandable, and it fits into history.

The great danger for all experts communicating with the public, and museum experts are no exception, is that the fact of being expert makes it difficult to realize how little the average person knows. The good communicator understands that most people know very little about most things, but that people do like to learn if the learning process is pleasant, and he can see the essence of a thing so his message goes to the heart of the matter directly. In interpretation, an eye for the unusual, the exciting, the dramatic, the glamorous is perhaps the most useful asset of all, provided that honesty and accuracy are involved, for without these, interpretation is meaningless.

If anyone ever asked me for my best and briefest advice to museum people wishing to communicate with the public, I would say only five words: "Watch people in several museums." This should be essential training for every museum employee. I once watched people beside a large display of old bottles. These were just rows of bottles in a glass case, and they were labelled only as old bottles from that region. Not many visitors gave them much time. A few did, and these were obviously people who already knew something about the fascinations of old bottles. They made comments to companions like:

"Hey, look at the shape of that hand-blown one."

"That one looks oriental."

Other people mostly glanced and moved on. To them, the bottles were just bottles, and that was as far as their knowledge went. Some did have brief comments:

"Hey, look at all the bottles."

"Why do they show so many?"

"Just empty bottles."

"Are they whiskey?" Another voice answered: "Yeah, your grandfather's collection."

"If they want bottles, I've got lots at home."

"They need one of the new beer bottles."

"Man, what a row they would be for target practice."

"Big deal. Bottles!"

"Look, my old man's been here."

"Just bottles" is not enough for most people. At the very least, the back of the case could have had diagrams showing how bottles differ from one another by showing very simply how they were made differently. Or there might have been a few words on where they came from so the viewer might glimpse the commercial trade of the time. Or, since bottles are not very important except as containers, the story might have been about what was in those bottles that was important to early settlers. This would fit bottles into pioneer life. Just showing advertisements of the time behind the right bottles would do this job, and do it well. One display cannot tell all about bottles, but three or four kinds of bottles can be compared in a dozen interesting ways.

It improves the staff too

Interpretation is not only good for museum visitors; it is also good for museum staffs. The person constantly involved in interpreting is on constant hunt for *facts* about things. This, to me, is the lure of this work. I am continually being led into new and fascinating fields of information. Without this prodding to know about things, one is apt to sit back comfortably and remain happily ignorant. I am constantly startled by my own ignorance, and frequently amazed at how much some people know of things I know nothing about. Take water, for instance.

Water is so common in our lives that most of us take it for granted. That is a mistake. Water is the most important stuff on Earth. It is also the most amazing stuff on Earth.

Water is a mineral. Strictly speaking, ice is a rock, and water is liquid rock.

Water is everywhere in our lives. It is the stuff that lakes are made of, and oceans and rivers and trout streams and springs bubbling from the Earth. Water is the reason for bathtubs. Water is the stuff of snow and fog and clouds and the ice cube in your drink. Water is the stuff of life. A tree is 75 per cent water. You are 75 per cent water.

Over 75 per cent of the Earth is covered by water. It is a coincidence that you are water and that the world appears to be, and this is what confused two angels. One was a scientist, and the other was a young angel only a few thousand years old. By chance, while the young angel was watching a girl angel on a nearby cloud, the scientist was looking in another direction and caught sight of the planet Earth. As they looked in different directions, their conversation went something like this. The scientist spoke first:

"Look at that heavenly body."

"Yeah!"

"Interesting topography."

"Yeah!"

"Are those mountains?"

"No, about right."

"Seems to be a live one."

"Yeah!"

"Looks a bit icy though."

"Could be."

"You know, bodies like that are mostly water."

"Man, that's the best-looking water I've ever seen."

And the moral of this story is that water can be beautiful, but it's better in some forms than others.

We are here tonight as living things because water is unbelievably queer stuff that rarely behaves according to the rules. Water is nearly a universal solvent, for it dissolves almost all other substances. Water has an enormous capacity to store heat. And ice floats, which is an astounding feature, for according to the rules it should sink like a rock, for remember, it is a rock. We are here, and the world is like it is today, because of water dissolving things, holding heat and floating when solid. If these were not so, life would be impossible; the world would be half oven, half deep freeze; and lakes, oceans and rivers would be mainly solid ice at all times with water only on the surface. Also, your gin and tonic would stay warm at the top, a really serious state of affairs.

Water is beautiful. Look how clear and sparkling it is. We treasure diamonds and fine glass for their water-like properties.

When water is abundant we can take it for granted, but when scarce or absent it can become the most valuable stuff on Earth. Byron once wrote:

> Till taught by pain
> Men really know not what good water's worth.

I think Byron has a message for the Okanagan.

Water is the cradle of all life. Water causes wars. For want of it, or from too much of it, men have died in millions.

You use about 60 gallons of water a day or, in other words, you use a ton of water every four days. Cities use about 130 gallons per day per person. To refine 1 barrel of oil requires 18 barrels of water. It takes 250 tons of water to make a ton of paper. We use huge amounts of the stuff, not only for personal needs, but also in manufacturing, and most of all for irrigation in drier climates.

You can see that plain old water is not very plain, and there seems to be no end to the amount of interesting information on it. I have given only a few morsels here, but I wanted to show you that everything has a story, and often many stories—even the water in your tap. And with a little practice you soon learn where to find what you want along with much more that you didn't want because you had no idea it existed.

There is really nothing new about interpretation. It has been in good teaching for centuries. Any communication that shows real things in action, or that lets you use real things, is interpretation of the best sort. The car salesman that talks you into road testing a new car is using the power of interpretation to help him make a sale.

Words alone can be interpretive, provided that the words are about something right there. But, strictly speaking, words alone are not interpretation, they are information. We live in a world filled with information. Our lives overflow with informative words, both printed and spoken, to the extent that we are apt to tune most of them out of our lives. But interpretation is different. Real things are involved, things you can see or smell or feel or operate, and this difference is the factor that separates interpretation from other kinds of information. When I talked about water that was right here as I talked, that was interpretation.

Searching for "how"

Interpretation is fun, and one of the more pleasant parts is the first steps, when you are brainstorming for ideas. Let us examine a few.

To repeat a matter mentioned previously, use old ads, and the line drawings so common before photographs in newspapers and books and magazines, to bring old things to life. These pictures usually blow up well, and your town will have someone who can do it, or who knows who can. It costs a bit, but what doesn't?

Many museums show firearms. Each kind had a major or famous use, whether military or sporting or food getting or tide hunting or to go under a lady's garter. The possibilities here for visual interest are rather obvious. The guns can come to life through old pictures or modern sketches, models or paper scenes simply done.

Rocks and minerals on display are difficult to make eye-catching and interesting. Don't show too many, do use dramatic lighting, and a small turntable revolving part of the display can add interest. Turntables, large and small, are in the stores of your town, making sales. Why not include a few in your museum, underlining one or two exhibits, or simply turning around something, like clothes, that people want to have turned around.

Clothes were made to enclose people and are apt to be uninteresting if empty. Homemade 2D shapes can be effective (simply cut them from plywood), but rough 3D forms made from wire—maybe just crumpled chicken wire—can be easy to make and can do a good job. Clothes relate to the general needs and tastes of their times. Show clothes with a few home furnishings to give a rounder picture and to show that simple pioneer clothes went with a simple life, or that heavy, ornate Victorian clothes lived in heavy, ornate homes.

Old cars, wagons, sleighs and other such large items are interesting, but beware of them. They do consume space. If you have them, try to make them live in people's minds as they once actually lived on the countryside. It is your job to counteract how out of place they look on a museum floor. Why not combine a car with clothes of its time? Why not a background with scenes of its time; or an ad of that very model; or a cartoon, blown up to car size, that lampooned motoring in those days?

Indian things, such as arrowheads, are apt to just sit in rows. They are small, and their detail is not easy to see, so why not a big, sharp, contrasty photo of an arrowhead as a centrepiece? Show a few different shapes, or show chunks of what they were made from, or show how they were attached to a shaft, using an oversized model. Just a little drawing skill is needed to interpret a number of possible themes on arrow points.

Stuffed birds and mammals are a problem in most museums. Frankly, there seem to be only two kinds of quality here: the good, which are very scarce; and the bad, which seem to be everywhere. Most are decidedly sorry specimens. But if you do show them, do it so people might remember these were living things at one time, alive in living places. Suggest habitats with simple shaped coloured papers. One of the most effective stuffed grouse I have seen was in front of yellow and green paper, with ellipses of yellow paper, suggesting leaves, about its feet. A dusty grouse skin plus coloured paper plus imagination equals a grouse in the woods in the fall, like a grouse should be.

Just showing birds' eggs can be rather dull. Why not fewer eggs, but telling more? Show size variation (hummingbird and gull), show camouflage on pebbles (sandpiper), show that hidden eggs can afford to be white (woodpecker), show that some eggs roll in a circle (auks), and so on. All of this has been in good bird books for over half a century, and there are lots of naturalists now to answer your questions. Dig a bit and the information appears.

The same with butterflies. Long rows can be deadly. Why not show how butterflies differ from moths, show camouflage, show the brightest local species, show the famous travellers, show simply ten local kinds that are often seen, so just worth knowing. Butterflies lend themselves easily to the use of paper, paint and pen to catch eyes and help tell stories.

Brainstorming like this is fun. It is a waste of time, however, if you have a habit of saying, "Oh, but we couldn't do that in our museum." When I catch myself thinking this, I think of someone I know who gets things done, and I ask myself if he could do it. The answer is usually "yes." I then decide that if he can, I can. Of course, you may not like the idea, or it may truly be beyond the resources of your museum and its circle of assistance, but never parrot "We can't" without exploring the matter.

Artwork frightens most people. That is nonsense. Even I can do some arty things for exhibits, and that means you can. The silhouette, for instance, is available to everyone. Silhouettes are evenly coloured outlines, and they can be very effective at setting the mood behind an exhibit. I have made dozens of silhouettes. The hardest part is finding photographs or drawings that will give a dramatic outline of what you want. Trace that outline, blow it up using a pantograph or a projector or a camera, or just by ruling squares, and you can be well on the way to an eye-catching exhibit.

The silhouette is like interpretation itself in that each tries to be accurate, simple, dramatic and attractive. Both outline something rather than getting involved with it. Other media are better able to dwell on details. Use silhouettes. They can be good interpretation, they are really easy and they will open up a new role for you to play in your museum. And they frequently remind you what interpretation is, which is the first thought at the start of this paper, so at the same time we seem to have gone back to the beginning and have arrived at the end.

New Fields for Interpretation (1970)

Paper presented at a short seminar given by William Barkley and Edwards to a class from the University of Guelph at Wye Marsh Wildlife Centre, January 31, 1970.

SINCE THE TURN OF THE century, park interpretation has been perfecting techniques for communicating with the public outdoors. These methods have been spectacularly effective. Only recently, however, has interpretation been taken out of parks and used to involve the public with other kinds of land use. I have seen it used, for example, by a forest products company to interpret a forest, and by an electricity agency to interpret a large power dam site.

The potential of interpretation is enormous, not so much in the overrated aspect of volume exposure, which is the strength of media advertising, but rather in its *effectiveness*, simply because it involves people with real things.

For example, I can think of nothing more easily interpreted than forest management. Here is a beautiful and visible balance between man and nature, and what better way for a forest management company to get people to appreciate its problems?

Interpretation aims at getting people *involved*. Can you think of a better way to consolidate public concern over pollution than to show it to them? Many people have not the slightest idea what pollution really is. To them, it's something on TV or in the newspaper. But you make an impression forever if you show it to them, right in their neighbourhoods. It's not enough to know only your own garbage can and your own toilet bowl. By contrast, the community sewer and municipal garbage problems are real shockers.

Is there a better way to persuade landowners to improve their soils to produce better crops, to manage woodlots properly, to create beauty on the land, than by showing what is the right way, by showing how to do it by showing that the right way is often the easiest way? Of course, this idea is not new. We have had demonstration farms and demonstration woodlots for years. But they have not been as effective as they might have been. Demonstration is the start, but effective demonstration involves first the effective attraction of people, followed then by effective communication.

And as my final example, there is the interpretation of wildlife, which is partly the story of this centre.

The CWS Plan

The CWS liked what it saw some of us doing in park interpretation and decided that this approach was needed in Canada to get the Canadian people involved with the Canadian landscape and with the wildlife in it. This idea is about ten years old, and it sat around, gathering strength, for about five years before it began to generate action.

The plan that emerged was exciting in both its geographic scope and in the message that was to be given to the public.

The plan calls for about ten wildlife centres across Canada, each centre being in a distinctive part of Canada and confining a large part of its message to the region it is set in. Some of the regions could be, then:

- The Atlantic Coast
- The Maritime Forest
- The Northern Hardwoods
- The Boreal Forest
- The Prairies, and so on

Each centre is to consist of a sizable parcel of land of high quality for demonstrating the regional message. On that land is to be a building, with theatre and exhibits and a staff of biologist/naturalist interpreters. Outside interpretation facilities are to be emphasized, like outdoor signs, outdoor exhibits and demonstrations, trails and self-serve nature trails, lookouts and towers with optical aids, boardwalks over delicate and/or wet habitats, conducted walks, outdoor workshops and projects, and so on.

The audience aimed at is to be in three parts with no priorities: tourists, locals, school classes.

So far, the greater plan is unique, but the plans for each centre have rough counterparts elsewhere. Only having a national chain is new. The United States has lots of individual centres, many of them municipal, which roughly duplicate the centre we are in right now, for instance.

The Canadian Wildlife Service, however, proposed an exciting new dimension in its message. Most interpretation everywhere has been about nature as a thing quite apart from man. This is a legitimate enough approach. Most interpretation was *park* interpretation and so in areas where nature is emphasized and man is not. Many centres near cities were, by definition, interested in natural science, which to most people means leave man out. The CWS, by contrast, wants to interpret the *total* landscape, warts and all. And anyway, if you are after an understanding of landscapes in southern Canada, man is the reason these places look as they do today. Man is part of the landscape, and that is the way CWS wants to tell the story. This does not mean that we avoid the natural history things. It means that we can talk about wild orchids in wild places in one breath, then switch in the next breath to talk about pollution of streams, or about why barns look like they do, or about why that town is located and laid out as it is. This is the exciting new dimension that has attracted us to this program. We have not moved very deeply in this dimension yet, because it has been easier to do other things first, but for the next few years we will be exploring this new and very exciting area.

So Wye Marsh Wildlife Centre is the first of a chain of such centres. Each one, I hope, will look different, and will do things differently, besides having its distinctive regional message. But together they will get people involved with Canada.

This is important, we think, because we are becoming a citified nation that considers the important part of the world to be paved in blacktop, where the natural scenery is potted trees beside buildings that look like egg crates. If we want to survive, we had better keep some good earth under our fingernails, and some understanding of the good earth among our common knowledge.

Sign outside Wye Marsh Wildlife Centre, Midland, ON, 1970. Edwards family photo.

The text reads:

Now see the real show.
The exhibits inside are only a preview.
The real show is out here.
Come on out.
The place is filled with living things.

The Canadian Wildlife Service Interpretation Program (1971)

Paper presented at the 35th Federal-Provincial Wildlife Conference, Toronto, ON, July 6, 1971.

Introduction

YOUR LIFE AND MINE ARE filled with contradictions and paradoxes that are routine and accepted without question. Labels cause the most trouble. The "freeway" through my town is the slowest way to the office in the morning; the "quality of our lives" is revealed to statisticians by how much water we waste, especially via our toilets; and the apple known as "Delicious" is the most tasteless apple on the market. A problem I live with daily is that my business of involving people with their living, fascinating world is saddled with the dull and colourless name "Interpretation." But none better has appeared, for "naturalist program" is as vague a term, and "outdoor education" is education, not interpretation. We seem to be stuck with a stuffy word. Perhaps the solution is to "unstuff" the word by simply having our program give it a new image.

What is interpretation?

Interpretation gets its name from being a method to "interpret" to people the language and knowledge of science and technology. But it is also a lot of other things, depending on how closely you look at it. Its parts are simple enough, but the sum of its parts is complex, because there are a lot of those parts. As a general description, think of interpretation as a communication system that can use any appropriate method of communication, but it is communication that has two essential characteristics. First, interpretation communicates about real things that must be right there, adding to the message "in person"; second, interpretation aims at introduction, at inspiration, at motivating its audience to seek more information. To put the matter more candidly, it seeks "to turn people on" so they become involved. It stops short of depths approaching education. Interpretation concentrates on opening doors into minds, and it lets things tell their own stories, communicating first-hand information by just being right there.

Interpretation aims at giving people new understandings, new insights, new enthusiasms, new interests. Not everyone gets the message, of course, but it is successful often enough that working at interpretation can be an unusually rewarding occupation.

A good interpreter is a sort of Pied Piper, leading people easily into new and fascinating worlds that their senses never really penetrated before. He needs three basic attributes: knowledge, enthusiasm and a bit of the "common touch."

The two requirements of interpretation that distinguish it from information and education are also its strengths. On-site communication, talking about a Douglas fir with a fir right there, is first-hand experience. Most communication these days is second-hand experience, whether via schools, radio, books, newspapers, television or conversation. The advantages of interpretation are that in our man-made worlds of fakery and unreal things, people are hungry for first-hand experience; and in seeking only to open the doors in people's minds, leaving other sources to fill up the spaces inside, interpretation concentrates on making converts, not experts.

What good is interpretation?

This sort of question about anything usually leaves me groping for words. How do you cope with such complete lack of understanding? Here I asked the question of myself because I wanted to see how convincing I could be.

Interpretation has been a service mainly associated with parks—national parks, state and provincial parks, and municipal parks. The term "park interpretation" is in many minds a generic term for this approach to communication with the public. Most people who have experienced interpretation have done so in parks. The method evolved, matured and became popular in the United States National Park system beginning about 1920, and in the past 20 years has spread abundantly throughout other park systems in North America. More recently it has taken root in Great Britain, Australia and New Zealand. Without doubt the remarkable strength and popular appeal of large parks today in the United States and Canada is the result, in part, of the years of pleasure and inspiration that park interpretation has given to millions of people using parks.

The methods of interpretation that evolved through 50 years of trial and error are completely effective at involving people with the land.

Oddly enough, park people have been the only land managers to carry their story to the public via widespread interpretation programs, yet the methods evolved in parks are available to other resource managers for equally effective communication. With North Americans swarming the highways every summer, seeking hungrily for new experiences, one wonders that the opportunities have been ignored by people in forest management, mining, watershed management, agriculture, fish management, water storage and hydro projects, and other fields that are suitable. Many resource fields talk at the public, but they use the traditional media, joining the second-hand information methods dominated by soap, deodorants and how to be suddenly shapelier, where the din is so loud that it is nearly impossible to be heard. The usual communication media are very costly, highly competitive and, in the resource field, not very effective. Cornflakes fit into a video tube, but not a managed forest. How can so small a window show the space and mass vitality that is the very essence of understanding a marsh or a lake or a forest?

Resource managers outside parks are now beginning to experiment with interpretation. I have seen several timid programs by forest products firms in Washington State, in California and in Quebec. Someday someone who can do something about it will realize that interpretation and forestry were made for each other. What more dramatic, well-rounded, ecological story of man and nature exists than a well-managed forest?

One of the best bits of interpretation I have seen was done by people whom I suspect were quite unaware of interpretation as a communications system. The Bennett Dam on the Peace

River was under construction, and high on the lip of the canyon, overlooking the construction far below, was a small building, its windows giving a superb view of the action, its interior comfortably filled with lucid models and diagrams explaining the show and its full plot from start to finish. Buses on a regular schedule took you right into the action. It was beautiful interpretation creating understanding and involvement, while the scale of the show helped with the inspiration and revelation that interpretation strives for. And it is not sour grapes, but just the way it was, that as an engineering story it had a straightforward message that could be simply told, and this natural simplicity was what gave it special effectiveness.

So what good is interpretation? I suppose the answer is simple enough. It is outstanding at communicating understanding to the public about natural resources, their structure, their ecology, their management and their values.

The CWS plan

In 1967 the Canadian Wildlife Service entered the interpretation field, convinced that a major need of wildlife preservation and management was an informed, involved public. The great strength of wildlife as a resource in competition for money and space is that people like wildlife. It is no accident that baby seals can cause an international uproar, that a bear by the highway can cause a traffic jam, or that Point Pelee every spring is crowded with people that have come to see birds. People "dig" wildlife. Interpretation is a logical way to deepen and broaden such public interest.

The CWS interpretation plan aims at establishing a wildlife interpretation centre in each biotic region of Canada. These regions, from east to west, can be variously defined, but our labels for them are Atlantic Coast, Maritimes Forest, Hardwood Forest, Canadian Shield, Prairie, Mountain Forest, Mountain Tundra, Great Basin Desert, Fraser Delta, and Pacific Coast. Each should have a major centre. In addition, there will be smaller, more seasonal centres serving the public need at National Wildlife Areas and at wildlife spectacles of national importance, such as the world-famous seabird colonies on Bonaventure Island in the Gaspé. To increase their effectiveness, major centres may look after signs or outdoor exhibits at stops of interest beside highways or in other suitable places outdoors frequented by the public.

These interpretation facilities will tell the total story of the Canadian landscape, specializing, of course, in the land that is close at hand. By "total story" I mean ecological story. Any idea that begins with spreading an understanding of wildlife is doomed to failure if it just stays with wildlife. A robin is not, like a porcelain figure on a shelf, a complete thing in itself; a robin is a living, breathing node in an ecological web of some size and complexity. To understand a robin there must be some understanding of the ecological forces that support it—or erase it—so to talk of robins is to talk of trees and weather, of lawns and earthworms and 2,4-D,* of cherries and cowbirds and maple trees and insects and migration, and men doing many things. So the CWS wildlife centres will, of necessity, have a general ecological message, but with heavy emphasis on wildlife.

Our thinking began with interpretation oriented mainly toward tourists, much as is park interpretation in federal

* 2,4-D "is a systemic herbicide which selectively kills most broadleaf weeds by causing uncontrolled growth in them, but leaves most grasses such as cereals, lawn turf, and grassland relatively unaffected.... 2,4-D is one of the ingredients in Agent Orange, an herbicide that was widely used during the Vietnam War." Wikipedia, s.v. "2,4-Dichlorophenoxyacetic acid," last modified July 29, 2020, https://en.wikipedia.org/wiki/2,4-Dichlorophenoxyacetic_acid.–Eds.

and provincial parks. But when our first centre opened near Toronto, we had already felt heavy pressures from quite another sort of audience. School boards were literally lining up to use the centre. This put a new dimension on the program and gave wildlife centres the opportunity to communicate for twelve months instead of four. So we set up a year-round service for groups, available by reservation. With school groups the main users of this service, our first centre is quite unable to meet the demand, except in summer holidays and mid-winter. We are confident that we can erase the winter lull, if we want to. To date we have used mid-winter to write, create and hammer together exhibits, signs and other interpretation facilities, for we believe that top quality comes from doing it ourselves.

Why CWS interpretation?

To become philosophical for a moment, the basic reason for CWS entry into interpretation seems to be that most Canadians know very little that is important about their wildlife resource. This is a worsening condition. As more Canadians become urban, and as our cities become larger and spread longer urban shadows across their surroundings, most Canadians are in danger of total unawareness of why the hinterlands are important. A nation dominated by urbanized ecological illiterates is on a sure road to disaster. Wildlife is the component of land most vulnerable to improper landscape management, so concern for this social trend is understandably great in wildlife circles.

I suppose you can sum this up by saying that in a democracy, urban citizens ignorant of their ecological role on the landscape are not going to make the right decisions at home, in the office or at the polls.

To me personally, the CWS interpretation plan had one great new dimension that lured me off my Pacific island. Most interpretation to date has been in parks, and quite properly the story there is preservation of the wild terrain. The CWS story is about the face of Canada, with man and his activities a major influence on that face. This is new. This is therefore a unique challenge, and this is interpretation finally facing its full potential to involve people with their land.

How is interpretation done?

Perhaps the easiest way to explain how we interpret is to describe the program at Wye Marsh Wildlife Centre. Your initial experience there is an approach to a building while passing some outdoor displays. Inside, a movie or slide show introduces the land outside the building, and a display hall motivates people to go outside to see the real show. Outdoors on the landscape there are trails, signs, outdoor displays, self-guiding nature trails, a window looking into the water of the marsh, a boardwalk giving access to the centre of the marsh, trained staff to answer questions, spontaneous talks and demonstrations by the staff, and regular guided walks through surrounding lands. We also offer helpful literature for use outside on trees, flowers, birds, tracks and other subjects. Guidebooks are sold. We also offer special lectures, special films and slide shows, seasonal displays, space for appropriate meetings, space and facilities for workshops and courses of study. We plan to have public elevated platforms overlooking the marsh, literature or tape cassettes to encourage the exploration of nearby Ontario, and more winter use of the marsh and its environs by schoolchildren, since we believe that most Canadians are ignorant of what winter is really like. Our vaguer plans are many, but perhaps the picture is now sufficiently complex.

We charge for use of the building. At 50 cents per adult, we suspect we could have tourists paying for our summer operation by 1975. We are encouraging a slow rise in attendance so we can learn to keep nature intact near the building in spite of all the trampling feet.

We charge groups as well, but at present we have no plans for groups to pay their way. In fact, we wonder if summer visitors should. After all, we have an important message, and we know we have more effective contact with people than most giveaway literature flowing from most public agencies does. We do not have as much volume, but we are confident that we lead in effectiveness.

When I came to Ottawa to launch this program, Expo was in flower and everyone had "Expomania."* Everywhere I was told that Expo had shown the way, and that I was expected to turn people on with Expo methods. It was a tough fight, but I seem to have outlasted these pressures.

Expo was terrific. It was lights and images and projectors and canned sounds and architecture. It was fast-paced, at times almost a pathologically exciting experience. It was also just that. It was an end in itself, and it was a stupendous in-turning of man upon man. I can think of few more ineffective ways to interpret the landscape than to use Expo methods. Everything we do to people in interpretation is aimed at placing them with nature while sharpening their senses and opening their minds so they will look with new understanding on a tree, a leaf, a bird, water and a great sweep of not-very-active-looking land. The last thing we need is a prior experience of audiovisual

* Expo 67 was a world's fair held in Montreal in conjunction with Canada's 100th birthday.–Eds.

frenzy before we take them into the peaceful green world. Most of them are already wound up too tightly to get our message easily.

Future centres

The general plan has been outlined, so I will add here a more specific account of places currently high in our interest.

Wye Marsh Wildlife Centre, 90 miles north of Toronto at Midland, Ontario, is alive and well with a staff living in frantic activity. This centre is on land donated for interpretation purposes by the Ontario Department of Lands and Forests, and Wye Marsh itself is owned and managed by that provincial department.

We have approval and funds to build a centre on our Cap Tourmente National Wildlife Area, about 25 miles east of Québec City. This centre will feature the greater snow geese, which are there in numbers in spring and fall.

We have approval and funds to build a centre at Percé, in the Gaspé, to feature the Atlantic coast in general and the seabird colonies of Bonaventure Island in particular.

A major wildlife centre building is designed for Last Mountain Lake National Wildlife Area in Saskatchewan.

Across Canada we have chosen other high-priority areas, all tentative:

- The Chignecto Isthmus, at the head of the Bay of Fundy, on or near Tintamarre National Wildlife Area.
- The Fraser Delta near Vancouver, to feature wintering waterfowl.
- The Okanagan Valley in British Columbia, to specialize in the Great Basin Desert conditions found there.

- The Ottawa region, where a national story of national wildlife should be told. This centre would, of necessity, involve more information and less interpretation than other centres, so here the Expo enthusiasts, including me, might have their day.

The list ends here, with some important and exciting site possibilities unlisted.

The CWS interpretation program is off the ground and flying. Because of austerity it has built up only limited momentum through the past four years, but the two Quebec centres will almost put it back on schedule. In the meantime, using our one large centre as a guinea pig, we have been aiming at increased effectiveness from realistic costs achieved by avoiding the inflexibility and overhead of commercial audiovisual and exhibit-producing services. We do it ourselves, and this also lets us be spontaneous in our approaches to the public. Spontaneity is essential to good interpretation.

Last words

I want to end on a philosophical note, and both time and words have run out. So I stole these final words from someone else because they summarize my thoughts on what interpretation should try to do: "The one miracle is to bring Man down from the clouds of his egoism and replace his passion for destruction with the desire to understand."[1]

Notes

1 From J.O. Curwood, *God's Country: The Trail to Happiness* (New York: Cosmopolitan Book Corporation, 1921), 10.

Observation blind, Wye Marsh Wildlife Centre, Midland, ON, 1970. Edwards family photo.

On Planning and Building a Nature Interpretation Centre: Some Notes (1971)

Paper written for the Canadian Wildlife Service, Ottawa, ON, September 1, 1971.

IN THE FINAL ANALYSIS, PLANNING an interpretation centre is a matter of making decisions, a long series of decisions. But the problem is that there are so many, and that often they must be made with the help of no guiding experience, and that there are a million things to think of and decide upon while the building is still a phantom existing only in the mind.

These guidelines will help—not much, perhaps, but they are a kind of checklist of reminders, set down in a logical order. If those that use it will pass on to me brief details on where the list failed to guide or got them lost, then we can make it more helpful for others.

1. We assume that you have land—suitable land—and a building budget.

2. Think through what the centre is to do and to whom. Write it down. Take these two basic analyses by repeatedly asking "how?" and "why?" Write down answers. Summarize them. You now have a statement to help you plan a functional, useful building.

And it is not too late to consider what is done best outdoors rather than indoors, nor whether a nature centre building, or a cluster of buildings, is really needed.

Have an experienced interpretation planner from a good program help you. Start with: Do we need a building? Why? Which of these "whys" really needs a building especially built for interpretation?

3. Relate money available to floor space possible. An architect can help here with his rule-of-thumb costs per square foot of floor space for several kinds of construction. The result is an approximate idea of building size, and some indication of the size variation possible within the budget. (One pitfall here is for habit or "prestige" to result in a type of construction that is unnecessarily costly. Rough, uninsulated construction, for instance, may be not just adequate but appropriate for a summer-season interpretation program.)

4. Decide what the building must do, considering size, appearance, location, surroundings and what is to be inside—foyer? lounge? cloakroom? information desk? sales desk? pay wicket? exhibit room? theatre? projection room? observation deck? restrooms? conference room? classrooms? furnace room? workshops? offices? library? storage? projects room? combine some of these? movable walls?

For each room desired, build a mental picture of what it should be like. List desired attributes. Consider dimensions, materials, colours, textures, locations relative one to another.

Each room is a box. Consider walls, ceiling and floor, then doors, windows, lights, sockets, taps, built-in storage or furniture.

Try seeing needs for special features: slanting floor (theatre), high ceiling (exhibits), good acoustics, extra electrical outlets (exhibits), spotlights, water system (exhibits), sound system (to page groups, etc.), public window (winter birds, etc.).

It helps to have someone experienced handy, but it is *your* project, so *you* must make final decisions, if only, in many cases, to decide to see what the architect proposes. There is no magic formula. The process here and in many other steps requires as much thought, fact and experience as you can assemble. Then the need is for a long series of courageous decisions.

5. Visit a few good interpretation centres of appropriate size to see different solutions to the interpretation needs of others. Talk to the people using them, not just to the boss at head office. Go visiting with a checklist of things to look for (but, of course, stay mentally alert to everything), the main points being those in your project that are undecided, deferred or open to think about because you cannot decide.

6. It is your building. You should make most decisions. Take your own plans as far as possible on room sizes, floor plans of building, materials, textures, appearances, character, details of surrounding and approaches to the building, if necessary again turning to experienced help before going to architects and landscape planners.

Interpretation calls the tune; know what is needed, but also give architects and planners as much scope for input as is possible. They are creative people. Let them create, and solve some of your problems, within the limits of what you lay down as needs.

7. Select your architect, and your landscape architect or planner. You will get best results, other attributes being equal, from people involved already with the rural landscape, wild lands, natural history or interpretation. Beware of people completely urbanized and not already, therefore, even partially involved with what the building is to do.

8. Spend time with the architect and the planner. If possible visit comparable centres together. Insist on lengthy, relaxed discussions (at least two) on what interpretation is, why it is important, what will go on in the building, etc. Put them in the picture as much as possible.

The object is for *you* to educate *them*. *They* must do the listening. Make sure that they do. It will save time and money later.

Unfortunately, you will be lucky if these people really understand your objectives and methods. These creative people seem to fill up easily with their own misconceptions. It helps if you communicate thoroughly, covering aesthetics, images, philosophy, enthusiasms, all from your viewpoint, as well as giving the mechanics of building use.

9. Fix about three formal meetings to review partially completed plans. These are the occasions to approve or reject progress details as the detailed plans unfold.

Three logical meeting and inspection times are:

a. at the end of general concept planning, which will include approximate details on building appearance, floor plan, room sizes and shapes, traffic flow and tentative thoughts on materials; landscape needs and first thoughts on parking, roads, trails, patio areas, views and how best to use them, etc.

b. when you have detailed concepts, as above, with plans to scale and final but for your objections. Materials, colours, etc., where not of prime importance, may be still undecided.

c. when plans are nearly complete. Last-minute adjustments are settled. Details are approved (or changed and approved) on colours, materials, textures inside; the same outside if not already done; materials, plant species, fixtures in landscape area.

After each meeting put in writing for file and for the use of architect and planner the change you desire. There is no reason here, or anywhere for that matter, to detail why you want them. There may be no reason beyond a simple preference. Do give reasons verbally, when you can, at meetings. Conflicts here are normal. Give way when it does not matter. Do not argue when you must have your way. Simply, as the client, state how it will be. Do, however, give opportunity to be shown wrong or improved upon.

Do not be stampeded into major changes in your thinking. They can be disastrous when accepted quickly. Take overnight to think them through.

10. Frequently and informally, if possible, review the evolving plans. It is best to do this often, making brief visits in a casually curious way. The architect and planner may not like it—who would?—but you have to live with the results, and you represent the customer, who calls the tune.

Put all required changes and suggested changes in writing.

11. Finally, plans and written specifications will be ready for final approval. Carefully study plans and specifications. This is not your last chance to catch errors or to make changes, but doing so later is much more awkward—and expensive.

You must be fair. It is proper that you insist on changes to meet your variously listed requirements, all of which you should be able to produce in writing. Do evaluate the alternatives before you with the thought that they may be as good as, or better than, what you specified.

It is late in the game to suggest other changes, but do so if the results will be important enough as compared to the time and money required to change the plans. Do remember that idea changes and new ideas from the client (and you are the client) at this stage indicate, on his part, failure to think previously, or poor previous co-operation on the plans, or poor communication between client and architect.

12. Approve building plans and specifications. Approve landscaping plans and specifications (see Appendix B).

13. You are now ready to proceed with planning inside the building (furnishings, exhibits, equipment—see Appendix A) **and outside** (trails, interpretation structures, outside exhibits, signs and other facilities). No further comment on these procedures will be given here.

14. At this point the need is urgent for the full-time to half-time services of a person skilled at overseeing construction, and knowledgeable on building materials and methods. Depending on costs, etc., such a person could have been profitably used to help you as early as step 4. This person will help choose your contractor, and through construction he will act both as advisor to the contractor and as the client's agent, protecting the client's interests during construction.

15. Before construction begins, mark clearly and as permanently as possible the limits of landscape damage to be allowed on the land.

- Use iron posts holding brightly coloured tape.

- Encircle trees with coloured tape.
- Encircle shrubs with coloured tape.
- Anticipate "end runs" by delivery trucks (lumber, cement, etc.).
- Go over these limits, once they are clearly established, with the contractor or his agent. Be reasonable. He needs elbow room, but less than he thinks. Work out compromises when he demonstrates hardship.
- Inspect and be equipped to repair these markers several times daily.

16. Relax while your agent keeps his eye on construction. He has three things to watchdog: construction, landscaping, protecting natural values nearby.

17. Take possession when the building is acceptable. There will be a money holdback on the contractors to ensure their action on repairs or errors requiring their attention in the first year or so.

18. The building is still far from functional. We suggest at least six months before a formal opening.

19. Our philosophy is to lean heavily toward simple boxes of rooms from the contractor, then to plan—right in the rooms with our own (temporarily employed) carpenters—the location and nature of partitions, work counters, cupboards, etc. At the same time, we have the carpenters to make simple outdoor furniture (waste boxes, benches) and to make framework and other structures to support exhibits.

We find it best in all ways to plan rooms in the rooms, with the new staff that will use the rooms. This is only possible to a degree, but that degree can give better planned rooms.

20. Finally, displays, furniture and equipment should begin to appear and go into place. Nature trails, if not done during construction, should now be constructed—preferably by small groups under your control. Signs and other outdoor features should be made and installed.

Appendix A

Furnishings

- public chairs, benches
- theatre chairs, benches
- office furniture
- outside benches
- coat racks (public)

Exhibits

- Too much detail here.
- Separate instructions needed.
- Ditto for outdoor interpretation plans

Equipment

- theatre screen
- slide projectors
- movie projectors
- tape recorders and players
- lab supplies and equipment
- workshop power tools
- office fans
- typewriters
- intercom (office)
- television
- telephones
- record player
- movie films
- fixed telescopes
- duplicating machine
- printing press
- water processing for aquaria
- stove and some kitchen things
- refrigerator and/or freezer
- paper-folding machine
- automobile or truck
- ladders
- cleaning equipment
- grounds care equipment
- flag

Appendix B

Landscape planning got lost in the details of the building. Consider planning, now, only the immediate vicinity of the building. Later you can plan to do outdoor interpretation planning beyond this area. Landscape planning and action near the building serves mainly to repair the landscape wreckage caused by construction.

Architect and landscape planner must work together. Again, you should make the decisions. Formal? rough? flowers? weeds? shrubs? trees? native species? soil quality? concrete? asphalt? parking lot? flagpole? patios? traffic patterns? where do trails take off? grass? regular mowing? stones? exhibit areas? bulletin boards? Some of these decisions can wait, but some cannot.

There should be agreement to replace plants that die.

Here, as in the building, my guiding philosophy is to plan, when possible, so that the result erases as few options as possible on future kinds of uses. And most of the trails, etc., away from the building should be planned by an interpreter, not a landscaper, and should be of such light construction that they can often be made by your own people with temporary help.

Smiling Gods and Fierce Scarecrows (1971)

First published in *Museum Roundup* 42 (1971): 48–50.
Reprinted with permission.

AFTER AN INCREDIBLE SERIES OF blunders and disasters that shook my faith in men in both business and government, Wye Marsh Wildlife Centre at Midland, Ontario, opened officially in June 1970. My first Ottawa project was just two years and one month behind schedule. But if it had a turbulent gestation and a difficult birth, its subsequent life as a public centre has been a smooth and happy experience. Of course, it should have been, for we had lots of time to get ready while the engineers, red-tape weavers and construction people performed their slow-motion comic opera.

The gods began to smile the day of the opening. The sky was a fleckless blue, which foiled the final act of the opera. The company that was to bring the canvas shelters to protect the VIPs "in case it rains" had never heard of us when we phoned that morning, mildly curious where our canvas was. We could chuckle happily at their indifference as we rang up $75 saved for Canada and wildlife. Later, as the Hon. Jean Chretien said dramatic words about conservation and the passenger pigeons that once filled Ontario skies, a bunch of scavenging gulls, pure white against pure blue, came low over the crowd, crying to one another as they scouted for partly used picnic lunches. Never was a wildlife centre better blessed at a better moment by a prettier miracle. To add to the wonder of it all, they speckled no spectators.

When the vigorous and youthful minister officially opened the main doors by lifting a long and weathered fence rail from old cedar posts, he turned happily to the crowd and the cameras, with the ends of the rail cutting two murderous arcs across the patio. But the gods still smiled. The cedar rail was light, his strong arms involuntarily shot aloft, and the old rail cut only air above all the heads. And it seems that when he saw inside, he smiled with the gods. Three months later the Canadian Wildlife Service was given money to build two more wildlife centres.

The construction of the building involved me only as a frustrated spectator. Once it was finished, what went inside was entirely my concern. Those of you who know British Columbia's nature houses would see their stamp inside the Wye Marsh building, and it is cared for under exactly the same philosophy that Ted Underhill, Dave Stirling and I evolved at Manning Park and Miracle Beach.

As most of you know, a clean, crisp, unmarred interior to a museum building is no accident but results from careful planning, a million details under constant review and daily attention to fussy housekeeping. The danger of all this is an air of grim formality that repels people, and this we try to avoid. But to send a recently acquired Vancouver story back west, there may occasionally be some point in overdoing things, as when the farmer made his scarecrows so fierce that the crows brought back all the corn.

A feeling of comfortable informality is the result of proper interior planning. We keep it fresh and like new by dusting and polishing every day. In the public area we give top priority to repairs, especially the minor ones. The public should not be insulted with the slovenly maintenance that sometimes is found in even our biggest museums. Equally disturbing are poorly chosen furnishings, like the plastic cases that housed a travelling exhibition of famous treasures some years ago in Vancouver. The lighting in the clear plastic boxes glowed brilliantly on abundant fine scratches in the plastic, and bits of dust held electrically to the plastic were dazzling little jewels of intense light. New ideas or new materials can have unexpected problems, so it is wise to experiment before rushing them onto the exhibit floor.

I designed the original exhibits at Wye Marsh, and now I am letting the staff there see what they can do about improving them. When 40 exhibits are designed and made in a hurry, there are certain to be failures among the success. And when a new staff assembles to eventually replace or modify the failures, I am astounded at the rich harvest of ideas. But not many are new, although in the new setting they may appear new. Most are ideas long ago discarded by anyone experienced after their trials have produced disasters of various sorts and sizes. Following years of happy experimentation with exhibits, to be suddenly asked to design and make exhibits for a large area is to call forth a bunch of ideas heavy with those proven successful and weeded of those that failed. The second wave of ideas from those new to the game is therefore a weedy lot, since they are the lot absent from the exhibits, and the neophytes have no means to recognize them as weeds. When an enthusiastic exhibit proposal is a long-rejected idea, I am tempted to shoot it down in flames, but I always wonder, too, if another mind might have the magic to make it work. So at Wye Marsh I have let some of my old disasters be repeated, and we have also tried some things that had all the earmarks of failure when they were still quite untried. I'm glad we tried them. It gave the new hands experience, I have learned more, and a few of the ideas seem to have unexpected promise. Within reasonable limits of cost and time loss, I think it wise to let people with promise as exhibit designers try turning known failures into successes. One of the best ways to spread around experience seems to include spreading around some of the painful lumps. The rest of my role, as I see it, is to suggest, to guide the lost, to prevent really major catastrophe, then pray that talent blooms.

Mechanical and electronic devices form a major portion of the failures, theirs and mine, referred to above, and at Wye Marsh we have amassed an impressive array of them. We have telephones with taped messages, push-button slide shows, push-button movies, push-button answers to questions, and pull-the-cords-to-change-the-pictures- in-the-windows. We have backlit pictures, pictures lit in sequence by time switches, and sounds as "background noise" throughout the building. We have closed-circuit television bringing the outdoors indoors, and recently we experimented with a column of sound audible at only one exhibit. I suspect that it all sounds impressive and modern and touched with Expo-ish glamour, but there is not an unqualified success in the lot. In many cases the tricky mechanism gets mentally in the way of the message, and in most of the rest we suspect that the same failure is present but difficult to see. For instance, we can see the push buttons pushed repeatedly to see answers for which the questions are never read. Here the brain is obviously turned off. And when people listen for minutes to the message telephones, it is difficult to know what is sinking in, but we suspect the worst when their eyes should be following the details of an exhibit to which they have turned their backs!

We are discussing an old problem. About 1960, Ted Underhill and I knew that our job was not just to pack people in and entertain them. That would be easy. "All it would take is free beer and dancing girls." We had the more difficult task of attracting and entertaining people with only the messages we were paid to communicate. Individual communication methods, like exhibits, demand the same approach. The method itself must not be consciously attractive and interesting, and therefore a distraction, if the message of the exhibit is to have the viewer's undivided mind.

Last summer we did a study of visitor distribution in our exhibit hall. At random times we quickly mapped where people were in the hall. The maps are easy to do but are very complex to understand. We cannot begin to explain some results yet. But one obvious fact is that those exhibits with mechanical or electronic features are good at attracting and holding people. It seems that our need now is a magic device to switch on brains so they can receive our message. Attraction and hold are essential to any successful exhibit, but there can be no success if they end at an unreceptive mind.

Or could it be that people are smarter than we think, and they are getting our word in spite of appearances to the contrary?

A Plan to Appreciate Canada (1971)

First published in *Journal of Environmental Education* 3, no. 2 (1971): 11-13. Reprinted by permission of Taylor & Francis Ltd.

THE CANADIAN WILDLIFE SERVICE IS a branch of federal government concerned entirely with ecology. In 1967 it entered the field of conservation interpretation. For years its biologists had been impressed by the success of park interpretation throughout North America, and they saw a need to use the methods of park interpretation to tell about wildlife in Canada outside parks. The need was caused by a poorly informed public that was allowing its wildlife wealth to deteriorate from lack of knowledge and concern.

This idea to interpret wildlife to create a more understanding public grew into a larger idea. This was to also inform Canadians about the total face of Canada. At first glance this seems a bit grandiose, but, ecology being what it is, you must understand the face of Canada if you are to understand Canada's wildlife, so we might as well state what we are doing and not be coy about it. As many Canadians now know because of their new ecological understanding, animals are the product of rock and soil, of water and air, of weather, sunshine, plants and other animals, including man, who can be among the most important factors of all. To understand wildlife, one must understand the total landscape. So the Wildlife Service found that it needed not wildlife interpretation so much as it needed ecology interpretation with a wildlife emphasis.

This word "interpretation" is a problem. It creates confusion, but there seems to be no substitute. This is not language interpretation, as in interpreting German to a Russian. This is ecology interpretation, in which the specialized ideas and language of science are explained in easily understood ways to the public. The people own the landscape and are supported by it, so it is obviously in their interest to understand it so they can care for it properly.

To tell someone about something is information. To tell them about something with that something right there to help tell its own story turns information into interpretation. Good interpretation includes first-hand experience.

The plan for interpretation put forth by the Canadian Wildlife Service was as follows: A wildlife interpretation centre would be established in each of the major regions of Canada, and each centre would tell an ecological story of the region it was in. These centres might be located in about ten places, such as on the Atlantic coast, in the north woods, on the prairie and in the West Coast forest. All of these would be located across southern Canada near large numbers of Canadians, and as many as possible would be near the Trans-Canada Highway, where travelers could be helped to understand the Canadian landscape and so to increase their enjoyment of it.

In addition to this regional chain of centres, there might be a few smaller centres in special places. For example, there could be interpretation of the seabird colonies off the Gaspé where the birds are already a major tourist attraction, or of the waterfowl in British Columbia's Creston Valley which is already a wildlife spectacle of some renown. These would interpret small situations instead of large regions, but would use the methods of the larger centres changing only their scale. Together, they would all form a trans-Canada chain of ecology centres.

The suggested plan of each major centre was as follows: Each would consist of a building located by an extensive area of public land that was well suited to the purpose of the centre. The land would be used for demonstrations in conservation, ecology, natural science and nature study. The building would be the focal point of activity, containing an office and workshop, and offering the public information through films, slide shows, exhibits and helpful people.

Near the building, outside, would be trails, nature trails, outdoor exhibits, information signs, conservation demonstrations, observation points and other inducements to use and enjoy the outdoors. The staff of interpreters would be the most important part of each centre. They would not only be required to help create and maintain the facilities just described; they would also make personal contact with as many visitors as possible. Much of the secret of park interpretation's success is due to the abundance of personal communication between park naturalist and public. There is no hope for a machine pleasing, inspiring or even informing with the effectiveness of an enthused and versatile human being. The plan specified that, in the building, an interpreter would always be visible and looking helpful. Interpreters would also offer daily activities outside such as demonstrations, talks and conducted walks, each enabling prolonged personal communication.

These centres were not to be museums in the usual sense, but in some ways would be similar. There would be no indoor collections in the normal museum way, for instance, because the "collection" was outside, being the parts of the landscape. The centre's task would be almost entirely that museum function of serving the public directly, through attracting and informing people, and through helping them use the collection. In fact, the major effort was to be directed at persuading people to become personally involved with the collection.

It is possible, of course, to carry too far this idea of the countryside being the collection. The countryside is also what Canada is, people and all. The whole purpose of the plan was to get more people involved with the living, breathing face of Canada, which is not just the wealth of Canada. It is Canada. This was a plan to spread ecological awareness, with wildlife the very appropriate vehicle for doing so. Inevitably, although we would talk specifically of ducks or cranes or bluebirds or bears or caribou, quite unavoidably we would be in the very thick of telling people how Canada works, and why it works, and how to keep it working as best we can. The central focus was to interpret the ecology of wildlife. Because ecology is a web of interrelationships, wildlife would lead inevitably to water and soil, to trees and wheat and fences, to cattle, the shapes of barns, the plans of towns and the activities of men. To talk of the ecology of wildlife is to talk also of the ecology of man.

That was the need, and that was the plan. In 1967 the action began. The first wildlife centre is now in operation.

Wye Marsh Wildlife Centre is located near Midland, Ontario, about 90 miles north of Toronto, where it interprets the hardwood region of southern Ontario and Quebec, a region now largely agricultural. This centre is within a day's drive of the homes of about 50,000,000 people. It is located in a popular tourist area centring on Georgian Bay. The schools of Toronto are less than two hours away, while most schools in southern Ontario are potential visitors. We have had classes from Windsor, Cornwall and Sudbury, which are at the limits of heavily populated Ontario. We are also within sight of the much-visited Roman Catholic Martyr's Shrine, and of the Ontario government's historic and religious attraction at Ste. Marie. We will have no lack of audience.

Beside the centre are 2,500 acres of public land owned by the Province of Ontario and managed by the Fish and Wildlife Branch of Ontario's Department of Lands and Forests. The primary purpose of these lands is wildlife management and public hunting, but many other land uses are compatible with these, among them public recreation such as hiking, photography, nature study, educational sessions and so on.

The federal government's role at this first centre is to interpret three overlapping areas: the hardwood region of Canada; the conveniently close part of that region, which we take to be Simcoe County; and Wye Marsh, which dominates the immediate vicinity. Our story is not about what most people call nature. In all three of these areas, man has heavily modified the countryside. We feature nature and man, warts and all. This means that our story about Wye Marsh will be largely the story of how the provincial government manages that area to increase public benefits.

The facilities now established at Wye Marsh Wildlife Centre are many. There is a building with a floor area of about 10,000 square feet containing a foyer, offices, washrooms, workshops, laboratory space, an exhibit hall and a theatre. The last features films or slide shows hourly through the busy tourist season, all shows being inducements to go outside and see for oneself that the outdoors is a place with interesting action. The exhibit hall contains about 40 exhibits, again most of them designed to motivate the viewer into looking for the real thing himself, outside. Some exhibits have slide shows or taped messages or 8 mm movies or aquariums with fish or other wet things.

Recently we began to experiment with closed-circuit television. Here we wonder if we can use TV to bridge the gap between indoors and outdoors by bringing choice bits of live action from the marsh into the foyer. We might feature, for instance, a duck nest, turtles sunning on a log, or fish underwater.

We are very careful about gimmickry, however. It can easily become an end in itself to both staff and audience. But when thoughtfully used, it can be useful. Most of it falls into the category of being a necessary evil. These machines, and also the very building itself, must remain a sort of mental gateway to prepare the mind for the real attractions, outside, on the face of Canada.

Some of our structures and gimmicks spill outside the centre to ease the transition from building to landscape. There are trails and nature trails, signs and outdoor exhibits, and blinds from which to spy on wildlife. At the edge of a pond we are constructing now a sort of public underwater window

Marsh window at the Wye Marsh Wildlife Centre, Midland, ON, September 1970.
Edwards family photo.

looking into the waters of the marsh. The real marsh is under water, and we want people to see that real marsh. We are also ready to construct a tower that will help the public see more of the marsh from the low shore, and a long boardwalk into the marsh will be in operation next year.

In these days of high costs and poor workmanship, we feel that the secret to success is self-sufficiency, versatility and the ability to seize quickly on an opportunity to communicate. Our theatre can be converted into a classroom or an exhibit room or a conference room in half an hour. We can make our own exhibits and can turn out an effective exhibit in a day. All exhibits can be quickly repaired on the premises. We can print our own temporary leaflets and booklets on our own machinery, and we have devised an inexpensive outdoor sign that is easy to make, and that we think is good-looking. Aside from the general advantages of being flexible, a major advantage of this self-sufficiency is that we can cope quickly with groups coming to us on short notice and, more important, we can keep up a changing interpretation program that is dealing with a constantly changing outdoors. The different seasons need different signs and leaflets, and if purple beetles suddenly become abundant, we can interpret the situation in several ways almost at once. Perhaps even more important, this constant change encourages people to return again and again. Our show is not static.

Wye Marsh Wildlife Centre opened quietly and unofficially last July. It has now had a trial run, the rough edges are gone and it is ready for its first full season. We plan an official opening in June. A one-minute film for television will publicize the centre in the greater Toronto area. A new and colourful pamphlet is aimed at tourists already near the centre. We will have to be careful about the level of visitation, however. We are so close to so many people that the atmosphere of the centre, and the nature around it, could be destroyed by too much success.

We have ideas on locations for the next wildlife centres. Between Regina and Saskatoon at Last Mountain Lake is one of the great wildlife spectacles. We hope our next centre will be there. We are interested also in the Tantramar marshes at the head of the Bay of Fundy,* and in Cap Tourmente, near Quebec City, where most of the world's greater snow geese spend their springs and falls.†

We have other sorts of plans as well. We like the idea of guidebooks pointing out the natural wonders and the wildlife spectacles in each region of Canada. Travel can be fun, and it should be periodically exciting, but it takes some help to make it that way. We are thinking of courses for people on how to read the landscape, or on how to use that camera outdoors, or on how to name that bird and tree and flower. We want to give short courses to teachers. We would like to give workshops for outdoor writers. But all of these are what we call "thinking big." We must never forget that our really important task is to think small. The real measure of our success is the child who, because of us, has a lifelong interest in trees, or the grandfather who has new zest in his life because we opened his eyes to the beauty—and to the fun—of birds. In interpretation, thinking small is the difference between failure and success. We are trying to reveal the magic of the grassroots, and for this, thinking small will always be best.

---

* Now the Tintamarre National Wildlife Area (1978), managed by the Government of Canada through Environment and Climate Change Canada.–Eds.

† Now the Cap Tourmente National Wildlife Area (1978) on the north shore of the St. Lawrence River, managed by the Government of Canada through Environment and Climate Change Canada.–Eds.

Yorke Edwards while at the BC Provincial Museum.

BC Provincial Museum

Lest it be thought that the only significant staff changes during the year were at Federal expense, we should add that Yorke Edwards filled the Assistant Director's position after it had been vacant for 2½ years. Mr. Edwards' extensive experience in museums, interpretation, and display will be highly valued in the years ahead when our exhibit programmes will continue to be among our top priorities.

Department of Recreation and Conservation, Annual Report, 1972.

Yorke had, in some ways, never really left Victoria. He continued, while he was in Ottawa, to write for the BC Museums Association newsletter *Museum Roundup*, and he maintained close relations with people on the West Coast. In 1972, he returned to Victoria as the assistant director of the BC Provincial Museum, working with the director, Bristol Foster. Yorke was instrumental in the development of exhibits in the newly opened museum building. When Bristol left in 1975 to begin the Ecological Reserves Program in the BC Ministry of Environment, Yorke was appointed director. Yorke then brought Bill Barkley back to BC, from his position as Wye Marsh Wildlife Centre's biologist-in-charge, to be his assistant director. Bill had worked as an early interpreter in BC Parks.

The Message Is Our Measure (1972)

First published in *Museum Roundup* 47 (1972): 50–52.
Reprinted with permission.

DREAMS ARE NOT ALWAYS THE asleep kind. Some are consciously constructed and carefully controlled. Of late, my planned ones have featured museums and how to improve their communication with people.

Most museums are firmly stuck in the 19th century. To inform their public they display objects, add a label, then consider duty done. A label can save an object from being meaningless, but most do not. After all, the words "Indian Arrowhead" or "Greek Vase" may reduce confusion in separating vases from arrowheads, but by themselves are not likely to put new interests into lazy minds. This traditional sort of museum communication is the barest minimum. It puts all of the initiative to understand in the hands of the viewer, and not many viewers rise to the challenge.

My dream museum uses labels that inform. Long labels can be a bore, but a few choice sentences open doors to understanding. Some drawings of the objects in use may be essential, and when the natural habitat of the object is suggested by its museum surroundings, the object can begin to take on some meaning. While interest is stirring, the viewer can go further at once. Information sheets in a nearby dispenser round out the story—either on the spot or later by the fire at home—and each sheet ends by telling where to find further reading, see other exhibits, borrow films, purchase slide shows and so on. Sometimes this in-depth communication is done better by an inexpensive booklet covering several exhibits. All such printing helps most by being immediately obtainable near the inspirational object, not just at the sales desk near the front door. Germinating and growing new interests is a delicate process that needs constant tending, for interest withers fast if kept small.

The medium is not the message

I am continually meeting museum people who seem to be aware that much museum communication is a failure, and they all assume that the solution lies in electronic media like television and recorded labels at exhibits. While these new methods have a bright future, I believe there is no magic in them. The magic in any medium of communication is in how it is used. We have not put much magic into the old methods, not in several centuries, so I expect no magic to come easily with the new methods. We may be dazzled by a new means of communication, but a dull and inaccurate message remains dull and inaccurate no matter how communicated. I suspect that even in this space age, the communication medium with the most glittering future is still the printed word, whether label, sign or leaflet.

Half the secret of communicating effectively is to know your audience in order to cater to its needs. Most museum communicators are primarily experts in science, so full of their subjects for so long that they have trouble being understood by people not having much the same expertise. Small wonder that most people have not the slightest idea of what many museum experts are talking about.

The museum visitor is offered a series of experiences that are intended to be interesting. Most would be if only the visitor could understand the message. But usually the words he receives are put together by someone quite unaware that most visitors know almost nothing about almost everything, which is of course the standard human condition. It is largely true that most museums are showing meaningless objects with meaningless labels in meaningless surroundings.

A hobby of mine is visiting museums while disguised as a sightseeing tourist. I am impressed by how few museums have told me, quickly, clearly, impressively, what they are all about. Every museum front door should have near it, inside or outside, an inspiring statement of purpose that is so presented that it is impossible to ignore. The most obvious way to do this is to set the words, big and strong, into a large and commanding wall. My dream museum does this.

Having shared the secret of what the place is all about, my museum offers the standard museum attractions with the unusual aim of clearly communicating easily understood information about both the collection and the museum's activity. Exhibits carefully avoid the disturbing current trend for the message to be hidden by artistic expression. While artistic content is essential, it must not get in the way of the message that is the exhibit's whole purpose. Communication effectiveness must be the full purpose of exhibits. And the only exhibit themes acceptable are those appropriate to the purpose of the museum, its collections and its functions.

A theatre for interpretation

The museum in my dream has a theatre in frequent use, offering the most popular attractions in the building. It is the interpretation centre for the rest of the museum, breathing understanding and meaning into the objects in the collection. Museum objects are of necessity unused, "dead," rather meaningless things that are usually observed completely out of context. The magic of the theatre is the obvious way to put them into context by transporting people mentally through time and space as desired, using modern techniques and even pioneering new ones. Any museum featuring such a good interpretation theatre must, of course, have the full-time services of a very good movie photographer. In many museums the planetarium has shown that the theatre—even the highly specialized theatre—can be an impressively popular attraction while being successful educationally and financially as well.

The imaginative use of slides in the theatre is also important. Slide shows in the exhibit hall, on the other hand, must be considered cautiously, since their wide use in this way through the past decade seems to have been accompanied by much public disinterest. Expo 67 showed that the still-photo theatre can be exciting and informative, but outside the theatre the slide becomes just a picture, and usually a faded one at that since light interference is rarely under control.

Closed-circuit television has suffered from overenthusiastic claims for its communication values, but this must not prejudice against its several useful features. And to lay a general misconception to rest, it can be much less expensive than most museum exhibits. It has several uses in my museum of dreams. In the exhibit hall, the TV lens can sometimes see what the visitor cannot by looking from a difficult angle. More useful perhaps is using television to magnify small things or small details on large things to more visible size. I remember once looking at a beetle through a pocket lens and wondering how many people know what a fantastic creature it really is, head on and times ten. And the beauty of an arrowhead is often in its surface detail, where beautiful material has been lovingly shaped by skilful hands. To just display is not enough. The interesting message is often in the detail that untrained eyes fail to see, and which magnification reveals.*

Another use of television is as a window looking at museum function. There are activities going on behind the scenes in many museums which can fit regularly into a TV screen. My museum has a small lounge where for several hours a day there is television communication on a large screen from museum to citizen on the functions essential to museum success. The method has its pitfalls, of course. Improperly done, it can be dull. But creative thought and a bit of showmanship can produce a mix of activities—live if in the building, pre-recorded on tape if in the field—that results in more citizens sympathetic to the needs of their museum.

Museum publications should enable people to deepen the museum experience in the comfort of their homes. Inexpensive printed matter to extend the message in exhibits has been mentioned. My dream museum offers, in addition, a leaflet series,

---

* We are reminded of an expression that was attributed to the 19th-century naturalist Louis Agassiz: "The best aid to the untrained eye is a sharp pencil." For more on Agassiz's influence, see N. Lerner, "Drawing to Learn Science: Legacies of Agassiz," *Journal of Technical Writing and Communication* 37, no. 4 (2007): 379–394, http://oww-files-public.s3.amazonaws.com/6/6f/Draw2Learn_NLerner.pdf –Eds.

picture series, wall-chart series and poster series to enrich the atmosphere of home and school, office and retreat. Large museums quite properly concentrate on scholarly publication, but there should also be much energy put into capturing and changing the uninformed mind. This surely is the undeveloped area in greatest need of museum conquest.

Mass and more manageable media

To most people the mass media are the important communicators. Newspapers and magazines, radio and television are with us constantly. They are not much used by museums, and perhaps this is as it should be. Museums are in the business of showing people real things, and this advantage is lost if too much effort goes into communication divorced from first-hand communication. My dream museum is in the mass media periodically, but mainly because it is a place of frequent newsworthy action. When museums offer satisfying and sometimes exciting experiences that contain something new, the mass media then want to feature museums. In a way, I suppose, the frequency of newsworthy events in a museum is a rough measure of how well it is doing the job of touching directly the man in the street. It is a matter of museum vitality, people-oriented. But most important of all, perhaps, such museum vitality sets in operation the best medium of all for spreading word among the masses, and that is when friends tell friends not to miss it, because they saw it, and it was good.

The possible communication methods with their variations are almost endless. I can remember one museum in which the main attraction was a stage show complete with a pretty girl and a series of crowd-gathering demonstrations. My dream museum has used this approach only on special occasions. It

Yorke collecting aquatic invertebrate samples during the Brooks Peninsula expedition on the west coast of Vancouver Island, August 1981.

regularly uses guided tours, lectures that entertain, unusual field trips, a newsletter offering news with flair, pamphlets that are real lures to see the museum, advertising on public transportation that works ideas into idle travelling minds, and attractive travelling exhibits. Even small museums can increase their value to people by using a dash of showmanship and a sprinkle of enthusiastic experimentation to (1) attract people, (2) hold people and (3) "turn them on," so that (4) they tell their friends, who are attracted, held, turned on and so on and on and on...

A sadly neglected problem in museum communication is that of how a provincial museum can have a truly provincial audience. The National Museum of Canada has had the same problem and is now taking steps to solve it. Time will tell if Ottawa is capable of a wide scattering of fragile treasures at acceptable cost. The provincial solution cannot be similar, for there are, in each province, few buildings capable of giving suitable space to fragile treasures, which, come to think of it, is immaterial beside the problem of general poverty among provincial museums. Perhaps the function of the provincial museum is not to invade local areas with collections, but to do for them on film and paper the in-depth interpretation of locally held collections. This plan has the advantage, hard to beat, of leaving local collections where they have the most significant story to tell, and featuring them there. The provincial museum is thus busy telling the provincial story, with each chapter told in its proper environment. My dream museum would welcome help and money to bring its collections more alive.

It is not enough to be talking. It is not enough to have an audience politely trying to understand. It is enough, I think, to be understood by an inspired capacity audience. This is what my dream museum strives for. Can we be satisfied with less?

Interpretation—What Should It Be? (1976)

First published in *Journal of Interpretation* 1, no. 1 (1976): 13–16. Reprinted with permission.

FREEMAN KING OF VICTORIA, WHO devoted his life to nature interpretation, died recently. His concept of interpretation was what interpretation should be. He combined a lot of facts, an ability to use fiction to reveal truth, and a constant store of happy nonsense to instinctively relate things to people and to their lives at home. He had the common touch, he was interesting and he liked people, but above all he had an infectious enthusiasm, a boyish excitement about things that held people and inspired them. Even to his last year, which was his 84th, he captivated audiences of all ages. However, children were his special interest because he never lost the zest and wonder of his own childhood. Also, kids loved him, and I never believed the old story of the Pied Piper until I saw Freeman gather up and carry off a herd of children without touching one of them.

Indoors, Freeman seemed somehow a bit out of place, for it was the outdoors that was his home, and there, what he said fitted the wonder and beauty of the landscape. Instinctively, he chose to address the public from a stage where the props themselves communicated most of his message about nature.

After all, he might have said, words alone cannot do much toward understanding a tree. You have to experience a tree. Understanding must start with seeing it and hearing it and smelling it and feeling it and perhaps even tasting it.

Freeman didn't have too much faith in signs or leaflets or electric gimmicks. He talked to people, and I suspect, had he been asked, he would have said that is the best way to communicate with people.

For almost 20 years, with the help of many friends including Freeman King, I have been developing my ideas on interpretation. It still gives me trouble at times, but not nearly so much as I have seen others have when they have no concept of what makes interpretation effective, popular and different enough to be a distinct form of communication. Much of what I hear called "interpretation" I do not consider to be interpretation at all. It is simply information. And there is nothing wrong with that, except that information is everywhere; there is a huge and constant supply of good information available to all of us, but not much of it can be dignified by the term "interpretation."

My current concept of interpretation gives it four essential characteristics. It is attractive communication, offering concise information, given in the presence of the topic, and its goal is the revelation of significance.

Not many of you will accept this concept immediately, I am sure. So be it. You have yours and I have mine. But since I am asked to share my concept of interpretation, not much would be meaningful if I did not give my basic views first. So there it is; help yourself if you can live with it.

Understandably, perhaps, the part of my concept probably most difficult to accept on first encounter is to me the most important. Namely, that interpretation is possible only in the presence of the thing being interpreted. It took some years for me to be completely convinced of this. For about a decade it was vaguely disturbing to me, whenever I had time to think about it, that we seemed to use the word "interpretation" very loosely. Much of what we labelled "interpretation" seemed nothing more than information relabelled. We seemed to be selling an old product by using a misleading sales pitch. I had guilty feelings but never had time to isolate the difference.

But it did appear, first as the conviction that the best interpretive situation is in the presence of the real thing; then as the realization that only before the mountain can the mountain be interpreted. And it is, of course, the messages that your senses are receiving from the mountain that are interpreted by the interpreter. The very word "interpret" implies a message needing translation.

Once this is accepted, a flood of new understanding invades what most of us so loosely call interpretation. Much of it is not interpretation at all, but information. Most theatre shows and campfire programs are entertaining information but not interpretation. Most indoor displays and exhibits, as well as some outdoor ones, are simply information. Lectures and talks are often information. Most publications simply inform. In an interpretation program, these informing activities may be excellent preparation for interpretation, as people use what they know to interpret what they experience later. But information is not interpretation until it is used to interpret.

So while it is possible to impart good information about the Douglas fir almost anywhere, interpretation can take place only when a Douglas fir is right there, communicating its own complex messages to the audience. In order to understand a

Douglas fir, you must experience it. Words or pictures about it are not nearly enough. I recently read an article about blind people who see for the first time. Before, they had lived in a world of words, smells, sounds and touch. But the world of light, when they experience it, is nothing like what they imagined it to be. How can you imagine a fir if you have never seen one? And I suspect that smells, sounds and the feel of things would be even more difficult to imagine in the absence of being able to experience the real things.

Nothing else can equal the accuracy and clarity of experiencing the real thing. Everything else is replica or second-hand account, which are, incidentally, the predominant experiences of our formal education. People today are experience poor. It is this present scarcity of understanding from the real thing, from first-hand experience, that makes interpretation unique, impressive and successful.

It was exploring this real-thing dimension that led me from landscape interpretation to the city museum. The museum exists to collect, preserve and interpret real things. But after landscapes, the museum was both an unexpected disappointment and a unique challenge. The disappointment is that while the things in museums are real, they are set in meaningless surroundings that cause them to lose much of their significance. An arrowhead of black glass found on a beach beside a remote mountain lake has much more to communicate than an arrowhead in a museum room. Yet it is still a real thing and so, to some extent, can be effectively interpreted. The challenge is the large and accessible audience, and providing the magic to ignite their desires to understand the world.

"Why the real thing?" some will ask. "Why not pictures instead?"

Pictures can be dramatic, exciting, beautiful, educational and aids to interpretation, but they are not the real thing.

They smell wrong, sound wrong and may even look wrong. They are often in the wrong environment, and also the human mind receives them as something inferior. When museums such as this one have come to realize that even looking at something real through glass diminishes its communicated message, it is easy to understand that framed, electrified, two-dimensional images, even when they move, are poor substitutes for reality. I'm not depreciating the audiovisual miracle; I'm just saying that your own sensory equipment is time-tested and works better when not filtered through a Johnny-come-lately machine.

Once you accept the idea of using the real thing for maximum revelation, many hallowed interpretation practices become suspect. It was at Wye Marsh Wildlife Centre, north of Toronto, that I first experienced these disturbing ideas: I began to realize that nature interpreters do a lot of indoor communicating about how great it is outdoors, and that we had spent a million dollars on brick walls to isolate that indoor communication from the real thing outdoors. So with an imaginative architect, we talked and pondered for several days and filled up perhaps a mile of tape. It was mainly a post-mortem using hindsight to decide what we should have done at Wye Marsh. We came out thoroughly disenchanted with enclosed buildings as interpretation facilities in parks and park-like places, and suspicious of both theatre experiences and enclosed exhibit galleries. In our minds, we put all interpretation out in the warm green or cold white world where it should be; indoors we put administration, toilets, eating rooms and educational space for kids. We also put indoors the informational experiences that we felt were necessary upon returning from the marsh, experiences like a library, a bookshop and an audiovisual experience reinforcing and tying together the real experience just obtained from the marsh.

The plan involved less money and better interpretation. It incorporated a full range of devices used outdoors to make nature accessible and communication about it possible. We planned floating boardwalks, blinds, viewing towers, underwater viewing windows, outdoor exhibit clusters, signs, labelled nature trails, leaflet nature trails,* guided walks, guided boat trips, rented binoculars and magnifying glasses, fixed telescopes, flights overhead for the bird's-eye view, and others that I cannot now recall. It was fun. It was exciting. And I think we did something worth doing. This summer, Ottawa plans to build an interpretation complex by a slough in Saskatchewan, and it will use many of the ideas that we examined at Wye Marsh. There, it was an exercise in how things should have been done, but now others are putting those ideas to work elsewhere.

It is easy to misuse some of our media, and in my experience the movie film is often the most misused. In the early days, cost and lack of an appropriate theatre kept movies out of my interpretation planning, but two later experiences convinced me of the dangers of movies.

Years ago in Banff, I went to an outdoor theatre one evening expecting to learn about the spectacular national park that was all about me. The place was packed, and we saw a film that night on salmon canning on the Pacific coast. In fairness, I must say that the event was not billed as interpretation. It was put on by information people in the park. (In those days, interpretation and information had separate staffs. Maybe they still do.) But the content was still inexcusable, even if the aim was simply entertainment. In subsequent years, I was often under heavy pressure to show National Film Board films in British Columbia's provincial parks, and, needless to say, I was ready

* On leaflet nature trails, the walker is guided and informed by material in a leaflet. In 2020, an app using GPS might serve the same function.—Eds.

to lay my job on the line before park naturalists would project salmon canning or anything else inappropriate in our BC parks.

Later, in Ontario, I found myself planning the use of a wildlife centre by a marsh, and the centre had a theatre. This time the National Film Board had a good film, one about a typical southern Ontario marsh, and it seemed to do a superior job of communicating about nearby Wye Marsh. We showed the film every half hour as an introduction to our interpretation of the marsh. It was a good film by all of today's standards: imaginative, action-packed, exciting, accurate commentary and good photography. It was also a disaster. We wanted people to understand our marsh, and to get into it mentally and physically. To begin their introduction, we were showing them a highly entertaining film crammed with close-up action views of shy creatures—flying, swimming, diving, singing, mating, threatening, chasing, fighting, killing one another and gulping one another down. It was total involvement. The people came out of that theatre with their hearts pumping adrenalin into their farthest fibers, ready to experience the real thing. But when they got to the marsh, what a letdown—lazy clouds, still waters, cattails whispering, maybe a distant swallow, heat, buzzing insects, silences. They soon left for some action on the tube or in the nearest beer parlour.

Every bit of that film was true, but the selection of the bits and the way they were put together were pure and misleading fiction, as are most popular nature films that flood our lives today, even when the bits and the characters in them are pure fact.

Needless to say, I distrust the value of films in nature interpretation unless they are accurate in all respects. However, in contrast, I cheer for the slide show as a safe, effective and accurate media, since it is received by the audience (many of whom have cameras) as a biased selection of frozen glimpses of things worth photographing, and an honest narrative with it is clearly tying together isolated events into a quite unnatural composite experience.

So much for my distrust of some audiovisual techniques in interpretation. I began by saying that interpretation requires the presence of the real thing. I then suggested that some methods we use in the information part of our work are acting against us, instead of for us. Now I wish to extend the latter thought into our interpretation endeavours and point out that often our own carelessness makes our interpretive efforts a waste of time, and sometimes even results in our communicating loud, clear lies.

Interpretation is a kind of communication, and the word "communication" implies that not only is a message sent, but it is also received. I suggest that much of what we send in interpretation is never received.

The effective interpreter communicates in a manner that the audience finds easy to receive and understand. This art may be innate or acquired, but that makes no difference, for most of us must acquire it. Having it is a matter, I believe, of being able to put yourself in the audience's shoes, and to look at your communication from their viewpoint and in the light of their needs. Simply to have understanding yourself of a thing does not qualify you to interpret it. You must also understand how to interpret effectively. A great problem of being an expert of any kind is that you are, by definition and by thought processes, different from the non-experts who constitute most of your audience. Being different is apt to make you difficult to understand. Even more serious, once you are an expert it is very difficult to remember the needs you had as a beginner. Worst of all, once we are experts, we subconsciously want to show it, and this, for example, is why the communications of science are often meaningless to most citizens.

I suppose, then, that all this and some related communication failures result from incompetence or misunderstanding or indifference or combinations of these. Examples follow:

- A common one is saying too much, whether verbally or on a label.
- Also, common are messages loaded with words like symbiosis, urbanization, cortex, batholith, adaptation, *Pseudotsuga*.
- Another example is distracting attentions and therefore minds, and there are thousands of methods to do this, with pocket jingling, stage "dances" or phony mannerisms; with Scotch tape, nails, stains, distracting lettering; or with art getting in the way of information. The axiom here is "let the information have no competition."
- Related to the last, in signs and exhibits, what may be excellent design from the standpoint of art is often a disaster as information in interpretation. For the same reasons, a beautiful and imaginative interpretation structure (like a building) may be a negative asset, simply because it seizes attention away from the message it is supposedly aiding. It should be the message that stands out. The ideal vehicle of the message must be unremarkable, and perhaps even as close to invisible to the mind as possible. Most informative exhibits in Canada today have far too much art of the obstructing kind. They are design dominated. Surely information is the dominant purpose, and this should be design augmented at most, or at least design free to the casual observer.
- Again, last August, not far from Victoria, I walked a nature trail. The labels were good but their locations often made them completely misleading. A typical example was a label on western red cedar and Indians. The audience would consist, as do most of our audiences, of few people who

could confidently distinguish cedar from hemlock—or from any other conifer for that matter. Yet that sign was 20 feet away from a red cedar. It was touching ferns, and the nearest conifer was a small Douglas fir. I wonder how many people now believe that red cedar looks like sword fern. Carelessness? Who knows. Certainly there was no successful attempt to stand in the audience's shoes, and the result was destructive instead of constructive.

- Finally, the process of good interpretation requires the successful accomplishment of attracting the audience, then holding it, while informing it. If you are not attractive, not much happens. So the successful interpreter must have a touch of showmanship, a bit of the Madison Avenue touch, a bit of the medicine man flair. It is not so simple as that, however, for he must have with this a fine sense of when the art of attraction becomes dishonest misrepresentation. Nowhere is this attraction more necessary than in our titles, whether the title of a talk, a walk, a trail sign or a display. Compare these titles, but remember, they are not for you or your science-oriented friends. They are for Joe Jones, accountant, or whoever you choose as a typical audience.
    - "British Columbia's Industrialization and Urbanization"
    - "The City Takes Over"
    - "They Turned Trees into Houses"
    - "All About Conquering the West"

  Many possibilities, many connotations, but honest attraction must be in the good interpreter's large collection of skills. You live in a world of titles. Think about them.

I suppose that the common factor to all this is that for good interpretation to take place, a certain sequence of certain kinds of communication must occur, and any weakening of any part weakens the whole, just as any failure destroys the whole.

In my experience, one of the absolute necessities of a good interpretation program, whether it is a complex of media or one lone interpreter, is periodic inspections by an observer who is a very fussy tactful tyrant. He must arrive unexpectedly, with a fresh mind because he normally works elsewhere, and must take the head interpreter in tow to raise helpful hell about gum wrappers on the nature trail, dirty signs, sloppy workmanship, all other interpretation disasters great and small, and also about related matters like egg on the headman's shirt. A lot of "interpretation" is not interpretation at all, sometimes because the machine is using the wrong parts, but more often because no one is giving the machine thorough periodic tune-ups.

Unfortunately, one of the great limitations of our success is that most of us are forced to play the numbers game, in which the measure of our success is the number of people we touch. Some of us are voluntarily playing this game, but most of us have bosses that insist we play it. Too many people wreck much of our effort. How do you interpret the forest primeval when part of the show is a mob scene? So we do what is mistakenly called "the democratic thing." Instead of reducing the mob so that at least some get something of the truth from us, we turn to bullhorns, taped lectures and other electronic assurances so that we become even less effective to even more people. We have the same problems in museums as in parks. This museum on a summer day when 16,000 people come through the doors is so jammed that most people cannot see the exhibits, and those that do cannot possibly get the mood-message that many exhibits are designed to give.

I believe in quality. I believe that in interpretation, quality can be communicated to only small numbers at once. In another place, and to a museum audience, I not long ago urged that more of us try "the grandfather way" of interpretation. I urged them to protect a small part of their budgets, at least, for quality interpretation such as using warm and friendly grandfather types to lead a few children at a time into the wide-eyed world of understanding things. I believe that if we must have our mob scenes to please our bosses, we should also have programs, however small, of leading perhaps only one or two people at a time into new worlds, even if we do it only once a day.

I suspect that if you could measure the mob, and then the one or two, for interpretation benefits received, the quiet little program would win because many of the people in the mob must receive negative benefits.

That is what interpretation should be—people talking, one to one, over something real and made overwhelmingly interesting by the skill and understanding and magnetism of the interpreter.

National Education and the National Parks (1976)

Unpublished manuscript written for Gavin Henderson of the National and Provincial Parks Association of Canada, June 1976.

FROM WHATEVER BIASED VIEWPOINT, THE basic purpose of the national parks must be clear to everyone. The parks exist to preserve old landscapes for people, and the preservation part must be the top-priority purpose or there can soon be nothing worth preserving.

While the preservation is *for* people, obviously the protection is *from* people. This is the universal park paradox, which requires that only gentle kinds of park uses are acceptable, and that mechanisms for the easy control of park-use volumes are essential.

What do national parks give to people? It is all summed up in one word: experiences. The experience of beauty, of primeval timelessness, of knowing other lives, of understanding how the world's ecosystems work, of clear evidence that man does not own the scheme of things but is rather part of that scheme—these are what parks are for.

Experiences are a fundamental need of man. They are not only the factors that make life interesting and therefore worthwhile; they incidentally lead to the wisdom of how to survive. Modern man needs more of this wisdom.

New experiences are the spices in our lives. Our culture glorifies the "new," as the adman has discovered, but he did not invent the idea. The memorable events in all of our lives are the fresh excitements like new friends, new reunions with old friends, new jobs, new movies, new foods—an endless list in which the new experiences of travel to new landscapes for their endlessly new delights support a multi-billion-dollar world industry. People want new experiences; they may even need new experiences to maintain happy sanity.

All experience is educational, so most normal people's lives are filled with pleasant education, which may be as small as discovering a new toothpaste, or as big as learning that the light reaching Earth from the North Star is 50 years old.* For some reason, most Canadians assume that "education" must have a capital "E," and that it always takes place in schools, but the really important education could never take place there. Most education comes from first-hand experience with real situations and real things. This is where parks excel. Parks are real and are composed of thousands of things. As oases of natural landscape in a world changed by men, parks are essential to the educational process of illustrating the natural science of Canada, the history of Canada and what men have done to Canada. Parks are essential to citizen awareness of where we came from, where we are and where we seem to be going. More than that, parks

* Yorke didn't have this quite right. The North Star seems to be, based on current science, around 320 light years from the Earth.–Eds.

and other areas preserving the past are data banks needed for man's survival. It is know-how in technology that has made man an endangered species. It can only be know-how in ecology that saves man from his technology. Parks preserve ecological facts, so are priceless educational resources important to man's future.

The present educational gains from our national parks are impressive but superficial, the major efforts not going much beyond providing public access and tourist accommodation. There are also some interpretive signs and some low-cost information leaflets, but neither are evident or attractive to the average car-bound visitor. Park naturalist programs have an exciting potential, but usually it is easier to find a gourmet dinner or junk souvenirs than to learn why the rivers are milky or what name to give the blue flowers. There has been a solid base of information and interpretation in some national parks, but these services still miss most of the people, while those getting the benefits are mostly converts who know where to find the answers. For most of the visiting public, the national park experience is dominated by crowded commerce-hungry towns, expensive highways encouraging speed through distant scenery, and a few specific attractions like waterfalls. The main purpose of the parks has little influence on what the average visitor experiences.

National parks should not be just tourist traps offering superficial scenery glancing; the management effort within the parks should be dominated by educational goals making it easy and exciting for people to slow down and to really see what they are looking at, while almost automatically keeping in touch with a famous interpretation service that explains the parks' meanings while revealing their highly entertaining and often exciting nature.

The key to successful park use is interpretation so good that it has not just fame in itself, but is also a very part of the fame of the park simply because an exciting park experience needs both the park and its interpretation. The messages that parks alone offer are not received by most of us, nor could we understand them the first time if we did receive them. Interpretation is needed, and it has to be so attractive, and so easily encountered, that it is obviously the only "window" through which to get the most out of the park experience. Tomorrow's alternative to national park use for political and economic gains alone is an interpretation program dedicated to the future quality of Canadian life. It is as big as that.

These days Canadians appear to face many expanding problems, from dying lakes to poisoned fish, from rising costs to declining markets, from decaying cities to rising crime rates. Among the ingredients at the base of all these problems is a generous amount of environmental destruction.

For a century now, scientists have known that two forces mould the living organism—which term, of course, includes man. One is the internal legacy of genes inherited from parents; the other is the external environment which shapes the genetic base. It is genes that give us the capability to be human, but it is environment that determines the quality of our humanity. As Canadians become increasingly urban, escaping from the economic uncertainties of rural life into the protecting city, we are increasingly out of touch with the land of Canada, which is our basic wealth. This is a frightening condition. Parks have a major role to play in counteracting this trend. With attractive lands so presented to the people that the result has rave reviews, national park education through park interpretation should lead the national effort to keep Canadians in touch with Canada.

We are halfway there now. We have superb parks. Most receive numerous Canadians annually. A nucleus of interpretation already exists. All we need now is the national conviction that national parks are not an expensive luxury but a national need in ecology for education, and the national vision to know that Canada, by going the rest of the way, can make its parks a smash hit in educational experiences while still preserving them better than we have done to date.

The issue is national quality. The objective is the popular know-how to sustain the nation as a superior environment for growing people. The action proposed is national parks leading the way simply by telling with flair what shapes and sustains the living land, and telling it in parks to all comers.

The Object's the Thing (1979)

Paper presented to the Association of Canadian Interpreters at Naramata, BC, November 1, 1979.

THE SUBJECT IS OBJECTS, AND to get real things in real places fixed in our minds, consider with me some landscapes, some historic buildings and some museums.

Point Pelee Provincial Park is essentially a sandspit. On it is a largely Carolinian assortment of plants and animals. Man is among the animals. One of the features of this place is animal migration—a zoogeographic phenomenon. Here is a story of land and life; a story of the histories of land and life; a story of the processes in history that made what we see today; a story about objects—a lake, a sandspit, a marsh, wild cucumbers, orchard orioles, man.

Jasper National Park has the same sorts of attributes, but of course is very different in detail. Using the brief description of Pelee, I can turn it into Jasper by saying "mountain ranges" instead of "sandspit," and by saying "a complex of mountain biotas" instead of "Carolinian." I can then say exactly as I said for Pelee: "Here is a story of land and life; a story of the histories of land and life; a story of the processes in history that made what we see today; a story about objects." The objects involved are, of course, different: plains, mountain ranges, jackpine, bighorn sheep and man.

The Fortress of Louisbourg is a place; buildings and furnishings. It is a tangible bit of reconstructed history. The location of the fort makes sense only in the context of oceans and continents and the colonial territoriality of its time. Its feature story is, like Pelee's, therefore zoogeographic. And exactly as I said for Pelee, it is a story of land and life, the histories of land and life, the processes in history that made what we see today; a story about objects. The objects are again different, however: a bit of land, a fort, associated buildings, furnishings for living, equipment for fighting, an impoverished boreal biota, and man.

O'Keefe Ranch, an historic site near Vernon, BC, is, like Louisbourg, a story of land and life, of history, and of processes to explain objects seen. Its own specific objects are a leeward mountain valley, bunchgrass, exotic herbivores, man and his works. And like Pelee, like Jasper, like Louisbourg, the story is essentially one of biogeography. All are visual stories of land and life.

The Royal Ontario Museum is a place for collections of objects, and one gallery features medieval England. Using visible things, again it is a story of a time and place, of people, of their objects—a story of land and life.

The same is true of the Haida Indian objects shown in the Museum of Anthropology in Vancouver; the theme is land and life.

Natural parks, historic parks, museums all use interpretation while focusing on objects great and small, and while the details vary, all are part of the same story of a mineral foundation that sustains a smear of life on its surface.

But do notice the irregularity in the six examples. Pelee, Jasper, Louisbourg, O'Keefe Ranch were things, places, bits of environment in which lesser things belonged as part of the place. But the two museums were different. In them the medieval tapestry and the Haida rattle were quite out of place, quite out of context relative to their origins and uses. Museums are simply protective and informative vehicles for involving people with objects. In museums the current physical environment of the object is useless, even detrimental, to understanding what the object communicates when you look at it.

Note also that in all six places the story of land and life is the complete story. There is no other. On Planet Earth, this is always the complete story of all places. Where there is no life, the reasons why are necessary, and so is a consideration of life and its needs. But, of course, the total interpretation is not usually our theme, partly because few of us can tell it all with confidence, and also because it is easier to tell it in parts. One's story of the day may therefore interpret only the rock in a mountain, leaving stories of plants and animals for other times.

So academic pigeonholes may have labels that emphasize minor differences and biases in our views of the world, but as interpreters we are really all telling the same story, no matter from which pigeonhole. Understandably, the differences seem greatest at the everyday levels of detail—in other words, at the level of the familiar as seen with the pedestrian eye. It is when the view is unusually sweeping or penetrating that the sameness throughout is most evident. So far, we still have few academic biases when looking down from a satellite, or out from the lofty heights of Darwin's theory, or, alternatively, when seeing the world through a microscope or as revealed by chemistry in a test tube.

It is the new view that has fewest biases, has a minimum of misconceptions. This is why the perceptive stranger often sees best things as they really are. The lessons here for interpreters of objects are obvious. Discard biases, and listen hard to perceptive strangers.

Notice that a few minutes ago we accepted the dividing concept of "natural" and "historic" parks. But is natural history not history? Specialists have put a narrow view on the word "history." But history is not just 1066, Sir John A. Macdonald and 1914–1918. History is also the solidifying of gases to make Earth, and the scales of a reptile evolving into feathers.

A Red-winged Blackbird singing in my garden last October is history, and it was natural. I suspect also that the fight in 1066 and the trenches in 1914–1918 were both depressingly natural. (As to what history is not natural, and so, presumably, is unnatural history, no one seems willing to make clear.)

So history (which some would confine to man) and natural history (from which many exclude man) are simply two parts of history. The apparent difference is perhaps an illusion, with man inside his own history unable to see his forest for the trees, while he is outside the rest of history and so unable to see beyond his own part of the forest. But it is one forest.

To take an even broader view, history is the only knowledge we have because we certainly have none from the future, and the present is only the moving interface between past and future.

Consider now the object. By definition, I suppose an object is a tangible thing that is visible. An object has substance since it reflects light to be visible, and it is usually solid enough to be feelable.

To people with functional eyes or with operating skin sensors, objects therefore communicate information.

An object is a thing, but all things are not objects. An idea is a thing and is not an object, to give an example. There may be no fine line between the two concepts. You can feel temperature but cannot see it, although the results of temperature can often be seen. You can feel wind but cannot see it, although the moving air may move something visible, like leaves. You can neither feel nor see a high-pressure weather system, though there are many associated clues to be seen and felt.

So objects are things, most are visible, most are feelable and there are some problems out at the edges of the concept as to when things are not objects. This discussion is not just academic, for it is useful to interpreters to know when they are interpreting, and by definition, if the audience does not somehow sense a thing being talked about, it cannot be truly interpreted. Information about it is just ordinary information unverifiable at the time.

Objects do communicate. Using words, interpreters interpret objects. More precisely, with words we interpret what the object communicates. More precisely still, interpreters put the non-verbal communication of objects into words. Hence, we are truly interpreters in the usual sense of the word. There is real translation.

Not only do we interpret the object itself, but we also give meaning to the object by interpreting the environment in which the object occurs, and in which the object is meaningful.

A ponderosa pine in Kew Gardens is an object that can be interpreted, but there the tree is in an alien environment. It is in fact in a kind of museum. But a ponderosa pine in the Okanagan Valley, in a sweep of golden grass and with a backdrop of dark hills, is a much more meaningful object. In both cases the tree is a perfectly good botanical object. In its home environment, however, it is a more understandable ecological and geographical statement.

So because objects are to some extent products of their environments, the story of (and by) the visible object is in part the story of the visible—and invisible—environment of that object.

Interpreters therefore interpret objects and
their environments.

Remember also that there are often two environments. Consider a cottonwood tree, or an old corner cupboard. Each not only has an environment; each is also itself environment to other things.

Cottonwoods in the Cascade Mountains are confined to the deepest valleys, and in these valleys are further confined to the flood plains of the rivers. The trees form pure stands that follow the riverbanks in a double narrow band. Here is an environmental story of valley temperatures, abundant groundwater, and annual floods both killing off competing plants and fertilizing the soil with silt. But the cottonwoods are themselves environment to a special community of insects—wood borers, leaf eaters, root feeders—as well as part of the environments of Mule Deer, Downy Woodpeckers and Ruffed Grouse.

While we interpret, nowhere is it written that we must only interpret. As interpreters we translate the visible. These services I believe to be our strength because they are our uniqueness and therefore justify our name. But we can quite properly fall back from time to time, or even for long periods, on just giving background information like everyone else. How else, in the period house of a doctor, can you describe the uses of medical instruments—the more drastic ones at least? How else, before a tree, do you build in a person's mind a working diagram of a tree as a pumping, manufacturing, self-fabricating machine powered by atomic energy? And how else, when challenged in January to inform people in an auditorium about spring flowers, do you have anything to say? You tell them how it was last spring, and how it will be next spring. You can also show pictures, even interpret them, but that is no full substitute for the real thing. You are still not interpreting real wild flowers. But you do it.

All communication methods are at our command, with all their variations, all their tricks, all their problems and limitations, and all their range of suitability for the job. All should be considered for use by interpreters, but I believe that the extent to which we are really interpreters—and therefore stand apart from the great mass of other communicators—is the extent to which we successfully and simultaneously translate the sensory messages that people receive from real things.

So, usually, to an interpreter the object's the thing, and always the object in its proper environment will be the best opportunity to interpret the most complete and most meaningful message.

In short, the object's the thing, and it is most articulate at home.

Currently my consuming challenge is a museum, and I should make it clear that most days I have no time for thinking about interpretation. But interpretation being exciting and addictive, I do find time occasionally to feed the habit.

The museum has interpretation with a difference. If the object is most articulate at home, the museum object is at a disadvantage. It is, in a sense, incarcerated. In a museum, the collected is quite out of context. Data attached variously to the object may describe some details of the distant environment, whether of collected bird, arrowhead, shark or Kwakiutl mask.* But these data are at best general and incomplete. To almost everyone, the object in the museum stands alien and alone, as out of place as a whale at Portage and Main.

And being alone, it is on its own as a direct communicator. Its surroundings give no help to the visual story of its significance.

While the great limitation of the museum is that its most successful communication medium, the exhibit, features objects in exile, the great potential of the museum is its size and the proximity of its potential audience. I went happily into museum

* Contemporary usage would employ the term Kwakwa̱ka̱'wakw.–Eds.

work aware of these two challenges, looking forward to working with both.

To enlarge on these challenges, I found them as big and totally consuming as I suspected. With the object's museum surroundings usually meaningless, much more verbal background information must fill the void of the missing environment, although an alternative approach is to simulate the missing environments in various ways, or perhaps just suggest them with symbols. Examples are the diorama, or old wallpaper as a backdrop to a show of Victorian lamps.

The audience challenge is more variable from museum to museum, but most museums want to increase attendance in their galleries. In what seems to be desperation, some have gone wildly experimental, even to featuring drop-in centres for the elderly, daycare for the young, and door prizes. It is easy to lose sight of the museum's purpose here, for the challenge is to make the museum more attractive, not to turn the museum into something else that is more attractive.

These were the two great challenges. But now a third one is emerging, and I do not yet have it in sharp focus. It takes the problem of interpreting the object that is out of context, and instead of using words or pictures or whatever else to reconstruct something of the object's home environment, it ignores all that and simply seeks to do a good job of interpreting the object itself. It sounds deceptively simple. But while this approach is certainly not new, it is strangely rare in some groups of museum academics.

It is a case of concentrating on the object. There is no suggestion here of decreasing efforts to interpret and otherwise inform about the object within its proper environment. The need is to add a neglected perspective. In our preoccupation with relationships, our knowledge of the object itself can remain very superficial. The museum dedicated to the object (as most are), and possessing objects out of context, should be society's centre for understanding objects per se—centres of knowing more about what objects are. And the challenge is a case of turning a limitation into an opportunity to fill a need.

We have done much fitting of the historic object into wordy narratives of past situations and conditions, and this is not to be criticized. It is a valuable approach which should properly remain the most popular approach. But this is what I call revealing the "object-out." My point is that we have been neglecting the "object-in."

To some extent the same is true of the natural sciences, although when compared to human history, so-called natural history has many traditional areas of "object-in" specialization. As in history, nature interpretation has tended to offer the "object-out" point of view.

There is nothing new about the "object-in" approach. Museum people, or at least some of them, have always been able to demonstrate astonishingly detailed knowledge of the things in their care. Amateur collectors have at times been quite the equal of the museum professionals. Dealers, of necessity, have often been the most expert of all. But there is a strong trend away from such expertise in some museum circles today, and museum communication with the public—interpretation efforts included—rarely features this approach. In general, the "object-in" is considered to be too detailed. We have been taking the easier way.

Curators set the levels and directions of scholarship in museums. Past trends in education systems producing curators are strongly "object-out" oriented, if, indeed, objects figure in their education at all. Wide acceptance of the relatively new ecological approach in the biological sciences, as well as in anthropology, ensures an "object-out" emphasis. Often the teaching received is strictly bookish, or again may consist of viewing entire environments with no sharp focus on the objects within them. Much history as taught ignores historic objects completely, as if by design (except for people, which I suppose are historic objects). Curators entering employment in museums are often not object-oriented at all and continue to function professionally using the sweeping concepts received in their schooling. Most do turn to objects, but in a limited way. The object is used simply as an illustration inserted into the written or spoken narrative of larger concepts.

This common approach is not necessarily bad. It is bad in museums, however, to the extent that it is not balanced by scholarship focused on the object itself. The current predominance in museums of "object-out" curatorialism suggests that some correction is in order.

The "object-in" approach is a sort of finer and finer focus on smaller details. Much can, of course, be done with the unaided eye. A Kwakiutl mask has line and form, composition and colour, a number of materials, imperfections, and evidence of wear and accident. It is all there for a sharp eye, to be noted, pondered, translated and interpreted. And in many cases, this "object-in" detail can lead directly to new and exciting "object-out" understandings. While each mask is unique, most can be variously clumped into "species" and so to a degree are comparable. The carved detail has in it a sort of signature—or "fingerprint"—of the carver, and research can make this message readable and translatable to a degree. The kind of wood, the sort of hair attached, the metal or shell inlays have both inward and outward significance.

But the extent of inward looking only begins with the naked eye. The microscope reveals the species of wood, the origin of hair, sometimes the source of inlaid copper, and these can lead to more facts. X-rays and others reveal the hidden; chemistry offers many routes to new understandings.

While museum interpretation could have more to show and translate as a result of more inward looking, the smaller and smaller aspects of the approach do present problems in their visibility to the public. But help is already at hand. The needs of the classroom to see have resulted in useful ways to show groups what the researcher sees in his laboratory. We may inherit challenges to adapt these existing techniques for museum use, but many gallery problems are solved before we start.

In museums, the object's the thing, and revealing the details of the objects is the museum's new role (among other roles) in our culture. The museum curator may, as a result, become our unsurpassed scholar on what objects *are* (object-in) and *why* (object-out).

Looking ahead, the future of museums may hold increasing involvement with microscopy, with photography and drawing with the microscope, with energy-wave analyses of several kinds, with chemistry—in short, with the exciting detective work of interpreting the details of things.

Museum communications must always follow the curators. We enter here a world for the public in our museums of more visual enlargements, more chemistry, more exploded drawings, more interpretive line drawing. And for the public outside the museum, the museum will offer holograms on stage,* books that feature the object and its details, and television using techniques evolved and controlled by museums.

* "It seems that today more and more museums are embracing the digital challenge, but there is still not a real awareness of how to let virtual and real contents work together to enhance the experience of the visitors in and with the museum's collection. Real and virtual continue to be juxtaposed, but not combined together, in order to produce a powerful experience of mixed reality." (From E. Pietroni, D. Ferdani, M. Forlani, A. Pagano and C. Rufa, "Bringing the Illusion of Reality Inside Museums: A Methodological Proposal for an Advanced Museology Using Holographic Showcases," *Informatics* 6, no. 2 (2019): 1–43.)–Eds.

So interpretation museum-style, like interpretation any style, is the business of interpreting what objects communicate about history, and all history is the story of land and life, or, to be more precise, is the story of Earth—unique because it is green.

But the museum has a special interpretation emphasis on its horizon. Coming soon is not just "object-out" thinking, but "object-in" too, for we need both to really know what objects are saying.

In Park Interpretation, Small Can Be Beautiful (1981)

First published in *Parks* 5, no. 4 (1981): 1–3. Reprinted with permission. *Parks: The International Journal of Protected Areas and Conservation* is published by IUCN World Commission on Protected Areas (https://portals.iucn.org/library/node/5646).

MY FIRST INTERPRETATION PROGRAM PLANNED for a park began with establishing a nature centre which I believed necessary as a focal point to attract park users. The lure to the centre was imaginative exhibits which explained the natural history of the park, and a park interpreter (we called him a park naturalist) was there at all times during the day to answer questions and to interpret the park's landscape so that it had meaning as well as scenic beauty for the receptive visitor. The idea of a focal point worked well in this case, for 25 years later there is still a nature centre in a small building functioning successfully on the same site.

While it is not necessary for a park interpretation program to have a building as a focal point, this particular program with its tent "building" did experience immediate success and evolved rapidly into offering a series of daily experiences for the public away from the centre, such as short walks and long hikes, each with a leader-interpreter who introduced groups of people to the geology, flora and fauna in a variety of life zones in the mountains; and evening talks and slide shows in an open-air theatre. As planned, the nature centre became the logical and successful meeting place and coordination centre for all interpretation activities. It helped, too, that the centre was located in the best site possible, since both park users and travellers on the highway were attracted in numbers to the only supply centre selling food and fuel for many kilometres, which was nearby. But as new interpretation programs were established in other parks in British Columbia's park system, many were successful while using simply well-placed notice boards as their focal points. Here the notice board was the information centre directing people toward periodic interpretation events, as well as the initial gathering place for people taking part in some organized activities.

The smallest programs had only one interpreter, and these were sometimes the best. Take one inspired and informed park naturalist, put him in a park, big or small, that has park users to challenge him and landscapes to illustrate his stories of land and life, and there is no necessity for buildings, exhibits or slide shows to create good interpretation. One medical student [Frank Buffam], who came to interpret every summer until his first year of internship, preferred a coastal park where each day he led people on informative walks that featured either heavy forests or intertidal life at the edge of a rich sea. Each night his theatre just above the waves was made of driftwood to sit on, and as the sun settled into the sea he told the assembled audience true tales of whales, of waves carving into shores, of passing Indian canoes bent on war, and of early European explorers "discovering" land that other men had called home for thousands of years.

Another small park, little more than a camping ground in a setting of large trees, was interpreted to campers by a man [Freeman King] of so many years that a law in British Columbia made it necessary each year to obtain a special government order so we could hire him. Again, a well-located board was the coordination centre of the interpreter's program. Children loved him because he had somehow never lost the curiosity and delight in discovery that is part of childhood, and every morning his walk with campers along the forest trails—with frequent stops to talk of plants or animals, stones or clouds—were occasions dedicated mostly to the children present. Yet others enjoyed them too. Everyone is at least a bit of a child, no matter how old, and anyway, this interpreter's simple yet clever messages were really for everyone. His other walks were for adults; his evening gatherings for families on a circle of benches around a brisk open fire were times for ecological stories partly of his own creation, like the tale of a raindrop making its long journey back to the sea—a yarn of good, sound science made so exciting that all ages hung on every word.* As the night grew black, the orange firelight danced on the huge trees enclosing the circle, and those very trees were, of course, part of the raindrop's adventure. The old man was a superb interpreter who always talked about objects or noises or smells that the audience could experience at the time. He interpreted what they were sensing.

These one-man programs were run by people with special talent, some of it obtained earlier, but most of it perfected as

* Aldo Leopold, one of the "fathers" of modern ecology, published a similar story in 1942 about the odyssey of an atom travelling from a limestone ledge to the sea. (See Aldo Leopold, "Aldo Leopold's Odyssey," *Audubon* [1942]: https://www.audubon.org/magazine/may-june-1942/from-archives-aldo-leopolds-odyssey.)–Eds.

interpreters by the self-training of simply doing it. Most people have useful knowledge and talent to start on. Add a few days of preparation for a topic, then talk to groups while experimenting with improvements. The only way to learn how to do it well is to do it, and to do it better every time.

One important lesson learned from these small programs was that our modern fixation on the need for audiovisual support may not involve a need at all. The electronic methods have their places, of course, but some beginners at interpretation communication, even those afraid at first to talk without the help of electricity, can be put "naked" (as one frightened beginner described his feelings) into an interesting landscape containing a potential audience, and with what they have as normal skills, plus some science background, plus the things everywhere that illustrate their own stories, plus a few reference books to check the facts, they can evolve an entertaining interpretation program that no canned show could ever equal in accomplishment. I have watched many people create such programs, in the process discovering unexpected powers and talents in themselves. The best communication is still a person talking to people, especially when right among the very things being talked about.

That last sentence is almost my definition of interpretation. The landscape—our surroundings—is constantly sending us messages that our senses can receive, our eyes, our ears, our noses, our sensitive skins. We do not receive most of those messages, for our receivers are turned off. Those we do receive, we often do not understand. Park interpretation, like all kinds of interpretation, explains these messages to us; and, of course, good park interpretation is also attractively entertaining, because if it not it will not attract an audience.

Before becoming a park interpreter, I was a wildlife biologist in the provincial parks of British Columbia, Canada's mountain province. I worried over the future of those scenic places teeming with wild living things, for few people seemed to know what a park really was. Most park visitors only glanced at the scenery as if it was so much scenic wallpaper, then rushed on. This was use totally without understanding. Without knowing it, such people can in a few minutes trample more living miracles than anyone could fully see and appreciate in a lifetime. Only from some understanding of what is underfoot can there be much appreciation of the drama and excitement in a sweep of mountain scenery. Assuming that those who understood parks would be those most likely to defend them from enemies, I pressed my director for a chance to experiment with park interpretation. After some years I got my chance.

An immediate result of the new interpretation program in British Columbia's parks was increasing numbers of people much more aware of their surroundings, much more able to appreciate and understand what they were looking at, and with far more enthusiasm for the priceless public treasure that parks preserve. Almost from the beginning there were more people on their knees seeing the details of flowers, more cameras focused on butterflies, more people using printed leaflets to work out the names of trees, so more people pleased to know that the great tree sheltering them was the famous species called Douglas fir. Even more important, there were more people wanting to do their part to protect and to keep wild these newly found places that interpretation had helped them discover.

Interpretation programs need not be expensive. Often they do evolve into expensive buildings, large staffs and sophisticated equipment. These may satisfy the needs of giving information to large crowds or may seem to enhance prestige, but in doing so, such programs can be poor examples of interpretation. Good interpretation must be mostly a grassroots method of taking people into the grassroots. Living land lives mostly as small forms of life. Expensive man-made facilities, in contrast, can lead people away from the insight that good interpretation strives for. Such devices can form a real mental barrier between the audience and nature.

A sophisticated wildlife centre in Canada's province of Ontario dominated my thinking some years ago. The focus there was on a brick building complete with exhibition hall and theatre. Trails led away from the building to self-guiding nature trails, to a steel tower overlooking a marsh, to an underground chamber with a window into the underwater world of the marsh, and to a floating boardwalk that was a foot trail well out into the marsh. All of these facilities were variously successful, especially the outdoor facilities that enabled new viewpoints into the natural world. Even these, however, had an element of making the observer feel like a stranger looking into a world that had not been really entered. The worst offender in this respect was the brick building. It was necessary, perhaps, for its washrooms and offices, its woodworking shops and a library, but the exhibit hall and theatre in it were to some extent out of place. There was something wrong about bringing people indoors to tell them about the highly interesting mysteries and wonders and beauties to be found outside. If "outside" was so interesting, why bring them inside?

It is difficult to know the relative successes of the many approaches to interpretation. Perhaps it is sufficient to know that most of them can be surprisingly effective when used with a little wisdom and sensitivity. Some of the success is clearly visible and audible from audience reaction, although the total success never is. The educator never knows how much he affects the future, nor how far his message will go in time and distance.

When there are small funds, however, thoughts of expensive sophistication are purely theoretical. Looking back at the medical student in the seashore park, I suspect that his program gave the most interpretation with the most influence on the most people at the least cost.

That student's efficiency was perhaps rivalled by the first experimental nature centre in the first park where British Columbia tried park interpretation. For that centre I was given a university student to help and enough money to buy only nails, paint and materials for handmade labels and signs. We salvaged two wooden tent floors from a deserted construction camp and found two discarded tents in the local forestry station, and these we made into the first "nature house." The local refuse dump yielded treasures like boxes, pails and tubs with repairable leaks, bits of wood for signs, and other free supplies. A distant artist friend sent rough paintings of local birds for an exhibit. We photographed things, made diagrams, created catchy titles, found objects in the wild surroundings and combined all these into exhibits. Each simple message was somehow illustrated by objects or pictures, and each one featured some aspect of the natural world just outside the tent. Our success was soon apparent. Gratifying numbers of people came to see, and a gratifying proportion of them went to look closely at the green world outside, for this nature centre was planned not as an end in itself, but as an experience which in almost every exhibit encouraged the visitor to go outside to see something interesting for himself.

The first centre got results at small costs because it could only afford to be as simple and as creatively effective as possible. Creative thinking in a garbage heap or in a nature centre need not be costly.

Landscape interpretation has spread around the world as a widely known approach to building public understanding of the land and of the life on it that makes our living world possible. For some years I have had much pleasure from being able to experiment with many interpretation methods, and much pleasure too from being involved with a dozen interpretation programs in as many kinds of places. I have also experienced numerous programs created by other people. Only recently have these experiences come together into the question: if interpretation can be so effective, why is it not even more widely used than it is? Part of the answer may be that small, effective programs tend to grow into larger, ineffective ones. If this is so, the solution is to favour simplicity in order to sustain maximum results.

There is no doubt that small interpretation programs can have outstanding successes. Small funds often yield high-quality successes. Here, two thoughts from Fritz Schumacher are slightly out of context, but still sum it all up rather well: "Any third-rate engineer or researcher can increase complexity; but it takes a certain flair of real insight to make things simple again" and "Man is small, and therefore small is beautiful."[1]

Yorke Edwards is director of the British Columbia Provincial Museum in Victoria, BC, and is widely known in the field of interpretation in Canada and abroad. His recent book The Land Speaks: Organizing and Running an Interpretation System *was reviewed in the last issue of* Parks.

Notes

1 Both quotations are from E.F. Schumacher, *Small Is Beautiful* (London: Sphere Books, 1975).–Eds.

First Years of Park Interpretation in British Columbia (1987)

First published in *Heritage Communication* 1, no. 2 (1987): 17–20. Reprinted with permission. *Heritage Communication* was a short-lived venture initiated by Canadian interpreter John McFarlane.

IT IS NEVER CLEAR WHERE to begin a "history," because all history is a continuum. Interpretation in Canada's westernmost province perhaps began on June 29, 1957. That day, the nature house in Manning Provincial Park first opened its tent flaps to the public. Possibly interpretation in national parks took place in British Columbia before that date, but that would be another story. In any event, that 1957 opening began British Columbia's most extensive chain of interpretation programs.

From the start, I accepted the name "Park Naturalist Program" because, unable to do better, I was determined not to have Nature "Centres." Endless kinds of centres were everywhere. It was a cold, unimaginative term when the need was for warmth and a friendly beckoning to a place where people belonged. "House" gave my boss a verbal explosion when I first proposed it, but in a few weeks he agreed to a one-year trial. British Columbians were soon using "Nature House" comfortably, and still do after 30 years.

The first nature house opened on a cold day in the Cascade Mountains at 1,219 metres above sea level, 240 kilometres by road from Vancouver. That old tent with new exhibits resulted from over two years of promoting interpretation in Parks Division's head office.* I had seen the beginnings of interpretation in Ontario's Algonquin Park—little more than a tent containing a summer student and stuffed birds, plus periodic walks and talks—and from reading was familiar with the success of interpretation in many national parks in the United States. After observing that most British Columbians in their own parks were unaware of the fascinating wild lives all about them, and that their park experiences therefore ranged somewhere between bewildering and boring, I kept up pressure on my boss, and with the help of allies finally gained a hollow victory.

Cy Oldham was not one to mince words.† "Edwards," he said, "you want it, so you do it. You have $300 for supplies and one summer student." I was both elated and dismayed: elated to have won—if that was the word—but dismayed because I already led an array of programs in wildlife research and management that was overflowing with exciting projects. After ineffectual resistance, I accepted victory from fear of losing

* Parks Division was created in the late 1940s as a division of the British Columbia Forest Service, but became a branch of the Department of Recreation and Conservation in 1957.–Eds.

† Oldham was the chief of Parks at the time Yorke was trying to establish an interpretation presence in Manning Park.–Eds.

the whole campaign, then asked Donald Smith,* a university student, to help with preparations and later to take charge of the program from late June to early September. That summer, the wettest and coldest on record, was not the best choice for a trial run. Our most popular display was a small wood stove demonstrating some properties of local woods.

The tent was not large, about 4 metres by 5 metres, and had inside on its walls nine hastily assembled exhibits designed to be dramatic while delivering brief messages. Their two overall purposes were to create new interest in the natural history easily seen in nearby subalpine forest and alpine tundra, and then to encourage viewers to walk and enjoy the real thing outdoors.

Never was a beginning more humble. The tent was much stained from use and came mildewed from the basement of a distant forest ranger station. A tent floor with attached tent frame, found in an abandoned survey camp, was hauled into place, then repaired and strengthened. The frame's eaves were elevated to make head room inside to the tent walls; then old boards from other floors sheathed the gap between floor and canvas. A counter, 65 centimetres wide, was built around three walls, leaving a wide entrance. Plywood sheets and half-sheets rising from the counter held display graphics, and these were illustrated by natural objects placed on the counters below. A tent fly (simply a large canvas sheet placed over all) ensured a watertight roof once holes in the fly did not coincide with those in the tent's canvas roof.

The entire building was made of salvaged materials. Materials for exhibits and signs came from two sources. In a local garbage dump we competed with scavenging black bears to find wooden boxes, large glass jars, a pail or two and a washtub

* D.A. Smith, a mammologist, was later a professor at Ottawa's Carleton University.–Eds.

with only one hole which later held a display of living bog plants. In the nearest village we stretched scarce dollars in small stores offering few supplies to buy paper, paint, stencils, glue, wire, cloth, plywood and a small aquarium.

On the July 1st "weekend," Canadians begin two months of filling their highways with summer's vacation traffic. That weekend in 1957, the little tent nature house was alive with people, and a week later it had received a thousand curious visitors. The public interest was then proven beyond doubt. Interpretation was in British Columbia's provincial parks to stay.

With only one person on duty in 1957, the program was limited to maintaining exhibits, and to personal interpretation in or near the Nature House. In 1958, the program expanded. J.E. "Ted" Underhill joined me at head office, and through ten years until I left Parks Branch he was my energetic and creative co-worker. Ted was a good botanist, his camera captured fine pictures, every summer he organized and led popular park programs, and in winter he was a magician in the interpretation workshop, where he worked making low-cost exhibits and other communication aids.

The Manning Park Nature House was twice as large but remained under canvas for two more years. Three tent floors were attached in a row, and tents were erected, facing one another, over the two end floors. A tent fly over each floor then had the two tents opening onto a roofed breezeway. Student assistants for summer staff gave us time to plan and experiment with nature trails offering informative labels, with taking groups of people on short and some long hikes to interpret the passing scenes, and with evening talks indoors but later in an open-air theatre. About this time we began producing a series of printed leaflets, simply folded sheets with contents ranging from a list of the park's birds to a key for naming local trees.

Meanwhile, in 1959, a second nature house was opened in Miracle Beach Provincial Park with David Stirling in charge.* At first in one tent, but soon in two, it backed into tall timber near a popular ocean beach. A nature trail with small signs featured the forest behind the house, while inside an exhibit with large aquariums displayed a colourful array of sea creatures, all seined from park waters. Evening talks and conducted walks were popular daily events.

In 1960 and 1961, these first two houses were replaced by rustic wooden buildings. Each had one large exhibit room with a cement floor, and a smaller area adjacent served as office, library and workshop. Low eaves front and back settled them visually into their surroundings. Skylights lit the exhibit areas with daylight. These buildings were spartan yet attractive, with a floor plan designed to keep visitors in touch with interpretation staff.

The early program used Manning and Miracle Beach Parks for proving grounds, where standards were tested and modified, techniques were evolved, purposes and objectives were clarified. At that time I was also in close touch with George Stirrett, naturalist and former federal entomologist, who was forming plans for the extensive use of interpretation in Canada's national parks. He included me in several of his annual seminars on interpretation held in Jasper National Park, where interpreters working in national parks and visitors like me exchanged ideas and pooled experiences on how to interpret effectively. These were exciting days, with enthusiastic people talking mostly about how to do simple, effective interpretation

* David Stirling soon became permanently employed as the second assistant in interpretation and remained active and engaged as a naturalist and a mentor to naturalists into his 90s.–Eds.

in the best ways possible. As enunciated in Parkinson's Law,[†] the beginnings of many organizations are characterized by energetic dedication, inventiveness and high productivity. It was all wonderfully satisfying.

In those first years I evolved much of my philosophy about interpretation, based then on three main principles: true interpretation actually interprets things seen, heard, smelled or felt (like a tree, a bird call, a flower's perfume or the rough surface of a leaf); the best interpretation usually comes from a skilled and informed person communicating "live," body language and all; and it is far better to add an enthusiastic new dimension to one person's life through interpretation than to just add dull information overload onto a dozen people. Perhaps above all was the thought that interpretation at its best offers revelation.[‡]

In 1963, the provincial program expanded in a different direction. British Columbia's Okanagan Valley extends north from the Canadian–American border as a dry strip of grassland, steppe and pine savannah. Large lakes add to the area's fame as a vacationland, and a series of small parks up the valley floor are designed for dense populations of campers. Undeveloped fringes in these parks, and much terrain around them, are largely wild land. Three of these camping parks (through 126 kilometres, from north to south, Ellison, Okanagan Lake and Haynes Point Parks) were served

† Parkinson's Law is the adage that "work expands so as to fill the time available for its completion." C. Northcote Parkinson wrote at length about organizations and bureaucracy, and Yorke may be referring to another of Parkinson's findings rather than the more familiar eponymous law. However, we really have no idea what he meant here.–Eds.

‡ Yorke noted in a footnote: "This was inspired by our bible of the time, Freeman Tilden's *Interpreting Our Heritage*, University of North Carolina Press, Chapel Hill, 1957. This book was our revelation."–Eds.

all summer by one park naturalist in a camper which served as vehicle, bedroom, diner and office. The naturalist interpreted in each park on a weekly schedule. Programs consisted of guided walks by day and a campfire talk each evening, the latter in makeshift outdoor theatres. Here speakers were quite on their own, unable to use slides or movies because the parks had no electricity.

When naturalists were first confronted by having to present these talks, of necessity without slides, in some panic they proposed using portable generators so they could have electronic support. My two reasons for "No slides" left them partly unconvinced, but later all thanked me for standing firm. I believed that noisy generators would be ludicrous background for a talk on the joys and values of wild places, and I believed that once they learned to address audiences without leaning on slides as a crutch, they would be much more effective communicators. It worked as predicted. At first, only the noise factor had made sense to them, but with experience they also agreed that, although slides have their uses, they can also be third-rate communication when compared with listening to good talk as the sun colours the world at sunset, or with sitting around a fire at night, the trunks of pine aglow all about, while nighthawks call and a breeze breathes through countless leaves in the blackness above. After this experience, we used rough outdoor theatres in most parks that had electricity. The old and simpler way was better communication, as well as vastly more appropriate to the purposes of the program.

The third nature house was built on Shuswap Lake in the dry forest of the Interior Plateau. A summer-long population of campers filling all 260 family campsites to capacity gave this small park heavy use. It was an ideal place for interpretation to accentuate basic geology and biology rather than unusual features, which were rather scarce anyway. A rustic nature house built there had half the floor space of the others on the theory that it would be used frequently but briefly as a reference facility. This was a park with reliably good summer weather and natural vegetation scattered throughout, convenient almost everywhere for use by interpreters. Here, "basic" geology and biology indicates the more fundamental features found in most landscapes, such as shapes of hills, functions of leaves, purposes of bird song, names of weeds, and small ecological dramas staged by wasps, butterflies, flies, hummingbirds and sapsuckers attracted to the sap oozing from sapsuckerwells drilled into birches. The small size of this nature house simply reflected my growing conviction that if the outdoors is to be promoted as a pleasant place for enjoyable hours of discovery, interpretation should re-examine the common tendency to take people indoors to promote the outdoors.

Yet another form of program was tried and improved through the 1960s. One park naturalist was placed in summer residence in each of two parks having campgrounds as well as much wild land. These parks, and the naturalists working in them, could not have been more different. A young medical student returned annually to lead walks and give talks in Wickaninnish Provincial Park, now part of Pacific Rim National Park on the rugged and rather remote west coast of Vancouver Island, the two natural landscapes there being a long and superb beach of sand and a forest that was partly stunted coniferous rainforest, partly treed bog. In contrast, Goldstream Provincial Park near Victoria, the provincial capital, had an energetic man in his 70s who led walks and gave evening talks almost daily in a park featuring a salmon stream and an old forest, partly rainforest, partly the dry Mediterranean-like forest found close to the Strait of Georgia. I have two vivid images of these programs in action.

Like all ocean beaches in British Columbia, Long Beach (Wickaninnish Provincial Park*) is strewn with logs moved about by high tides. Before every evening talk, Frank Buffam arranged logs into seating so his audience faced west. Then, as the sun set into the Pacific Ocean, and the surf foamed onto the beach in endless processions, he told tales of the great whaling canoes that local Indian hunters once paddled over that horizon, or told of the improbable animals that swarmed in that world of water stretching to Japan, and in the wet sand beneath their very feet.

Freeman King [in Goldstream Provincial Park] talked in a different setting. He chose a grove of huge conifers in a little valley in which he built rough benches in concentric circles for seating, and there in firelight, with the giant boles of trees soaring into the night, he told stories perfected at countless fires. A favourite was about a raindrop on its endless journeys from sky to wet forest, through organisms, into soils, transporting solutions, travelling rivers, returning to the sky again and perhaps having other adventures. The possibilities were endless. He could have told a new raindrop story every night through July and August, the time of heavy park use, and every time the tale would have held the full attention of young and old.

I was in charge of this provincial program from 1957 to 1967. Those were years of scarce money, so services offered were spartan. Nature trail labels were made on our small printing press, while exhibits and signs were made in our workshop. Electronics had limited use, partly because costly, partly because prone to embarrassing breakdowns in remote places, but mostly because considered to be inferior communication.

* In the early 1970s, Wickaninnish Beach Provincial Park became part of the newly created Pacific Rim National Park Reserve on the west coast of Vancouver Island.—Eds.

When I left in 1967 to work in Ottawa, Kerry Joy took command through ten good years of increased funding. Four more nature houses were created, and programs without houses began in about 13 more parks. Through the recent decade, interpretation programs have survived but with severe economic restrictions and under decentralized administrations.

Interpretation is satisfying work, often pure pleasure. The rewards most memorable were the pleasures of watching the dawn of understandings on people's faces, and the satisfactions of observing people find delight in discovering the details of the Earth's surface. Even so, such feedback is fragmentary. Like all educators, interpreters never can know how far the ripples travel from where they have dropped new understandings.

Chronological Bibliography of Interpretation-Related Speeches and Writings

Naturalist Trevor Goward has gathered over 250 reports, papers and books pertaining to Wells Gray Provincial Park that will form the basis of the Edwards-Ritcey Online Library, honouring the contributions of both Yorke Edwards and Ralph Ritcey, whose early work on Wells Gray Park's wildlife created a solid foundation for future research.

The articles listed below are those by Edwards that primarily or exclusively focus on interpretation and related topics. Some of the papers not included in this book will be available at the Edwards-Ritcey Online Library.

▼ *Indicates works included in this volume*

1942

▼ "Six Wood Warblers." *Canadian Nature*, March/April.

1962

▼ "Interpretation Ideas." Unpublished, Parks Branch, Victoria, BC.

▼ "Interpretation in British Columbia's Provincial Parks." Paper presented to the Third Annual Naturalist Workshop and Training Course of the National Parks Branch, Banff, AB, June 9.

1963

- "Canada's Approach." Paper presented at a panel discussion on the topic "Outdoor Interpretation through Land for Learning" at the 59th annual meeting of the National Audubon Society, Miami, FL, November 9–13.

1964

- "Interpretation in our Parks." Presentation to BC Parks Branch training school, Manning Park, BC, February 11.
- "Naturalists and Parks." *Ontario Naturalist* 2, no. 2: 3–6.
- "The Role of the Park Naturalist in Park Inventory, Planning and Management." Paper presented to the Third Federal-Provincial Park Conference, Victoria, BC, October 1.
- "The Scientific Basis of Natural History Interpretation." Paper presented to the Fifth Annual Naturalists Workshop, held at Palisades National Parks Training Centre, Jasper, AB, July 5.

"Some Do's and Don'ts of Planning a Museum." *Museum Roundup* 15: 4–7. Reprinted 1966, in the Ontario Historical Society newsletter #107 (Museum Section).

"Why Wilderness!" *B.C. Digest* 20, no. 5: 20–21, 41–43.

1965

- "What Is Interpretation?" Paper presented to the BC Parks Training School, Manning Park, BC, January 27, 1965.

"What Is a Park?" *Canadian Audubon* 27: 137–43.

"Confessions of a Lazy Gardener." Western Homes and Living 16, no. 8: 34–35.

- "Park Interpretation." *Park News* 1, no. 1: 11–16.

1966

"The Words on Labels." Paper presented to the BC Museums Association, Duncan, BC.

1967

“Naturalists and Nature Interpretation.” Talk given at the annual dinner of the McIlwraith Field Naturalist Club, London, ON, December 1.

“The Impact of Recreation on the Landscape of the Mountains of Western Canada.” *International Union for Conservation of Nature Publications*, New Series 7: 125–26.

“The Preservation of Wilderness.” *Canadian Audubon* 29, no. 1: 1–7.

1968

“The Future of Recreation on Wild Lands.” *The Forestry Chronicle* 44, no. 3: 24-29.

“Interpretation and the Public.” Paper presented at the annual meeting of the Canadian Society of Wildlife and Fishery Biologists, Ottawa, ON, January 10.

“Interpretation in Your Museum.” Paper presented at the annual banquet of the BC Museums Association, Vernon, BC, September 13. Published in *Museum Roundup* 32: 68–74. Reprinted 1977, in *Interpretation Canada* 4, no. 2: 2–11.

“Something New: Conservation Interpretation.” Trail and Landscape 2, no. 3: 81.

“A Museum Watcher in Ottawa.” *Museum Roundup* 30: 50–51.

“Museums and the Importance of Things.” *Museum Roundup* 32: 75–76.

“Wild Naturalists I Have Known.” Ontario Naturalist 5, no. 3: 13–15.

“Two Museums: The Bad and the Beautiful.” *Museum Roundup* 33: 53–54.

“Educational Measures Dealing with the Conservation of the Natural Environment.” Paper presented to the International Federation of Landscape Architects at the Bonaventure Hotel in Montreal, QC, June 20.

1969

"Life Is a Long Walk." *Ontario Naturalist* 1: 11–14.

"Make Your Own Exhibits." *Canadian Audubon* Magazine March-April: 1–8.

"The Nature of Naturalists." Paper presented at the annual meeting of the Federation of Ontario Naturalists, Toronto, ON. Published in *Ontario Naturalist* 3: 23–25.

"Interpretation—Something New." *The Journal of Environmental Education* 1, no. 1: 17–18.

"Conservation and Naturalists." *Canadian Wildlife and Fisheries Newsletter* 26, no. 4: 2–3.

1970

"A Mustering of Museums." *Museum Roundup* 37: 59–60.

"Science and St. Augustine." *Museum Roundup* 38: 55–56.

"Museums: The National Prestige." *Museum Roundup* 39: 55–57.

"The Proof of Wildness." In *Wilderness Canada*, edited by Borden Spears and Bruce Littlejohn, pp. 149–56. Toronto: Clarke, Irwin.

"New Fields for Interpretation." Paper presented at a short seminar given by William Barkley and Edwards to a class from University of Guelph at Wye Marsh Wildlife Centre, January 31.

1971

"Say It with Museums." *Museum Roundup* 41: 55–57.

"Man and the Prairie Landscape." *Canadian Audubon* 32, no. 4: 111–15.

"Smiling Gods and Fierce Scarecrows." *Museum Roundup 42: 48–50.*

"On Buildings and a Book." *Museum Roundup* 44: 66–68.

"The CWS Interpretation Program." Paper presented at the 35th Federal-Provincial Wildlife Conference, Toronto, ON, July 6.

"On Planning and Building a Nature Interpretation Centre." Paper written for the Canadian Wildlife Service, Ottawa, ON, September 1. Published in *Museum Roundup* 46 (1972): 49–54.

"A Plan to Appreciate Canada." *Journal of Environmental Education* 3, no. 2: 11–13.

1972

"The Many Sources of Conservation Information." *Wildlife Crusader* 18, no. 2: 14–15.

"The Message Is Our Measure." *Museum Roundup* 47: 50–52.

1973

"The Grandfather Way." *Museum Roundup* 51: 50–52.

"Thoughts While Walking." *The Bulletin of the Ontario Conservation Council* 20, no. 3: 3–5. Reprinted 1974 as "While Walking." *Wildlife Review*, Summer.

1975

"Canadian Cities in Search of Nature." In *Proceedings of the Symposium—Wildlife in Urban Canada*. Guelph, ON: Office of Continuing Education, University of Guelph, May 26–30.

1976

"Interpretation—What Should It Be?" *Journal of Interpretation* 1, no. 1: 13–16.

"What Good Is a Museum?" *Canadian Museum Association Gazette* 9, no. 3: 10–12.

1977

"Tomorrow's Museum." *Canadian Museum Association Gazette* 10, no. 1: 6–11.

1979

The Land Speaks: Organizing and Running an Interpretation System. Toronto: National and Provincial Parks Association, http://parkscanadahistory.com/publications/nppac-cpaws/the-land-speaks.pdf.

"The Object's the Thing." Paper presented to the Association of Canadian Interpreters, Naramata, BC, November 1. Published in 1981 in *Heritage Interpretation: Making Interpretation Relevant*, *Heritage Record* No. 11, edited by W.D. Barkley, 1–5. Victoria, BC: BC Provincial Museum.

"The Unnatural Natural History in Museums." *Canadian Museums Association Gazette* 12: 14–17.

1981

"In Park Interpretation, Small Can Be Beautiful." Parks 5, no. 4: 1–3.

1987

"First Years of Park Interpretation in British Columbia." *Heritage Communicator* 1, no. 2: 17–20.

1988

"The Canadian Wildlife Service: Interpreting Across a Continent." *Heritage Communicator* 2: 3–7.

1991

"Environmental Museums?" *Museum Roundup* 164: 7–8.

1993

"Science and Technology in Our Museums." In *Science and Technology in Canadian Museums: A Neglected Heritage*. Proceedings of a Workshop Held March 19 and 20, 1987, Hotel de la Chaudière, Hull, QC, 2–11. Ottawa, ON: Canadian Museum of Nature.

Reference List

Works mentioned in the text.

▼ *Indicates works included in this volume*

Atherr, T.L. "The American Hunter-Naturalist and the Development of the Code of Sportsmanship." *Journal of Sport History* 5, no. 1 (1978): 7–22.

Bailey, L.H. *The Nature-Study Idea: An Interpretation of the New School Movement to Put the Young into Relation and Sympathy with Nature*. New York: Macmillan, 1911. https://www.biodiversitylibrary.org/item/62717#page/19/mode/1up.

Burnett, J.A. "A Passion for Wildlife: A History of the Canadian Wildlife Service, 1947–1997." *Canadian Field-Naturalist* 113 (1999): 1–183.

Cannings, R.A. "Yorke Edwards: A Natural Thinker." *Cordillera* 4, no. 1 (1997): 7–12.

Carson, R. *Silent Spring*. Boston: Houghton Mifflin, 1962.

Ceballos, G., P.R. Ehrlich, A.D. Barnosky, A. García, R.M. Pringle and T.M. Palmer. "Accelerated Modern Human–Induced Species Losses: Entering the Sixth Mass Extinction." *Science Advances* 1, no. 5 (2015): 1–5, https://doi.org/10.1126/sciadv.1400253.

Curwood, J.O. *God's Country: The Trail to Happiness*. New York: Cosmopolitan Book Corporation, 1921.

Edwards, R.Y. "British Columbia." In *The Enduring Forest*, ed. R. Kirk, 109–39. Seattle, WA: The Mountaineers and the Mountaineers Foundation, 1996.

Edwards, R.Y. "Chester Peter Lyons." *Cordillera* 5, no. 1 (2000): 3–4.

Edwards, R.Y. "Comparison of an Aerial and Ground Census of Moose." *Journal of Wildlife Management* 18, no. 3 (1954): 403–04.

Edwards, R.Y. "The Concept of Carrying Capacity." *Transactions of the North American Wildlife Conference* 20 (1955): 589–98.

Edwards, R.Y. "Fire and the Decline of a Mountain Caribou Herd." *Journal of Wildlife Management* 33 (1954): 521–26.

Edwards, R.Y. "First Years of Park Interpretation in British Columbia." *Heritage Communication* 1, no. 2 (1987): 17–20.

Edwards, R.Y. "Hawks Migrating over Vancouver Island." *Cordillera* 1 (1994): 30–33.

Edwards, R.Y. *The Illustrated Natural History of Canada: The Mountain Barrier.* Toronto: N.S.L. Natural Science of Canada, 1970.

Edwards, R.Y. *The Land Speaks: Organizing and Running an Interpretation System.* Toronto: National and Provincial Parks Association, 1979.

Edwards, R.Y. "Landform and Caribou Distribution in British Columbia." *Journal of Mammalogy* 39 (1958): 408–12.

Edwards, R.Y. "The Living Prairie." *The Young Naturalist* 12 (1970): 1–2.

Edwards, R.Y. "The Measurement of Tracks to Census Grizzly Bears." *Murrelet* 40 (1959): 14–16.

Edwards, R.Y. "Migrations of Caribou in a Mountainous Area of Wells Gray Park, British Columbia." *Canadian Field-Naturalist* 73 (1959): 21–25.

Edwards, R.Y. "Naturalists and Nature Interpretation." Talk given at the annual dinner of the McIlwraith Field Naturalists, London, ON, December 1, 1967.

Edwards, R.Y. "Notes on the Gulls of Southwestern British Columbia." *Syesis* 1 (1969): 199–202.

Edwards, R.Y. "Notes on Two Captive Meadow Jumping Mice (*Zapus hudsonius*)." *Canadian Field-Naturalist* 59 (1945): 49–50.

Edwards, R.Y. "Oaks in the Grassland." *The Victoria Naturalist* 57, no. 1 (2000): 16.

Edwards, R.Y. "A Plan to Appreciate Canada." *Journal of Environmental Education* 3, no. 2 (1971): 11–13.

Edwards, R.Y. "The Preservation of Wildness." *Canadian Audubon* 29 (1967): 1–7.

Edwards, R.Y. "The Reindeer That Vanished Forever." *Discovery* (Friends of the Royal BC Museum newsletter) 21, no. 3 (1993): 7.

Edwards, R.Y. "Research: A Museum Cornerstone." In *Museum Collections: Their Roles and Future in Biological Research*, ed. E.H. Miller, 1–11. Victoria, BC: BC Provincial Museum, 1985.

Edwards, R.Y. "Science and Technology in Our Museums." In *Science and Technology in Canadian Museums: A Neglected Heritage. Proceedings of a Workshop Held March 19 and 20, 1987, Hotel de la Chaudière, Hull, P.Q.*, 2–11. Ottawa: Canadian Museum of Nature, 1993.

Edwards, R.Y. "Six Wood Warblers" (illustrations by J.A. Crosby). *Canadian Nature* (March/April 1942): 13–14.

Edwards, R.Y. "Snow Depths and Ungulate Abundance in the Mountains of Western Canada." *Journal of Wildlife Management* 20 (1956): 159–68.

Edwards, R.Y. "Some Early Finds and Follies." In *Reflections of the Past: Manning Park Memories*, 45–47. Victoria, BC: Ministry of Lands and Parks, 1991.

Edwards, R.Y. "Tomorrow's Museum." *Canadian Museum Association Gazette* 10, no. 1 (1977): 6–11.

Edwards, R.Y. "Tropical Birds on McMicking Point." *The Victoria Naturalist* 48, no. 5 (1992):18–20.

Edwards, R.Y. "What Is Interpretation?" Paper presented at the BC Parks Training School, Manning Park, BC, 1965.

Edwards, R.Y. "Wilderness Parks: A Concept with Conflicts." In *Endangered Spaces*, ed. M. Hummel, 21–29. Toronto: Key Porter, 1989.

Edwards, R.Y. "Your Live Exhibit, the Native Plant Gardens." *Discovery* 24, no. 3 (1995): 7.

Edwards, R.Y., A.T. Cringan, C.D. Fowle, R.C. Passmore, A.J. Reeve and D.J. Robinson. "Forestry and Wildlife Management — Dual Endeavours on Forest Land." *Forestry Chronicle* 32 (1956): 433–43.

Edwards, R.Y., and I. McT. Cowan. "The Fur Production of the Boreal Forest Region of British Columbia." *Journal of Wildlife Management* 21 (1957): 257–67.

Edwards, R.Y., and R.W. Ritcey. "The Migrations of a Moose Herd." *Journal of Mammalogy* 37 (1956): 486–94.

Edwards, R.Y., J. Soos and R.W. Ritcey. "Quantitative Observations of Epidendric Lichens Used as Food by Caribou." *Ecology* 41 (1960): 425–31.

Gilson, J., and R. Kool, "The Place of Inspiration in Heritage Interpretation: A Conceptual Analysis." *Journal of Interpretation Research*, 24, no. 1 (2019): 27–48.

Intergovernmental Panel on Climate Change. *Global Warming of 1.5°C: An IPCC Special Report on the Impacts of Global Warming of 1.5°C above Pre-Industrial Levels and Related Global Greenhouse Gas Emission Pathways, in the Context of Strengthening the Global Response to the Threat of Climate Change, Sustainable Development, and Efforts to Eradicate Poverty*, ed. V. Masson-Delmotte, P. Zhai, H.-O. Pörtner, D. Roberts, J. Skea, P.R. Shukla, A. Pirani, et al. Geneva: World Meteorological Organization, 2018.

Leopold, A. "Aldo Leopold's Odyssey." *Audubon* (1942), https://www.audubon.org/magazine/may-june-1942/from-archives-aldo-leopolds-odyssey.

Leopold, A. *"Conservation Blueprints," American Forests 43, no.12 (1937): 596–608.*

Lerner, N. "Drawing to Learn Science: Legacies of Agassiz," *Journal of Technical Writing and Communication* 37, no. 4 (2007): 379–394, http://oww-files-public.s3.amazonaws.com/6/6f/Draw2Learn_NLerner.pdf.

Lothian, W.F. "Park Education and Interpretation." Chap. 11 in *A History of Canada's National Parks*, vol. 4 (Ottawa: Parks Canada, 1987), http://parkscanadahistory.com/publications/history/lothian/eng/vol4/chap11.htm.

Merilees, B. "The Beginnings of Interpretation in BC's Parks." *British Columbia History* 47, no. 2 (2014): 16–22.

Miller, R.G., R.W. Ritcey and R.Y. Edwards. "Live-Trapping Marten in B.C." *Murrelet* 36, no. 1 (1955): 1–8.

Peart, B. "The Definition of Interpretation." Paper presented at workshop of the Association of Interpretive Naturalists, College Station, TX, 1977.

Pietroni, E., D. Ferdani, M. Forlani, A. Pagano and C. Rufa. "Bringing the Illusion of Reality inside Museums: A Methodological Proposal for an Advanced Museology Using Holographic Showcases." *Informatics* 6, no. 2 (2019): 1–43.

Ritcey, R.W., and R.Y. Edwards. "Parasites and Diseases of the Wells Gray Moose Herd." *Journal of Mammalogy* 39 (1958): 139–45.

Ritcey, R.W., and R.Y. Edwards. "Trapping and Tagging Moose on Winter Range." *Journal of Wildlife Management* 20 (1956): 324–25.

Roy, P.E. *The Collectors: A History of the Royal British Columbia Museum and Archives*. Victoria, BC: Royal British Columbia Museum, 2018.

Schumacher, E.F. *Small Is Beautiful*. London: Sphere Books, 1975.

Steffen, W., J. Grinevald, P.J. Crutzen and J.R. McNeill. "The Anthropocene: Conceptual and Historical Perspectives." *Philosophical Transactions of the Royal Society A* 369, no. 1938 (2011): 842–67, https://doi.org/10.1098/rsta.2010.0327.

Steffen, W., K. Richardson, J. Rockström, S.E. Cornell, I. Fetzer, E.M. Bennett, R. Biggs, et al. "Planetary Boundaries: Guiding Human Development on a Changing Planet." *Science* 347, no. 6223 (2015): 736–46, https://doi.org/10.1126/science.1259855.

Thicke, J.C., D. Duncan, W. Wood, A.E. Franklin and A.J. Rhodes. "Cultivation of Poliomyelitis Virus in Tissue Culture. I. Growth of the Lansing Strain in Human Embryonic Tissues." *Canadian Journal of Medical Sciences* 30, no. 3 (1952): 231–45, https://doi.org/10.1139/cjms52-031.

Tilden, F. *Interpreting our Heritage* (Chapel Hill: University of North Carolina Press, 1957).

Trisos, C.H., C. Merow and A.L. Pigot. "The Projected Timing of Abrupt Ecological Disruption from Climate Change." *Nature* 580 (2020): 496–501, https://doi.org/10.1038/s41586-020-2189-9.

Udall, S.L. *The Quiet Crisis*. New York: Holt, Rinehart and Winston, 1963.

Index

Pages with illustrations are indicated in italics; "n" after a page number indicates the reference is to a note on that page.